THE COSTLIEST PEARL

BERTIL LINTNER

The Costliest Pearl

China's Struggle for India's Ocean

HURST & COMPANY, LONDON

First published in the United Kingdom in 2019 by
C. Hurst & Co. (Publishers) Ltd.,
41 Great Russell Street, London, WC1B 3PL

Printed in the United Kingdom by Bell and Bain Ltd, Glasgow

Distributed in the United States, Canada and Latin America by Oxford University Press, 198 Madison Avenue, New York, NY 10016, United States of America.

A Cataloguing-in-Publication data record for this book is available from the British Library.

ISBN: 9781849049962

www.hurstpublishers.com

CONTENTS

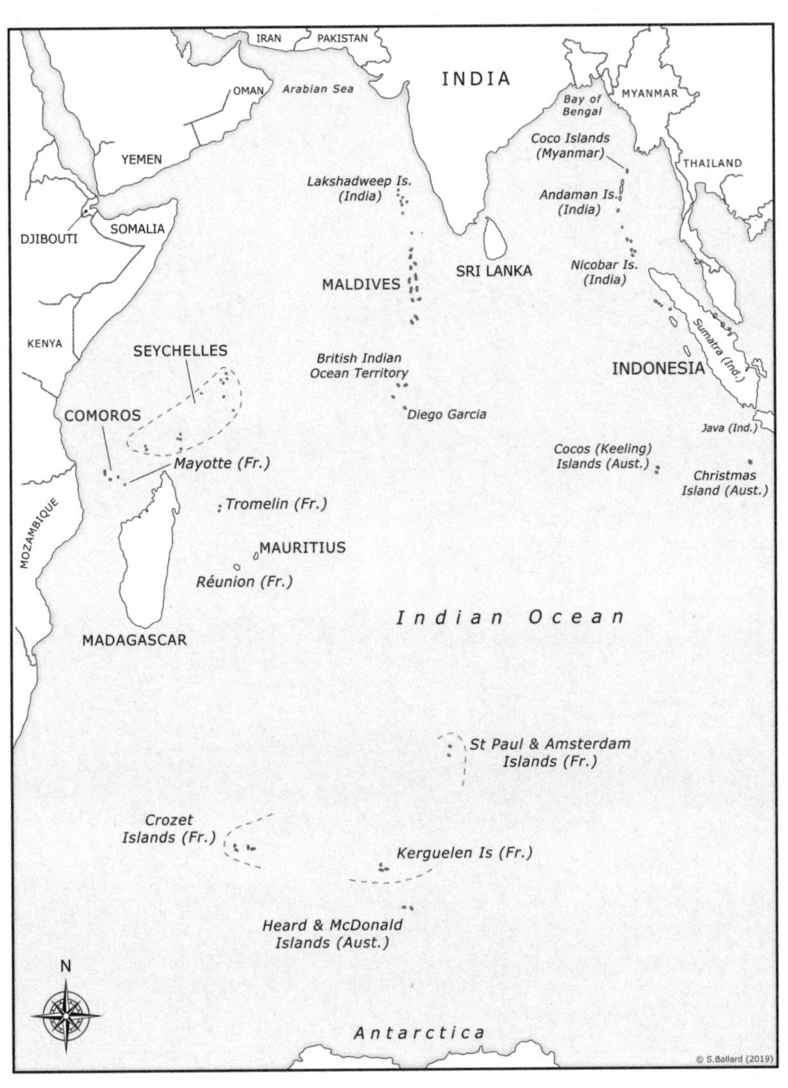
IRAN
PAKISTAN
INDIA
OMAN
Arabian Sea
Bay of Bengal
MYANMAR
YEMEN
Coco Islands (Myanmar)
THAILAND
Lakshadweep Is. (India)
Andaman Is. (India)
DJIBOUTI
SOMALIA
SRI LANKA
Nicobar Is. (India)
MALDIVES
Sumatra (Ind.)
KENYA
SEYCHELLES
British Indian Ocean Territory
INDONESIA
COMOROS
Diego Garcia
Java (Ind.)
Mayotte (Fr.)
Cocos (Keeling) Islands (Aust.)
Christmas Island (Aust.)
MOZAMBIQUE
Tromelin (Fr.)
MAURITIUS
Réunion (Fr.)
Indian Ocean
MADAGASCAR
St Paul & Amsterdam Islands (Fr.)
Crozet Islands (Fr.)
Kerguelen Is (Fr.)
Heard & McDonald Islands (Aust.)
N
Antarctica
© S.Ballard (2019)

INTRODUCTION

A giant monument showing four figures wheeling a circular object between them, their determined faces pointing directly south, stands where the road on the wide, concrete bridge that spans the Ruili River leads into Jiegao, a tiny sliver of Chinese territory on the other side. The Chinese characters on the base of the monument spell out the phrase 'Unite, Blaze Paths, Forge Ahead!'. Or, in more mundane terms: 'Southeast Asia, here we come!'[1]

What is striking about this monument is not so much where it can be found. Jiegao, a roughly hewn two-square-kilometre enclave completely surrounded by Myanmar, is a thriving commercial centre and the gateway to markets across the border and beyond. But the monument was placed there, with remarkable foresight, in 1993 when the bridge had only just been built and Jiegao consisted of little more than paddy fields with a few bamboo huts scattered between them. Today, 25 years later, there are high-rise buildings, luxury hotels, stores offering all kinds of wares, and a huge jade market where buyers from all over China shop for this precious stone, which is found in its imperial green form only in Hpakan, in northernmost Myanmar.

Every morning, caravans of trucks laden with Chinese consumer goods pass through the border post at Jiegao and into Muse on the Myanmar side. They are destined for Lashio, Mandalay, Yangon and other Myanmar cities and towns, and even places as far away as Tamu on Myanmar's border with India. From Tamu the goods are then brought into Moreh in India and from there on to Imphal, Dimapur, Kohima and Guwahati – the key cities in India's northeastern states. Not only Myanmar but also northeastern India is being flooded with cheap Chinese merchandise. For India, the road from Guwahati to Moreh is supposed to be its highway to Southeast Asia and part of what used to be called a 'Look East', and is now designated an 'Act East', policy. But most of the convoys of lorries head in the opposite direction; it is China, not India, which benefits most from the opening of new trade routes through the state formerly known as Burma.

The trade imbalance is not quite as pronounced as at Jiegao, where huge amounts of jade are imported from Myanmar. But that barely registers compared with the volume of Chinese exports heading in the opposite direction, through the border post. Apart from jade, there is little more than amber, petrified wood, seafood and fruit coming from the Myanmar side. A once thriving timber trade has dwindled to almost nothing since China imposed restrictions – and the forests of northern Myanmar are now almost depleted of trees.

The Jiegao crossing is of utmost importance to the export-oriented economic growth of China's landlocked, southwestern provinces. But not far from Ruili are newly laid pipelines through which oil and gas are being transported from the Myanmar coast to Yunnan, bypassing the vulnerable geostrategic choke point of the Malacca Strait. On the coast where the pipelines originate lies the port of Kyaukpyu, the construction of which was announced in 2007 and which is still being expanded and upgraded with Chinese assistance.

Once massive cross-border trade developed following the construction of the bridge at Jiegao in the early 1990s, and the subsequent proclamation of the enclave as a free-trade zone, the vision of a trade corridor through Myanmar became reality. China finally reached the Indian Ocean. China also soon emerged as Myanmar's largest trade partner, political ally, and supplier of military hardware to the military junta that then ruled the country. At the same time, Chinese companies became involved in the construction of several hydroelectric power projects in Myanmar that were to supply Yunnan and other southwestern provinces with electricity.

A map in one of the hotels in Ruili shows grand plans to build a maze of new highways and railways from Yunnan through Myanmar, down to the Indian Ocean. 'The Myanmar Corridor' has become one of the most important features of Chinese President Xi Jinping's 'Belt and Road Initiative' (BRI), which he launched in 2013.[2] Myanmar not only connects China with the markets of South and Southeast Asia; more importantly it provides China with an outlet to the Indian Ocean, thus bolstering Beijing's quest for geostrategic influence.

China's interest in the Indian Ocean was first articulated in an article written by Pan Qi, a former Vice Minister of Communications, for the 2 September 1985 issue of the official Chinese weekly *Beijing Review*, thus well before even the establishment of the free-trade zone at Jiegao.[3] Pan's argument was that China would have to find an outlet for trade for the landlocked southwestern provinces of Yunnan, Sichuan and Guizhou, with a combined population of 160 million people. He mentioned the railways from Myitkyina and Lashio in the north and northeast of Myanmar respectively, and the Irrawaddy River that flows through Myanmar down to the Indian Ocean, as possible conduits for Chinese exports.

Pan also mentioned in his visionary article that 'there was a road connecting western Yunnan with southeast and west Asia quite early in history: Zhang Qian, a Han Dynasty diplomat who lived from 202 BC to 220 AD, helped open a southern 'Silk Road' from Sichuan, and the artery was travelled for centuries.'[4] There is no doubt that Zhang Qian wrote extensively about trade routes, including the Silk Road, to and from China, Central Asia and beyond.[5] But his attempts to forge a route from Sichuan to India proved unsuccessful. No 'southern Silk Road' ever existed. In the past, China paid only scant attention to maritime ventures and it had had no presence in the Indian Ocean since the fifteenth century, when an explorer and trader called Zheng He sailed with his fleets to South- and Southeast Asia, the Indian subcontinent, the Arab peninsula, and even as far as the east coast of Africa.

Apart from Zheng He's voyages 600 years ago, there is no historical precedent for China's BRI, which consists of what the Chinese authorities call a 'Silk Road Economic Belt' and a '21st Century Maritime Silk Road'. Together, these are intended to connect China to Europe via Central Asia, the Mediterranean through the Persian Gulf, and South Asia via the Indian Ocean. According to official Chinese figures and statistics, the BRI encompasses 70 countries and estimates of what China will invest in it range from US$1 trillion to US$8 trillion.[6] It is the most ambitious development strategy in world history when it comes to one state supporting projects beyond its boundaries, surpassing even America's Marshall Plan, which helped Europe rebuild after World War II.

It is here that problems – and potential conflicts – become evident, as China's interests are bound to collide with those of existing Indian Ocean powers. Even other countries, which are dependent on Indian Ocean sea lanes connecting them with the rest of the world, have reason to be concerned about China's grandiose plans. Four-fifths of the container traffic between Asia and the rest of the world, and three-fifths of the world's oil supplies, pass through the Indian Ocean. And now comes the BRI, which, if successfully implemented, may establish China as the dominant power in the Indian Ocean region.

With such an enormous investment as the BRI entails, and given the importance of oil supplies from the Middle East and trade routes through the Indian Ocean, China undeniably requires a 'defence umbrella' to protect its interests. Military alliances have been and will be formed not only with smaller but strategically important countries such as Maldives and Seychelles, but also with Myanmar, Bangladesh, Sri Lanka and Pakistan. In 2017 China established its first overseas military outpost, in Djibouti in the Horn of Africa, ostensibly to combat piracy in the region. But the facility is also within striking distance of US bases in the region, including the facility on Diego Garcia and those in the Gulf Cooperation Council (GCC) countries.

And, judging from China's diplomatic overtures and the economic and political links it is establishing not only with Myanmar but also with other countries in the region, there are likely to be more bases established beyond that in Djibouti, strategic outposts in Beijing's new commercial empire. Apart from building a new port at Kyaukpyu in Myanmar, the Chinese are also involved in similar projects in Gwadar in Pakistan, Chittagong in Bangladesh and Hambantota and Colombo in Sri Lanka. For the first time in history, China is emerging as an Indian Ocean power.

Diego Garcia, an atoll in the British Indian Ocean Territory, Britain's last colonial outpost east of Suez, is one of America's biggest and most important military bases overseas. It is used by the US Navy as well as the US Air Force, and provides logistical support to United States forces deployed throughout the Middle East and Afghanistan. The base also houses signals intelligence equipment, satellite tracking facilities – and, it was alleged during the first years of President George W. Bush's 'War on Terror', a Central Intelligence Agency detention facility to which terror suspects from Afghanistan and elsewhere were rendered, held and interrogated. Not surprisingly, the United States is watching developments at the Chinese base in Djibouti and elsewhere with intense interest.

India, China's main regional rival, is also acutely concerned about its penetration into the Indian Ocean, which New Delhi has always considered its own 'lake'. Moreover Chinese submarine activity has been detected ominously close to India's Andaman and Nicobar Islands. There were also, in the 1990s, reports suggesting that China had helped the Myanmar navy install a signals intelligence facility on the Coco Islands, a Myanmar possession north of the Andamans. In 2001, India created a new military unit to protect its interests in the Indian Ocean: the Andaman and Nicobar Command. Significantly, it was set up as a result of a 1995 closed-door meeting in Washington, DC, between then Indian Prime Minister P.V. Narasimha Rao and then President Bill Clinton. Initially designated as the Far Eastern Naval Command, it was later expanded to include all three services of India's armed forces: the army, the air force and the navy.

Headquartered in Port Blair, the capital of the Andaman and Nicobar Islands, an Indian Union Territory, this joint command provides logistical and administrative support to Indian naval vessels in the region as well as ships which allied nations have deployed in the Indian Ocean. The Indian navy remains one of the strongest and most powerful in the Indian Ocean, and to counter China's growing influence, India has also announced that it intends to set up a naval base in the Seychelles. If the plan becomes reality, it will be India's first overseas military base.[7]

India's concerns are not confined to the waters south of Myanmar and around the Andaman and Nicobar Islands. Its main adversary,

Pakistan, has had a military and political relationship with China for decades, and long before the Myanmar Corridor was established the Chinese had built a highway over the Karakoram mountains, connecting Xinjiang in westernmost China with Pakistan. Construction began as early as 1959 and the highway was completed and opened to the public in 1979. Strategically it is an important route – Pakistan is the only country apart from Myanmar and India that borders China which also has an Indian Ocean coast – but for trade it cannot compare with the Myanmar Corridor. Xinjiang is too far from China's industrial centres, and the highway reaches an elevation of 4,714 metres above sea level, a dangerous climb for any commercial vehicle. On the other hand, China has helped Pakistan develop and upgrade the port of Gwadar on the coast, which, like Kyaukpyu in Myanmar – and Chittagong in Bangladesh and Hambantota in Sri Lanka, old ports which have recently been upgraded with Chinese assistance – forms part of the string of Indian Ocean ports China invested in before and after President Xi launched his Belt and Road Initiative in 2013.

Another, little known, Indian Ocean power is France. The islands of Réunion and Mayotte are French *départements d'outre-mer*, which means that French is the official language, the inhabitants are citizens of the French Republic and their islands are part of the European Union. France maintains a marine airborne regiment on Réunion and a detachment of the French Foreign Legion is based on Mayotte.

South of Réunion lies the huge Indian Ocean island of Kerguelen, which together with the Crozet Archipelago and the Amsterdam and St. Paul islands make up the *Terres australes et antarctiques françaises*, or TAAF, an overseas French territory. None of those islands has any permanent population, but they serve as bases for French scientists and contingents of military personnel. Kerguelen has a satellite and rocket tracking station, which goes to show how important France believes it is to maintain a strategic foothold in the Indian Ocean. Even more peculiar is the French presence on the so-called *Îles Éparses de l'Océan Indien*, five islets much further to the north which also belong to TAAF: Tromelin, north of Mauritius, and Juan de Nova, Europa, Bassas da India and the Glorioso Islands around Madagascar. Some of them have small airfields, and, occasionally, soldiers are stationed on those islands as well, although all of them are classified as 'nature reserves'. Put together, all these French possessions in the Indian Ocean give France jurisdiction over an Exclusive Economic Zone encompassing more then 2.5 million square kilometres of maritime territory.

France, a member of the North Atlantic Treaty Organization, or NATO, and therefore a US defence partner, has, however, kept a low profile to protect whatever hidden secrets there are on its far-flung islands. But the French have a very active military base in their former colony of Djibouti, where the United States has an air force base from which drones are sent to attack targets in the Middle East. Japanese and Italian forces are also present in Djibouti, which, with the latest addition to foreign military bases on its soil – the Chinese facility – has emerged as a nerve centre for espionage and clandestine activities in the Indian Ocean region.

Australia, another regional power, possesses Christmas Island south of the Indonesian island of Java, and the Cocos (Keeling) Islands further out in the Indian Ocean. Those are small dots on the map which together are home to fewer than 2,000 inhabitants, but the Cocos boast a 2,440 metre-long runway on its West Island, underscoring the lightly populated atoll's strategic importance. The rest of West Island is a tropical idyll, replete with coconut palms, white sandy beaches and a crystal clear lagoon full of tropical fish. There are signals intelligence facilities on the Cocos, and the Indian Navy has approached the Australian government to discuss the possibility of Indian ships docking there for maintenance and resupply.

To counter China's increasingly assertive stand in the region, a new alliance has been formed. It consists – informally, of course, so as not to upset Beijing – of the United States, India, France, Australia and even Japan, which is not an Indian Ocean power. Japan has territorial disputes with China, not here but rather in the East China Sea over a group of islands that the Japanese call Senkaku and the Chinese Diaoyutai, and is watching developments in the Indian Ocean with concern as well. China is Japan's main economic and political rival in the region, and relations between the two countries have long been verging on hostility. The Indians have also been apprehensive of, and even hostile to, China since the two countries fought a short but bitter border war in 1962, which led to a crushing defeat for India and a still unsettled border dispute.

Now, two nationalist prime ministers – Narendra Modi in New Delhi, and Shinzo Abe in Tokyo – govern India and Japan, and relations between those two countries have grown close and cordial under their leadership. Since 2007, India, Japan, the US, Australia and Singapore have, in different combinations, conducted joint naval exercises codenamed 'Exercise Malabar'. In the beginning, the annual exercises were held in the sea south of Japan, but they have since then been held in the Bay of Bengal, off the west coast of India, and in the Arabian Sea. In 2017, the United States, India and Japan participated, while Australia and Singapore did not, perhaps so as not to provoke Beijing into believing that there is some kind of grand anti-Chinese alliance in the region – which in fact there is.

Even if France does not take part in Exercise Malabar, its president, Emmanuel Macron, signed an agreement with Indian Prime Minister Modi in New Delhi on 11 March 2018 for the two countries to access each other's naval facilities in the Indian Ocean. Macron, who was on a state visit to India, stated that 'stability in the Indian Ocean region is very important to the stability of the entire region, and we are with India for freedom.'[8] China was not, of course, mentioned in his statement, while his host Modi simply said that 'both of us believe that in future the Indian Ocean will play a very important role in the happiness, progress and prosperity of the world. Whether it is the environment, or maritime security, or marine resources, or the freedom of navigation and over flight, we are committed to strengthening our cooperation in those areas.'[9] France may so far have kept a low profile, but it is becoming evident on whose side it stands in the new Cold War that is emerging in the Indian Ocean.

Then there are the smaller and often neglected independent nations in the Indian Ocean: Mauritius, Seychelles, Maldives and Comoros, whose territorial waters control huge exclusive economic zones through which pass regional trade routes – and which are vulnerable to Chinese penetration. Maldives, which traditionally has been close to India, is now for the first time establishing close contacts with China. Beijing and New Delhi are vying for influence in Seychelles and even Mauritius, an old Indian ally, is moving closer to China. Comoros, a politically unstable Islamic republic, has also found a new ally in the PRC.

Like many other small island nations, they have few if any natural resources and their production bases are minimal. Therefore, they have capitalised on their natural beauty to promote themselves, and very successfully so, as tourist destinations. But apart from accepting aid from China, they have also been involved in other, less legitimate ways of raising revenue. Mauritius and Seychelles have followed the example of several island nations and territories in the Pacific Ocean and the West Indies and developed themselves into financial centres for offshore banking, tax havens, and as bases for insurance companies.

In order to understand the dynamics of the Indian Ocean with its scattered islands, some belonging to countries in the region, others to distant powers, and several of which are independent nations, one needs to consider the history that shaped them into what they are today. All those territories have a tangled and politically turbulent past, with European colonisers using some as penal colonies, while importing labour from India to others, with slave traders bringing in people from Africa to yet others, and, in more recent years many playing host to pirates, gun runners, money launderers, coups and intervention by mercenaries – and now they are entering a new era, where Chinese investment and geopolitical power plays will determine in what direction these Indian Ocean nations and territories are headed.

Then there are countries on the African and Asian mainland like tiny Djibouti, turbulent Pakistan, war-ravaged Sri Lanka, and Myanmar with a decades-long, complex ethnic civil war adding to the uncertainties of China's designs for the Indian Ocean region. And it all began in the early 1990s with the construction of a new bridge on the Ruili River and a grand monument that stated China's designs for the future of the entire region.

1

THE NEW CASABLANCA

Many small countries with a limited population base and no minerals or manufactured goods to export have become tax havens or set up flags-of-convenience registration for global shipping. If they are fortunate enough to be blessed with beautiful beaches, they turn themselves into tourist paradises.

Djibouti has chosen a completely different path to earn badly needed foreign exchange, exploiting its strategic location at the entry point to the Red Sea and Suez Canal. It leases out its territory to foreign countries that want to set up military bases. Djibouti, the third smallest country on the African mainland after Gambia and Eswatini (formerly known as Swaziland), consists of little more than salt lakes, extinct volcanoes, limestone cliffs and rugged canyons, hence it is little wonder that Djibouti's leaders had the imagination to find a way of raising revenue in order to sustain its status as an independent nation. Even the straits off Djibouti are called Bab el-Mandab, Arabic for 'the Gate of Tears'.

The much written about Chinese base in Djibouti, which was formally opened in August 2017 and covers 36 hectares of land, is leased for US$20 million a year. In 2018, it housed about 1,000 troops, although there is space for 10,000 if necessary.[1] It may be Beijing's first military base abroad – but it is far from the only foreign military facility in Djibouti. The former colonial power, France, naturally, has the oldest bases in the country, now hosting some 1,350 navy and air force personnel. After the terrorist attacks in New York and Washington on 11 September 2001, the United States took over Camp Lemonnier, an old French Foreign Legion base, and turned it into a modern military facility. It is the only permanent US military base in Africa and it is there, it has been said, to combat terrorist threats emanating from Yemen and neighbouring Somalia. The United States has some 4,000 soldiers, including a large contingent of Special Forces, stationed at Camp Lemonnier along with aircraft, drones and naval ships. Japan's only foreign military base is also in Djibouti. The Italians have their own base, while troops from Germany and Spain are hosted by the French.[2] Most recently, Saudi Arabia and the United Arab Emirates have also announced plans to build military bases in Djibouti.[3]

All of them claim they are there to combat terrorists or Somali pirates, or both, or to carry out humanitarian rescue missions on the African continent. But, in actuality, Djibouti City, the capital with the same name as the republic, is beginning to resemble Casablanca of the 1940s: a Francophone place of intrigue where everybody seems to be spying on everybody else. Djibouti City, home to more than 70 per cent of the country's 942,000 people, is divided into a European Quarter with whitewashed colonial-style houses, cafés, bars and restaurants where the expatriates meet – and the more chaotic African Quarter with its mosques and busy local markets. A recent visitor to Djibouti recalls that he 'witnessed French and Japanese soldiers competing for the attention of local prostitutes in the... nightclubs, and the Chinese and Americans using every opportunity to take pictures of each other's equipment and logistics.'[4] A local Djibouti commander told the visitor that 'after Chinese sailors kept taking unauthorised photos of an American destroyer, he was asked to step in to provide some order.'[5]

Traditionally, Djibouti's economy depended almost entirely on trade, and that, besides the bases, remains an important source of income. 70 per cent of the activity in Djibouti's port consists of the import and export of goods to and from Ethiopia, which after the loss of its coastal areas in Eritrea in 1993 became completely landlocked. In that year, Eritrea became independent after a bloody civil war that claimed more than 100,000 lives. A UN supervised referendum ended that war, peace was restored – but it meant also that Ethiopia was separated from the sea by a new nation which saw its former overlords as enemies.

As a consequence, 95 per cent of all exports from Ethiopia had to pass through Djibouti, much along a new 756-kilometre railway from Addis Ababa. The governments of Ethiopia and Djibouti own the railway on their respective sides of the border, but until the end of 2023, two Chinese companies – the state-owned China Railway Group and the China Civil Engineering Construction Corp., a private business – undertake all operations. Those two companies also built the standard gauge railway, which replaced an older, metre-gauge line built by the French at the turn of the last century. The cost of the new project was US$4 billion, and China's Exim Bank provided a loan that made it possible.[6]

However, Djibouti's role as the sole conduit for Ethiopia's maritime trade may change. The leaders of Ethiopia and Eritrea met on 8 July 2018 to reconcile their differences, ending years of hostilities between the two countries. Border skirmishes continued even after Eritrea's independence in 1993, and the two nations did not have diplomatic relations. Now, as relations between Ethiopia and Eritrea appear to have been normalised, it could open an alternative route for Ethiopian exports. Eritrea's main port, Massawa, once served as the headquarters of the now defunct Ethiopian Navy as well as a thriving centre for the nation's overseas trade. If the peace between Ethiopia and Eritrea holds, Djibouti stands to lose from the rapprochement between the two former enemies. Currently, profits from Ethiopia's use of Djiboutian ports top US$1 billion annually, and are a key source of government revenue.[7]

Apart from its geostrategic location, which was easy to sell to foreign interests, Djibouti is also a haven of relative stability in the Horn of Africa, one of the world's most volatile regions. To the south Djibouti borders Somalia, or to be precise, Somaliland, a self-declared state. Somaliland is far more peaceful than the rest of Somalia, which has been devastated by civil wars or is ruled by terrorists and tribal chieftains. Somaliland has political contacts with Djibouti, Ethiopia, South Africa, Sweden and the United Kingdom, but is not formally recognised as an independent nation by any other country. Officially, it is only an 'autonomous region' of Somalia. Historically, Somaliland comprises the former British Somaliland which merged with Italian Somaliland to become the Republic of Somalia in 1960.

The French gained a foothold in the region in the 1880s and a colony called French Somaliland was established in 1896. It was known under that name until 1967, when it was renamed The French Territory of the Afars and the Issas, a reference to the two main ethnic groups in the colony. It was not until 1977 that it became an independent republic called Djibouti, the last of the French possessions on the African mainland to win freedom. But here, as elsewhere in former French Africa, France has maintained a high degree of political, military and economic influence.

North of Djibouti lies Eritrea, in effect a one-party dictatorship where no general election has taken place since it became an independent country after the UN supervised referendum in 1993. Once an Italian colony, Eritrea was occupied by Britain during World War II and came under Ethiopian rule in 1950. And to the west is Ethiopia, a huge country with a population of more than 100 million, which from 1974 to 1991 was ruled by a brutal, Marxist-Leninist regime. During the reign of the Dergue, at least half a million people lost their lives as a result of executions, forced deportations, and starvation. Now officially a democracy with one of the fastest growing economies in Africa, Ethiopia is still plagued by fraud during elections, severe human-rights violations, corruption, de facto authoritarian rule, and, in certain areas, regional insurgencies.

The Chinese declared when they opened their base in Djibouti in 2017 that the facility had nothing to do with military expansion and that it would be no more than a supply centre for their peacekeeping and humanitarian missions in the continent.[8] But to many others, the base signifies China's growing role in Africa and Beijing's determination to secure its expanding interests in the Indian Ocean region. As the Russian journalist Andrei Kots points out, China's People's Liberation Army Navy (PLAN) currently has more than 70 amphibious and military transport ships. Most of them are capable of operating far from China's shores, and Beijing plans to increase the number of its marines from 20,000 to 100,000.[9] Kots argues that new Chinese support bases and logistic hubs may soon appear in Tajikistan, Pakistan and Afghanistan to ensure the security of China's Belt and Road Initiative (BRI). That could also lead to the creation of new Chinese military bases in the Indian and Pacific Oceans, all to protect the 'Silk Road Economic Belt' through Central Asia as well as the '21st Century Maritime Silk Road' on the high seas.

China has already established bases on the Spratlys, tiny reefs that it has turned into islands in the South China Sea. China considers those islands its own territory but they are also claimed in whole or in part by the Philippines, Vietnam, Malaysia, Brunei and Taiwan. Although Beijing has denied it, Gwadar in Pakistan has been mentioned as a possible new naval base for China. In early 2018, reports in the Australian media suggested that the Chinese aim to establish a naval base in Vanuatu in the Pacific Ocean, which, again, was denied by China.[10] But it would be surprising if the facility in Djibouti was not only the first but also the last overseas Chinese base.

And rather than being a new Chinese centre for 'peacekeeping and humanitarian missions', it is obvious that Djibouti played a role in Beijing's designs for the wider region even before President Xi Jinping launched his BRI in 2013 and the base was decided upon. China and Djibouti established diplomatic relations in 1979, and, since then, China has financed in Djibouti a stadium, a hospital, new offices for the Ministry of Foreign Affairs, other public buildings, and a so-called 'People's Palace', a kind of cultural centre. Beginning in 1986, China has also provided scholarships for Djibouti students to study at Chinese universities and China has sent medical teams to work in Djibouti.[11] The Chinese have long been aware of Djibouti's strategic location and relative political stability, and the tiny country began to serve as China's gateway to Africa and part of the Arab world as far back as the 1980s.

The need for a Chinese presence in that part of the world became a matter of some urgency when China became a net importer of oil in 1993 and later of natural gas in 2007. Until then, energy had been provided by China's coal mines and oil fields, but the fast growing economy required more than the domestic production could account for. After spending most of the twentieth century virtually energy independent, China is now importing nearly 8 per cent of its coal, 22 per cent of its natural gas, and 60 per cent of its oil needs.[12] While a sizable share of China's oil imports come via pipeline from Central Asia, as much as 80 per cent originate in the Middle East and Africa.[13]

In December 2008, before the base in Djibouti was built, China dispatched a naval flotilla of PLAN ships to conduct its own escort mission off the Horn of Africa. It was said to be part of an anti-piracy mission, but it was also the first such foray into the Indian Ocean since the fifteenth-century explorer and mariner Zheng He sailed to Africa 600 years ago. It was evident that piracy was not the only thing on the minds of the Chinese when their ships were testing the waters off the Horn of Africa and the entrance to the Red Sea. Jeff M. Smith, a US observer, noted that the deployment gave the PLAN 'valuable experience operating in ports in Djibouti, Oman, Yemen, and Pakistan for resupply and refuelling and provided an ideal chance for the PLAN to practice and evaluate various blue water tactics, techniques and procedures in an environment far from the Chinese periphery, without generating significant political or military alarm.'[14] Plans for a permanent base in that maritime region must have been on the agenda as well. And reasonably stable Djibouti became the natural choice.

As Smith points out, 'securing and diversifying China's energy imports was one of the premier foreign policy initiatives of the Hu Jintao administration.' Hu, China's president from 2003 to 2012, oversaw a decade of consistent growth of the Chinese economy. It was also during his tenure that infrastructure was improved – and Beijing hosted the 2008 Olympics. He was seen as a moderniser and China appeared somewhat freer under his leadership. His successor, Xi, is a moderniser as well – but also a strict authoritarian. Censorship has been significantly stepped up under Xi. Pro-democracy activists have been arrested, among them Xu Zhiyong, the founder of the New Citizens' Movement, and Pu Zhiqiang, a civil rights lawyer. Many bloggers have stopped writing on social media for fear of being picked up by the authorities.

Xi is seen as having amassed more power in his hands than any Chinese leader since Mao Zedong. In March 2018, the National People's Congress, China's rubber stamp legislature, passed a set of amendments to the constitution including removal of term limits set for the President and the Vice President. Previously, they could serve only two five-year terms. Under the new law, there are no limits and

Xi can at least theoretically be president for life. In the days after the event, Chinese censors were busy tracking down and erasing references on social media to 'the new leader, Xi Zedong.'[15]

With such a strongman in charge, it is hardly surprising that China wants to protect its vital supply of energy from the Middle East and Africa as well as general trade routes across the Indian Ocean. And with economic growth comes visions of grandeur, a hallmark of Xi's presidency. While China has never before launched anything as extravagant and far-reaching as the BRI, it is the logical consequence of its economic expansion, and with it comes the need to forge alliances with countries in the Indian Ocean region. That policy actually manifested itself long before the BRI through the Karakoram Highway, the Myanmar Corridor, the military reach into the South China Sea, and even in engagement with the small but strategically important countries Comoros, Seychelles, Mauritius and Maldives which are all located in the Indian Ocean. And, for that matter, with Djibouti, a country closer to the sources of China's energy needs.

According to the Chinese foreign ministry's website entry on Djibouti, 'mutually beneficial cooperation between the two sides began in 1982'. Then came China's need to import oil from the Middle East and the desire for a firmer presence in the region. In 1998 China and Djibouti signed a trade agreement, and by 2002 bilateral trade stood at US$49.83 million, of which China's exports to Djibouti accounted for US$49.81 million and imports from the African nation stood at US$20,000.'[16] These are hardly amazing figures in a global context, but they are significant for a small country like Djibouti. And the trade imbalance between the two countries is also worth noting. Hundreds of contracts have been signed with Chinese companies, which, apart from the railway, have undertaken projects such as the construction of a school and bank in Djibouti.[17]

China's growing interest in the Indian Ocean region did not go unnoticed in Washington, where as far back as 2005 strategic thinkers began talking about a 'String of Pearls' – a series of planned Chinese bases, or bases which China would have access to – stretching from the Middle East to Pakistan, Sri Lanka, Bangladesh and Myanmar. The term was first used to describe China's emerging maritime strategy in a report published that year and titled 'Energy Futures in Asia' by US defence contractor Booz Allen Hamilton, a strategy which was elaborated in a more comprehensive paper written in 2006 by Christopher J. Pehrson for the US Army War College.[18]

Pehrson argued that the 'String of Pearls' would serve as a litmus test for the future course of US-China relations and went on to identify potential sources of conflict between the two superpowers such as the Korean peninsula and Taiwan. More importantly, Pehrson argued that 'as a maritime power, the United States cannot afford to relinquish its role as security guarantor in the "String of Pearls" region or any other area of strategic interest in Asia.'[19]

The United States needs its blue water navy in the Indian Ocean 'to project power from the sea,' Pehrson argued, 'as demonstrated by the US Navy's offshore bombing and cruise missile strikes conducted during recent combat operations in Afghanistan and Iraq.'[20] And, Pehrson wrote, 'today, the seas are no longer empty, and, as China develops its capabilities to venture beyond its shores, it is increasingly likely to encounter US maritime presence. China's growing interests and influence along the "String of Pearls", primarily driven by the need to secure energy resources and trade routes, present a complex strategic situation that could impact the future direction of China's relationship with the United States, as well as China's relationship with neighbours throughout the region.'[21]

Billy Tea, an Asian writer on regional security issues, dismissed those concerns as 'alarmist', arguing that there is still scant concrete evidence that China is 'currently or in the near future planning to build and maintain military bases along its SLOC (sea lines of communications). Indeed, to date the controversial theory is based more on speculation than fact.'[22] Tea listed the same Chinese port projects in the region as Pehrson did in his paper, but argued that those were meant only to facilitate civilian trade, and were not associated with any military activity.

But it would be foolish to assume that China would not be interested in defending its vital trade routes – and, especially, all the projects that come under the multi-trillion dollar BRI. So far, roughly 70 countries have joined the project which is supposed to run until 2049, the 100th anniversary of the founding of the People's Republic of China and Xi's target date for establishing the country as 'fully developed, rich and powerful.'[23]

Estimates of the exact sums China will spend on the BRI vary depending on who is calculating the cost. The lowest estimate, US$1 trillion, is based on promised infrastructure investment. The highest estimate, US$8 trillion, comes from a 2016 commentary in the *Hong Kong Economic Journal*, which stated: 'The financial experts at the State Council have estimated that "One Belt, One Road" would cost as much as US$8 trillion if it was fully implemented following Xi's orders.'[24] Xi himself has stated that, 'through the BRI, a peaceful, prosperous, open, innovative, and civilized world will be built.'[25]

The levels of Chinese investment also vary widely from country to country. Pakistan has been promised US$60 billion to upgrade its roads, railways and ports. South Korea has signed up for its share of BRI funding, but, as of 2017, it had no Chinese projects at all.[26] The haphazard nature of the BRI is also seen in India, a vocal critic of the plan and certainly not one of the signatories. Even so, a 2018 report by the Washington-based think-tank the Centre for Strategic and International Studies stated that 'an industrial park in Gujarat…would easily be branded as a BRI project elsewhere.'[27]

Work on a US$1 billion Chinese industrial park in Sanand in Gujarat began in 2016 under a Memorandum of Understanding signed the year before between the China Development Bank and the Gujarat government. And, not surprisingly, *the Global Times*, an official Chinese news site, also described it as part of China's broader plan for becoming the world's leading economic power: 'Led by the China Association of Small and Medium Enterprises (CASME), the China Industrial Park in India, a "One Belt One Road" pilot project, aims to build an international investment platform, helping Chinese SMEs go global…given the strategic opportunities brought by promotion of the "Belt and Road Initiative", Chinese small and medium enterprises are encouraged to actively explore the Indian market, said Li Zibin, president of CASME.'[28]

Gujarat, the home state of Prime Minister Narendra Modi, a staunch Indian nationalist, may, after all, be an exception. India's criticism of the BRI was articulated by India's Foreign Secretary Vijay Gokhale in his first public remark since he took over the post on 29 January 2018: 'The experience has been that while initially the appearance of free money or cheap money, as well as the quick execution of projects, which we have to admit, is very much a part of the Chinese modalities, was attractive to a number of those countries and they signed up very quickly to doing these projects.'[29]

Then Gokhale began to mention examples of China's controversial projects, and the effect those have had on the economies of weaker countries in the region. His first example was Sri Lanka whose government had to lease out land in order to service its loans to China. The result of the deal was that the China Merchants Port Holding company got a majority stake for 99 years in the Hambantota port for US$1.1 billion.[30] Gokhale went on to mention Bangladesh, where what were supposed to be soft loans from China for infrastructural projects are turning into something else. 'There has been some rethinking there,' Gokhale said. The Chinese loans turned out to be governed by 'interest rates comparable to international interest rates' coupled with an insistence on 'buying Chinese equipment rather than tendering on international basis.'[31]

Gokhale referred to a similar rethinking in Myanmar. The sheer size of the port of Kyaukpyu 'does not appear to be something that the Myanmar government is going to utilise in the next few weeks.'[32] Just before the 2015 election in Myanmar, China had granted the then government a US$100 million loan – but not a single dollar actually crossed the Myanmar border. The money was used to buy agricultural implements and machinery from China, which turned out to be useless. But the loan has to be repaid, which cash-strapped Myanmar can ill afford.[33] Although it has not yet happened, the fear in Myanmar is that China could drop the repayment of that loan in exchange for more trading and investment privileges in Kyaukpyu. That could also include a Chinese military presence.

On 3 May 2018, Takehiko Nakao, the president of the Manila-based Asian Development Bank (ADB), warned countries in the region against unsustainable borrowing to fund infrastructure projects, which he said could leave them stuck in a dept trap. Nakao referred specifically to the BRI, saying that although the ADB would cooperate with China when appropriate, caution would have to be exercised when borrowing money to cover infrastructure gaps.[34]

Nakao was not alone in warning countries about the dangers inherent in poorer countries' placing their hopes for a brighter future on the BRI. In April 2018, the International Monetary Fund director Christine Lagarde told a conference in China that the BRI could put a heavier burden on countries already saddled with a lot of public debt.[35] Where it will all end is an open question, but it is indisputable that China is not dishing out vast amounts of dollars in grants and loans simply because it wants to see other countries develop and prosper.

Pehrson's analysis of China's geostrategic aims in his aforementioned paper from 2006 was dismissed by many at the time as being overly pessimistic, but with the launch of the BRI he has turned out to be rather prophetic. While striving to assume for China a more significant, if not dominant, global leadership role, a crucial part of the BRI is to develop, and, if possible, seize control of, a string of ports across the Indian Ocean and beyond.

To endow China's new policies with some historical legitimacy, Beijing's policymakers and commentators have elevated Zheng He to the position of a national hero. A Muslim eunuch from Yunnan, he was largely forgotten until the 1990s when stories of his exploits began to appear in the official Chinese media. Statues of Zheng He have been erected in a number of Chinese cities, among them Jinning south of Kunming, the capital of his home province Yunnan, Nanjing, Shanghai and – and, with Chinese assistance, even in Malaysia and Indonesia. Zheng He has been made into a symbol of modern China and its maritime ambitions and given a prominence he never had until quite recently. As professor Timothy Brook of the University of British Columbia in Canada has put it: 'The West had Columbus and the Chinese needed one.'[36]

Zheng He's voyages have even been mentioned by Chinese authorities to justify their claims to the Spratly Islands in the South China Sea.[37] He was supposed to have sailed past those islands and therefore they should belong to China – but that is a remark that requires qualification. The detailed accounts and maps, which were compiled by Zheng He's aide Ma Huan, list more than 700 place names in Southeast Asia and the Indian Ocean, including remote islands in the Andamans, the Nicobars, Maldives and Lakshadweep.[38]

Chinese cartographers were no doubt aware of the existence and location of the Spratlys and Ma Huan mentioned them as well, but not in such great detail as other places in his logbooks. The reason is quite simple: the Spratlys are not actually islands, but treacherous shoals and underwater reefs, which the ancient navies – including Zheng He's fleet of wooden junks – sailed around to avoid being shipwrecked. But that has not prevented China from making its spurious assertions – and, most recently, literally cementing its claims. Any opposing view is branded an interference in China's internal affairs.

President Xi himself has brought up Zheng He in his speeches, referring to him as a 'friendly emissary' leading 'treasure-loaded ships' to build a bridge for peace and 'East-West cooperation'.[39] There may be little evidence to back up that claim, but China is forging ahead with its ambitious BRI regardless of historical realities. Besides establishing a military base in Djibouti, the Pakistani port of Gwadar is playing a crucial role in China's strategy for regional dominance. The construction of a deep-sea port at Gwadar began in 2001 and the first phase was completed in 2007. China both financed and constructed the port to open up a 3,000-kilometre long land route from the sea to the western city of Kashgar in Xinjiang.

In April 2015, China obtained 40-year management rights on the port and, as part of the BRI, will also invest in the construction of railways and roads, and, as has been suggested, even oil pipelines through Pakistan. But because of the long and difficult route over the Karakoram Mountains to Kashgar, it is doubtful whether it can be used to import oil from the Middle East. Moreover, given the treacherous terrain and remoteness of Kashgar, even bilateral trade would be limited.[40] The importance of the port at Gwadar lies in its location. It will firmly position China on the shores of the Arabian Sea and vis-à-vis 'the Pakistan Corridor' is of strategic rather than economic significance, irrespective of whether a free-trade zone is constructed near the port. Even Mushtaq Khan, an economist and former chief adviser at the State Bank of Pakistan admitted in an interview that China's primary interest in Pakistan is geopolitical rather than strictly economic.[41]

Gwadar was already seen as strategically important by early Arab seafarers as well as the Portuguese explorer Vasco da Gama, who tried unsuccessfully to occupy the town with its then rather rudimentary port. In 1783, the Khan of Khalat, a Baluchi ruler, granted sovereignty over Gwadar to the Sultan of Muscat, a seafaring nation on the Arabian Peninsula. Muscat, later known as Oman and Muscat before finally becoming only Oman, thus gained a foothold on the coast of today's Pakistan. Until 1856, its sultans also controlled Zanzibar on the coast of Africa, which was an important entrepot for the slave trade. As a reminder of the once mighty Muscat and Oman sultanate, there are still today small communities of Africans in southern Pakistan. They are called *siddi* and, apart from being descendants of slaves, they also trace their origin to African sailors, mercenaries and traders.

Muscat and Oman became a British protectorate in 1891, though it enjoyed a high degree of autonomy and the Gwadar enclave was never part of British India. But the sultan's interest in the enclave on the coast of what in 1947 became the independent nation of Pakistan began to decline in the 1950s. The sultan, who became the ruler of a fully independent nation in 1951, offered Gwadar to India, which may seem incongruous given its location. But ties between Muscat and Oman and India were strong in the past. The Indian rupee was actually Muscat and Oman's only currency until 1940. It continued to circulate even after that and it was not until 1959 that the Gulf rupee took over altogether. In 1970 Muscat and Oman finally got its own currency, the rial. In the same year, it also finally abolished slavery. In that year, the name of the country was changed from Muscat and Oman to simply Oman.

India, however, was not interested in taking over Gwadar so the sultan of Oman turned to Pakistan which in 1958 bought it for US$3 million. These days, as Gwadar is becoming an important trading post, Indian security analysts speculate, half-jokingly, what would have happened had India accepted the sultan's offer and acquired a foothold on the coast of Pakistan.

In 1954, when Gwadar was still under Omani rule, it was identified as a suitable site for a deep-water port by the United States Geological Survey at the request of the Pakistani government. However its potential remained untapped until the Chinese moved in with their construction crews in the early 2000s. And most of the workers on the port project were brought in from China, rather than being recruited locally.

But how secure is Gwadar? Pakistan seems to stagger from one political crisis to another and has never managed to become a functioning democracy like India, from which it was separated when British rule ended with Partition in 1947. Moreover Gwadar is part of Baluchistan, one of the most volatile of Pakistan's five provinces, which has been wracked by a low-intensity insurgency protesting the province's exploitation by the government in Islamabad and, later, by Chinese economic interests. When the American writer Robert Kaplan visited the area in 2008, ethnic Baluchi rebels told him that they 'would never permit roads and pipelines to be built there, until their grievances with the Pakistani government in faraway Islamabad were settled.'[42] Gwadar is where dreams clash with reality, according to Kaplan. And reality struck with a vengeance when, on 23 November 2018, heavily armed militants attacked the Chinese consulate in Karachi. Seven people were killed, including two policemen, two civilians and the three attackers. Separatist Baluchi rebels claimed responsibility for the attack saying that, 'we have been seeing the Chinese as an oppressor, along with Pakistani forces' which are 'destroying the future of Baluchistan.'[43] Pakistani prime minister Imran Khan described the attack as 'part of [a] conspiracy' against Pakistan's 'economic and strategic cooperation' with China.[44] But immediately after the attack, a Chinese foreign ministry spokesman stated that it would not affect relations between China and Pakistan. 'China and Pakistan are all-weather strategic cooperative partners,' the spokesman said.[45]

Pakistan may be China's most faithful ally in the region – and even more so after US President Donald Trump in one of his first tweets of 2018 accused Pakistan of deceiving his administration and harbouring terrorists while accepting billions in dollars in aid from Washington.[46] Some US aid to Pakistan was cut and it may be reduced even further, if Trump gets his way. The response to the tweet in the streets of Pakistan cities was swift: noisy demonstrations denouncing Trump. The Pakistan government also reacted angrily. Shahid Khaqan Abbasi, Pakistan's prime minister, called a meeting with the country's National Security Committee, which expressed its 'deep disappointment' over the president's comments.[47]

Pakistan-based terrorists are also a problem for the Chinese, perhaps even more so than some rag-tag bands of ethnic rebels in Baluchistan. In December 2017, China warned its nationals in Pakistan of plans for a series of imminent 'terrorist attacks' on Chinese targets in the country.[48] The concern is, of course, for the thousands of workers from China who have gone to Pakistan to implement the BRI, and whether they can be protected. In a surprise move in December 2017, following allegations of corruption, China halted funding of at least three major road projects that were part of the BRI. The announcement left Pakistani officials 'stunned', according to media reports.[49]

But China's alliance with Pakistan is far too important to be seriously disrupted by such concern. Andrew Small, an analyst of China and Pakistan, noted that 'Pakistan is the only friendship China has that has been tested over the decades, commands deep support from across the political spectrum and institutions of state, and has a base of public support that is so high that it is a striking outlier in any opinion survey of how China is perceived abroad.'[50] That said, if Islamic militants step up their activities in Pakistan, and, more importantly, link up with like-minded elements in Xinjiang, which has a huge, disgruntled Muslim population, China may have to reassess that friendship. Among Muslim activists in Pakistan and elsewhere, discontent is growing over China's treatment of the Uighurs, Xinjiang's Muslim population.[51] To what extent Uighur militants actually operate from Pakistani territory is uncertain and the government in Islamabad has always refuted such claims. But, in 2012, China urged the Pakistan government to expel Uighur militants who they said had sought sanctuary in Pakistan's tribal areas. China said such groups, with links to al-Qaeda, were responsible for the unrest in Xinjiang.[52]

International human rights organisations like Amnesty International and Human Rights Watch have released numerous reports on the treatment of the Uighurs. Amnesty's report for 2017/2018 says that numerous detention facilities have been set up in Xinjiang, 'variously called "counter extremism centres", "political study centres", or "education and transformation centres", in which people were arbitrarily detained for unspecified periods and forced to study Chinese laws and policies.'[53] Human Rights Watch reported that the authorities 'in recent years have increased mass surveillance measures across the region, augmenting existing tactics with the latest technologies. Since around April 2016, Human Rights Watch estimates, Xinjiang authorities have sent tens of thousands of Uighurs and other ethnic minorities to "political education centres".'[54] In some of those re-education camps, the inmates are forced to drink alcohol and eat pork, both of which are taboos in any Muslim community.[55]

The Pakistan government and the country's mainstream politicians, who usually speak out against the treatment of Muslims in Palestine, Kashmir and Myanmar, have been conspicuously silent on the repression of the Uighur population in Xinjiang. But that is hardly surprising given the importance of the geostrategic and economic alliance with China.

That alliance also includes military cooperation, and the two countries have agreed to 'safeguard the security of the China-Pakistan Economic Corridor'.[56] But whether that extends to letting China set up a permanent naval base in Pakistan remains to be seen. Bill Gertz, writing for the *Washington Times*, seems to think so. He says there are indications the Chinese have visited an area east of Gwadar on the Sonmiani Bay, a region known for its advanced computer centres, and 'there are signs the Chinese are ready to build another port facility at that location.'[57] Whether the base is going to be there or at Gwadar is not clear but 'Chinese construction and military activities in the port appear similar to what China did in Djibouti.'[58] If correct, China would soon have two military bases from which they could monitor and protect vital oil shipping routes from the Middle East.

It should also be remembered that China's BRI projects do not consist of direct aid. Even when it comes to a long-term friend and ally like Pakistan, Chinese investment is tied to loans and credits. China forces Pakistan to buy Chinese equipment for use in Chinese projects – then Beijing extends loans to cover the purchases, sending Pakistan's debt soaring. Pakistan's debt is now US$91.8 billion, and the public debt-to-GDP ratio is 70 per cent, far higher than among other countries in the region. And about two-thirds of the early loans from China have been extended at what has been described as a 'usurious rate of interest', seven per cent.[59] China and Pakistan may be close allies, but this is not, as an Indian commentator put it, 'what friends do to each other.'[60]

The next pearl in the would be string is Hambantota on the southern coast of Sri Lanka. A new port and a huge airport were opened there in 2013. Construction began with US$8 billion borrowed from China shortly after the government's victory in the 27-year-long war against the LTTE (Tamil Tigers) in 2009. The then president, Mahinda Rajapaksa, had a dream of turning his ancestral home into a tourism and business powerhouse.[61]

Both projects turned out to be huge white elephants. The Mattala Rajapaksa International Airport near Hambantota has been called 'the world's emptiest international airport', and not without reason. The 10,000 square-metre terminal with 12 check-in counters can handle a million passengers a year, but hardly any airlines fly there. Some of the empty hangars are even rented out to locals to store rice.

US$190 million of the total cost for the construction of the airport, which amounted to US$209 million, was provided by the Chinese government through the Exim Bank of China.[62] But the main problem is the location, far from the capital Colombo and any tourist centres. Passengers have expressed unhappiness with having to wait for hours in what they described as the middle of the jungle.

The airport project was evidently an abysmal failure from a commercial point of view, so why would anyone be interested in buying into it? Yet that is exactly what India did in 2017. It pledged to pay US$300 million for a joint venture granting it a 40-year lease. That would buy out Sri Lanka's debt to China – and India would be able to keep Chinese influence on the island somewhat at bay. In that case it is immaterial if the airport is empty or not. Currently, it handles about a dozen passengers a day.

A key element in any overseas naval base, and even a logistics facility, Australian analyst David Brewster argues, is easy access by air for people and supplies. A naval base also requires maritime air surveillance capabilities. Control over the newly-built airport will give India considerable oversight over how the nearby port is used.[63] From that point of view, India's purchase makes perfect sense.

The port at Hambantota has fared no better commercially than the airport. International shipping companies had no interest in docking at Hambantota as there is an excellent port at Colombo. Only a handful of ships call at Hambantota and then mostly at the insistence of embarrassed Sri Lankan agencies.[64] Then came the bill. The Sri Lankan government could not repay its loans to the Chinese bank so it was forced to hand over ownership of the port to China in a debt-for-equity swap. Although the Sri Lankan authorities claim to have retained control over management of the port, the details are, as Brewster says, 'suspiciously murky'.[65] Brewster also argues that the Hambantota port project 'is held up as proof that the Belt and Road often involves foisting uneconomic projects on developing countries with loans that can never be repaid. According to critics, these projects will only damage long term economic development and make countries politically indebted to China.'[66]

Hambantota may be an unsuitable location for an ordinary container port, but New Delhi's suspicion that it is destined for another purpose – a logistics point for an expanded Chinese naval presence in the Indian Ocean – could well prove to be true. According to Brewster: 'Although Colombo has repeatedly claimed that no Chinese naval facility will be permitted in Sri Lanka, New Delhi worries that China's influence will one day reach a point where the Sri Lankan government simply cannot say no.'[67]

Sri Lanka, traditionally an Indian ally and close to Western powers, began to turn to China during the war with the LTTE. When the Sri Lankan military was accused of committing serious human rights abuses in its campaigns against the Tigers, China prevented the UN Security Council from putting the issue on its agenda. When the US ended direct military aid in 2007 as a response to Sri Lanka's abysmal human rights record, China increased its aid to nearly US$1 billion, Beijing becoming Sri Lanka's biggest donor.

The Independent reported on 22 May 2018 that China gave Sri Lanka 'tens of millions of dollars' worth of sophisticated weapons, and making a free gift of six F7 fighter jets to the Sri Lankan air force. China encouraged its ally Pakistan to sell more arms and to train pilots to fly the new planes. Suddenly, thanks to China's diplomacy, the hectoring of the US and Europe didn't matter any more. After nearly 500 years under the thumb of the West, the immensely strategic little island in the Indian Ocean had a new sugar daddy – one with a very different conception of its duties.'[68] India also lost an ally, and can now do little more than observe China's activities from the world's emptiest airport.

Further up the Indian Ocean into the Bay of Bengal lies Chittagong, the largest port on the southeastern coast of Bangladesh. There and beyond the tug of war between China and its rivals is even more evident than in Sri Lanka. In 2016, the Bangladesh government cancelled plans to build a Chinese-financed port at Sonadia in Cox's Bazar, 127 kilometres south of Chittagong. India immediately expressed interest in helping Bangladesh develop a new deep-sea port at Payra at the mouth of the Ganges, or Padma, a river delta south of the capital Dhaka. At the same time Japan has expressed interest in developing another deep-sea port at Matarbari near Cox's Bazar. China's countermove in the port war is to build a 750-acre industrial park in Chittagong. State-run China Harbour Engineering Company will hold a 70 per cent share in the proposed joint venture, which is being set up for the park with the Bangladesh Special Economic Zone Authority.[69] Before that, in 2010, China had agreed to finance a US$8.7 billion development of the port of Chittagong but work is progressing very slowly. Bangladesh will prove a sterner test for Bejing than Sri Lanka, at least while the cautiously pro-India Awami League is in power in Dhaka.

China realises that – which is the reason why Xi went to Bangladesh on a state visit in 2016, the first such visit by a Chinese head of state in 30 years. The Chinese are on the move even here, and the Reconnecting Asia Project of the Washington-based Centre for Strategic and International Studies has identified three key BRI projects in Bangladesh: the Dhaka-Jessore railway, a power plant at Payra, and the Karnaphuli Tunnel – the country's first-ever underwater tunnel. Chinese banks dominate the financing while Chinese contractors have taken over the actual construction of those projects.[70]

Then there is Kyaukpyu, across Bangladesh's border with Myanmar, where the Chinese are busy constructing what may become the most important pearl in the string after Gwadar. Pakistan and Myanmar may be only friendly neighbours, which share a border with China, and can therefore be seen as China's only direct 'corridors' to the Indian Ocean. But that also means that China has chosen to depend for the success of the BRI on two of the most politically unstable countries in Asia.

China is apparently prepared to take huge risks but it could, and should, also be argued that it still has a long way to go before it can challenge the United States in the Indian Ocean region. China has for now only the base in Djibouti. The United States has Diego Garcia, a much bigger military facility, and maintains nearly 800 small and big bases in more than 70 countries and territories across the globe, including Afghanistan, Bahrain, Qatar and Kuwait, not to mention those in Japan and South Korea. When it comes to overall military spending, the United States spent more on its military in 2017 than the next seven highest-spending countries combined, and those were China, Saudi Arabia, Russia, India, France and the United Kingdom. Total US defence spending in that year amounted to US$610 billion while Washington's Cold War foe Russia spent as little as US$66.3 billion. But China is number two on the list with US$228 billion – and that is a 110 per cent increase since 2008.[71]

It is the trend that is important. And the fact that China is moving into areas such as the Indian Ocean where it has had no presence for centuries. And everywhere the pattern is the same: loans which have to be repaid and if that cannot be done, China expects other privileges in return. This is not traditional colonialism, but a modus operandi that leads to dependence and undermines the fiscal and therefore also the political sovereignty of the indebted nations. And what will happen when China's military presence in the Indian Ocean region reaches a point where traditional powers such as the United States and India really feel threatened?

What may happen with the rise of China is that the United States will lose relative power and be unable to assert its hegemony over parts of the world such as the Indian Ocean region. As Bruno Maçães points out, 'we are entering the first period in human history in which modern technology will be combined with a chaotic international arena, in which no single actor or group of actors is capable of imposing order.'[72] He speculates that the coming wars may be armed conflicts, but they could also take radically different forms: 'struggles to control infrastructure, propaganda battles, tech races in artificial intelligence and robotics, cyberwar, and trade and economic warfare.'[73]

Djibouti is the place where all those fears, challenges and intrigues converge in a small piece of real estate. Among the most bizarre stories to have emerged from Djibouti in recent years came in April 2018 when the US military released a notice to its airmen warning about 'unauthorised laser activity'.[74] The notice said that 'there have been multiple lazing events involving high-powered laser in the vicinity of N1135.70' – coordinates which point at a location 750 metres from the Chinese base in Djibouti.[75]

The allegations, including a claim that two US air force pilots suffered eye injuries during one of those laser attacks, were swiftly denied by China's defence ministry, which dismissed them as being 'in complete contradiction of the facts.'[76]

But whatever it was and where it came from, it certainly increased tensions between the Chinese and the Western powers that have bases in Djibouti. *Jane's Defence Weekly* had a more detailed account of what may have happened: 'multiple intelligence sources report that China's People's Liberation Army Navy (PLAN) is suspected of operating a high-power lasing weapon at the base or on a ship offshore. The use of lasers to temporarily blind pilots has been increasing over the years and dates back to the Cold War when US Navy pilots were periodically attacked by lasers emanating from Soviet naval vessels and spy trawlers.'[77] Intelligence officers who had seen reports of the Djibouti incident told *Jane's* that they suspected the use of what was described as a 'blue-coloured laser', which is consistent with the type of laser weapons that have been used on board Russian and Chinese naval vessels for years.[78]

The already tense situation in Djibouti deteriorated after the incident and prompted fears that any hasty move by one foreign military force or another there could precipitate a clash that might, in turn, lead to a wider conflict. This is an ever-present danger when so many foreign military bases are crammed into such a small place.

And then there is the possibility of economic and political turmoil in the tiny republic. The bases may provide the government with an income, but as Simon Allison, a South African journalist, noted in a visit in 2018: 'Djibouti is going to struggle to keep up with the repayments on the enormous sums it has borrowed from China to build [a new] port, as well as another airport, a fancy new railway line linking Djibouti with Addis Ababa, and a 120-km water pipeline bringing fresh water from Ethiopia. The loans are worth at least US$1.1-billion, according to the International Monetary Fund.'[79]

Allison also reported that 'having invested so much in Djibouti's stability, superpowers are all too prepared to overlook the abuses by the Guelleh regime – well documented by Freedom House and others – in an effort to guarantee that stability.'[80] That hear-no-evil, see-no-evil strategy might backfire, Allison wrote, and went on to quote a local opposition politician as saying 'go to the poor areas, you will see that this country is not satisfied.'[81]

Ismail Omar Guelleh, Djibouti's president since 1999, is also Commander-in-chief of the country's military forces and wields enormous power. Demands for more democracy, which came in the wake of the Arab Spring in 2010, were quickly suppressed. There is hardly any opposition to speak of and Guelleh was re-elected with 80 per cent of the votes in the most recent presidential elections in April 2016. The main newspaper, *La Nation de Djibouti*, and the broadcaster, *Radiodiffusion Télévision de Djibouti* are controlled by the government. An opposition newspaper, *Le Renouveau*, was shut down in 2007 after publishing an article claiming that a local businessman had bribed Guelleh's brother-in-law, the national bank governor.[82] Although the publication of some opposition media is still being tolerated, strict libel laws lead journalists to practise self-censorship.

As recently as the early 1990s, there was even an armed conflict in the country between the ruling party, *Rassemblement populaire pour le Progrès* (RPP, the People's Rally for Progress), and the opposition *Front pour la Restoration de l'Unité et de la Démocratie* (the Front for the Restoration of Unity and Democracy). The conflict ended with a form of power-sharing agreement in 2000, but Guelleh, who the year before had succeeded his uncle and the country's first president Hassan Gouled Aptidon, remained the country's seemingly undisputed strongman. It is also often forgotten that Djibouti was a one-party state under the RPP from 1981 to 1992, when the multiparty system was re-introduced after a referendum. Yet it is fair to say that the RPP has controlled the legislature as well as the executive since the party was founded in 1979. Opposition parties have boycotted several elections, citing government control of the media and intimidation of candidates from parties other than the RPP.[83] Corruption within the administration is another serious problem. It is widespread but, according to Freedom House, efforts to curb it have met with little success because public officials are not required to disclose their assets.[84]

Mainly thanks to income from the bases, Djibouti's GDP has doubled in the past decade, from US$848 million in 2007 to US$ 1.7 billion in 2015, but 23 per cent of the population still lives in extreme poverty and 60 per cent of the workforce are unemployed.[85] There is also rising discontent with the Chinese presence in Djibouti. Locals complain that they, unlike staff at the other bases, bring in their own drivers, cooks and guards. Guelleh has gone out of his way to explain that China is a good friend. In an interview with *Afrique* magazine, quoted in Allison's article, Guelleh said: 'China is a genuine partner; indeed; the only one today that functions on co-operation on a long-term basis. China is our friend... They are unrivalled investors in Africa. They believe in our future, our emergence.'[86]

Djibouti, the oasis of stability in the Horn of Africa, could just as well be described as a political powder keg. Guelleh's position is far from secure and internal turmoil cannot be ruled out, especially if the gap between the rich and poor widens, which is likely to happen as lease payments for the bases keep rolling in but benefit only a few. Nor should China take for granted its friendship with smaller countries. Heavy dependence on Beijing could even backfire – as happened in another country bordering the Indian Ocean: Myanmar.

2

THE MYANMAR CORRIDOR

The announcement came as a bolt from the blue. In a speech before parliament in Myanmar's new capital Naypyitaw on 30 September 2011, President Thein Sein announced that his government had decided to suspend the construction of a hydroelectric power station with a mega dam at Myitsone in the far north of the country. 'It is contrary to the will of the people', he said.[1] The US$3.6 billion dam would have submerged 766 square-kilometres of forestland – and 90 per cent of the electricity produced would have gone to China. It was a joint venture between the state-owned China Power Investment Corporation, the Myanmar government's Ministry of Electric Power, and Asia World Company, a conglomerate owned by a Sino-Myanmar business tycoon.

Before the announcement was made, many people in Myanmar had demonstrated against the project. Pro-democracy leader Aung San Suu Kyi, then in opposition, had spoken out against it and so had Myanmar intellectuals and scientists. The dam was to be built at the confluence of the Mali Hka and Nmai Hka rivers, which form the beginning of the mighty Irrawaddy River which eventually empties out into the Bay of Bengal and the Indian Ocean.

'Myitsone' means 'meeting of rivers' and for the Kachins, the local tribesmen who inhabit the far north of the country, the site is of near-religious significance. And the Irrawaddy, which flows through the entire length of Myanmar, is itself a national symbol for everyone in the country regardless of nationality. The Chinese could not have chosen a more unsuitable place to build a huge dam and hydroelectric power station to satisfy only its own needs for electricity. People of all nationalities in multi-ethnic Myanmar were bound to oppose the scheme.

But why would Thein Sein be against it? He was a retired general who had been prime minister in Myanmar's military government prior to an election in November 2010 as well as a leading member of the then ruling junta, which was above the cabinet. He became president in March 2011 as leader of a government dominated by the military's own party, the Union Solidarity and Development Party (USDP). Everyone knew that its landslide victory in that election had been rigged and the parliament that was elected as well as the new government consisted mostly of former military officers like Thein Sein. A quarter of all members of parliament were even serving officers, appointed by the military.

Thein Sein had, after all, made some overtures to improve still military-ruled Myanmar's tarnished international image by lifting the house arrest of Aung San Suu Kyi, who had been in and out of this form of detention since 1989, and releasing hundreds of political prisoners. But given his past as a general and a leading member of the junta that had held the country in an iron grip, Thein Sein had hardly shown himself to be a closet liberal before all that happened. Up to that point, Myanmar had also been perceived by many as a Chinese client state. Then, only six months into his term as president, Thein Sein suspended the Myitsone project, which was bound to upset the Chinese. Many were confused, but the move should be seen as an outcome of internal military politics rather than concern about 'the will of the people'.

In August-September 1988, a nationwide pro-democracy uprising shook Myanmar. It was brutally suppressed by the country's military. Thousands of pro-democracy demonstrators were gunned down in the then capital Yangon and elsewhere. The bloodbath led to condemnations, sanctions and boycotts by the United States and the European Union, and some countries in the region such as Japan and India also denounced the carnage.

China did not. Instead, Myanmar emerged as China's principal economic, political and military ally in Southeast Asia. The

Myanmar economy, moribund following the unrest and decades of mismanagement before that, was rescued by the cross-border trade in consumer goods from China and natural resources from Myanmar that began in the late 1980s. Beijing also provided the State Law and Order Restoration Council, the junta that had assumed power in September 1988, with generous loans, and blocked any attempt by the West to raise the Myanmar issue in the UN Security Council. Massive supplies of military hardware were also crucial to the desire of Myanmar's extremely unpopular military regime to consolidate its grip on power. Had it not been for China's economic, diplomatic and political support, it is plausible to assume that Myanmar's military government would not have survived the crisis of the late 1980s and early 1990s.

A seemingly insignificant event in the midst of the political turmoil that engulfed Myanmar in 1988 turned out to be an important watershed in Sino-Myanmar relations. During the decade 1968-1978, when it had actually been Beijing's policy to export world revolution, China had poured more military and financial aid into the insurgent Communist Party of Burma (CPB) than to any other communist rebel movement outside Indochina. The China-supported, heavily armed and staunchly Maoist CPB built up a 20,000-square-kilometre base area along the Sino-Myanmar border, which also served as training grounds for Thai and Indonesian communist militants while links were maintained with like-minded insurgents in Malaysia and India. China saw Myanmar as a springboard from which Maoist communism would spread to South and Southeast Asia.

The initial changes came following the death of Mao Zedong in 1976 and the once disgraced reformist Deng Xiaoping's return to the political fold. At home in China, a free market was introduced after decades of austere socialism, and Beijing's foreign policy turned from exporting revolution to promoting economic expansion through trade with neighbours such as Myanmar. But either way, safeguarding and even controlling the 'Myanmar corridor' has always been of vital importance to whoever was in power in Beijing and whatever the aim of the ruling power's foreign policy. And the event that heralded a definite change in China's Myanmar policy was the August 1988 agreement, which was concluded as mass demonstrations shook

Yangon almost daily and only two days before a general strike crippled the entire country.

Most observers at the time were probably amused to read in the official media in Yangon that China and Myanmar agreed to open their common border for trade. While the rest of the world was watching what they thought were the last days of the old regime, Beijing was betting on its survival. And that turned out to be a correct assessment.

The protests were suppressed, and the 'old' military-dominated regime only gave way to direct military rule under a tightly knit junta. For China, that was not a problem. In fact, it could take advantage of the West's human-rights oriented policies to promote Deng Xiaoping's trade-friendly, free-market oriented policies. Behind it were also the thoughts Pan Qi had articulated in the *Beijing Review* on 2 September 1985. But Pan had failed to mention in his article that the border areas were not then under central Myanmar government control. At that time, nearly the entire 2,192-kilometre Sino-Myanmar frontier was actually in the hands of the CPB and other ethnic rebel groups that also had ties to China, notably the powerful Kachin Independence Army (KIA) in the far north.

Following a previous border agreement signed in 1960, a joint Sino-Myanmar team had marked the frontier with stones and markers that covered the full length of the common border. When these had crumbled more than two decades later, new border stones were erected in 1985 in accordance with a new agreement. But this time, the Myanmar border stones, the location of which the Chinese decided, were conveniently located in open paddy fields and glades in the jungle, far from major rebel bases along the frontier.

The civil war raged on and, in early 1987, Myanmar government troops managed to recapture a few CPB strongholds along the frontier, including the booming border town of Panghsai, where the fabled 'Burma Road' crosses into China at Wanding east of Ruili. Although Panghsai was located inside the CPB's base area, freewheeling, black-market trade across the border had been brisk. With the 1988 border trade agreement in place, the business was legalised – and now under Myanmar government control.

At the same time, the Chinese had already begun to penetrate local markets through an extensive economic intelligence reporting system within Myanmar. This network monitored the availability of domestically manufactured Myanmar products, as well as the nature and volume of illegal trade from other neighbouring countries such as Thailand, Malaysia, Singapore and India. China could then respond to the market conditions by producing goods in its state sector factories. As a result, more than 2,000 carefully selected items began to flood the Myanmar market. Chinese-made consumer goods were not only made deliberately cheaper than those from other neighbouring countries, but were also less expensive than local Myanmar products.[2]

Then came another dramatic turn of events. In March-April 1989, to the surprise of many, the hill tribe rank and file of the CPB's army mutinied and drove the party's predominantly Bamar leadership into exile in China. The mutiny came after years of simmering discontent between the hill tribe foot soldiers, who had been forcibly recruited into the CPB's army, and the ageing intellectuals from central Myanmar who had spent years in exile in China before they, with Chinese assistance, crossed the Myanmar border and established a base there. In the beginning, most of the fighters were actually Chinese 'volunteers', but, gradually, local tribesmen from the hills had been recruited into the CPB's army. While the rank and file had little or no idea about communist ideology, the old leaders were still clinging to their orthodox Maoist ideals, perhaps much to the dismay of even the leaders of Deng Xiaoping's new China.

The government in Yangon quickly and shrewdly exploited the mutiny: the tribal leaders of the new forces who emerged from the ashes of the old CPB were promised that they could engage in any kind of business, if they agreed to a ceasefire with the government and refrained from sharing their vast quantity of weaponry, which they acquired from the Chinese from 1968 to 1978, with other rebel groups. And there were many ethnic, non-communist rebel armies in Myanmar that the CPB mutineers could have allied themselves with. After the crushing of the August-September pro-democracy uprising, thousands of urban activists had fled to the areas where the ethnic rebels were active, and they also wanted guns to fight the military regime in Yangon.

No such alliance between the former CPB forces and the country's other insurgents and dissidents was formed. Instead, a potent military threat to the regime was neutralised at a time when the military government was facing serious opposition from ethnic rebels as well as people who had belonged to the pro-democracy movement in the Myanmar heartlands.

The old CPB subsequently broke up into four regional, ethnic groups of which the United Wa State Army (UWSA) with at least 20,000 soldiers was by far the strongest. Alongside the UWSA, the other three groups also made peace with the government and, in accordance with the ceasefire agreements, all of them were allowed to keep their weapons and retain control over most of their respective areas.

In light of new policies in Beijing and improving relations with Myanmar, some had expected China to break off relations with the leaders of the UWSA and the other ex-CPB forces. But that did not happen. They were, after all, former military commanders in the CPB's army with whom they had maintained close relations for decades. And, given Beijing's new economic and foreign policies, the UWSA was a more trustworthy ally than the old Maoist intellectuals in the CPB would have been in the new era. As long as they eschewed any political activity, the ageing Myanmar communists were provided with government pensions and housing in Kunming. Myanmar's decades-long communist insurrection, which China had long supported, was over – with the Chinese overseeing its demise.

In the wake of the Yangon massacre of 1988 and the bloody events in Beijing's Tiananmen Square in June 1989, which provoked a similar international response, it was hardly surprising that the two isolated, condemned neighbours would move even closer to each other in the years that followed. This new, very special relationship between Myanmar and China was first articulated by the country's powerful intelligence chief, Lt. Gen. Khin Nyunt, a leading member of the then ruling junta. In an address to a group of Chinese engineers working on a project in Yangon, Khin Nyunt said: 'We sympathize with the People's Republic of China as disturbances similar to those in Myanmar last year [i.e. 1988] broke out in the People's Republic of China [in May-June 1989].'[3]

The importance of relations between these two bloodstained authoritarian regimes was marked by a 12-day visit to China in October 1989 of a 24-member military delegation from Myanmar. Commander-in-chief Gen. Than Shwe led the team, which also included Lt. Gen. Khin Nyunt, the director of procurement Brigadier Gen. David Abel, and the chiefs of the air force and navy. The visit resulted in a massive arms deal: China pledged to deliver US$1.4 billion worth of military hardware to Myanmar, including a squadron of F-7 jet fighters (the Chinese version of the Soviet MiG-21), at least four Hainan-class naval patrol boats, about a hundred light tanks and armoured personnel carriers, trucks, antiaircraft guns, rockets, a substantial quantity of small arms and ammunition, and radio equipment for military use.[4]

A year after the signing of the border-trade agreement in August 1988, Myanmar had also become China's chief foreign market for cheap consumer goods, and China became a major importer of Myanmar timber, forestry products, minerals, seafood and agricultural produce. At the time, World Bank analysts estimated that nearly US$1.5 billion worth of goods were exchanged along the Myanmar-China frontier, not including a flourishing trade in narcotics from the Myanmar sector of the Golden Triangle.

In addition to trade, China soon became involved with upgrading Myanmar's badly maintained roads and railways, as Pan Qi had suggested in 1985. By late 1991, Chinese experts were working on a series of infrastructure projects in Myanmar. That same year, Chinese military advisers arrived and were the first foreign military personnel to be stationed in Myanmar since the fifties.[5] Myanmar was indeed becoming a Chinese client state. What the CPB failed to achieve for the Chinese on the battlefield was accomplished by shrewd diplomacy and flourishing bilateral trade. It was at this time the bridge to Jiegao was built and the monument that urged China to blaze paths and forge ahead to the south, into Myanmar and beyond, was erected.

On the surface, the relationship was close and friendly, but it masked a deeper sense of unease within Myanmar's fiercely nationalistic senior officer corps. Many of those soldiers had fresh memories of fighting CPB troops armed by Beijing and there was deep-rooted mistrust of China's intentions. These tensions first became noticeable in ways that looked like internal power struggles but in reality were often spurred by disputes over China's influence. The first blow against China came as early as October 2004, when the intelligence chief Lt. Gen. Khin

Nyunt, who had by then also become prime minister, was ousted in an internal putsch. The Chinese at first found it hard to believe that 'their man' in Myanmar had been pushed out – but then quickly adjusted to the new conditions.

Despite the setback to China, relations appeared to be returning to normal. In April 2007, China's National Development and Resource Commission approved a plan to build oil and gas pipelines connecting China's interior to Myanmar's vast untapped on- and offshore petroleum resources. In November 2008, China and Myanmar agreed in principle to build a US$1.5 billion oil pipeline and US$1.04 billion natural gas pipeline from the Myanmar coast to Yunnan. And in March 2009, China and Myanmar finally signed an agreement to build that natural gas pipeline, and in June that year an agreement to build the crude oil pipeline.

The inauguration ceremony marking the start of construction of the pipelines was held on 31 October 2009, on Maday Island on Myanmar's western coast. Then, in the same year and without advanced warning to Beijing, Myanmar troops moved against a non-state armed group in the Kokang area in the northeast. More than 30,000 civilians sought temporary shelter in China. That armed group, the Myanmar National Democratic Alliance Army (MNDAA), was one of the four former CPB forces that had made peace with the Myanmar government in 1989 and, for the Chinese, Kokang was an especially sensitive area for a conflict because the vast majority of the inhabitants are ethnic Chinese. The Kokang Chinese speak the same Chinese dialect as people do in Yunnan across the border.

Not surprisingly Beijing felt compelled to express its unhappiness with the Myanmar military's attack on Kokang. But, ultimately, China took no steps beyond démarches. And, in order to smooth things over, China agreed in September 2010 to provide Myanmar with US$4.2 billion worth of interest-free loans over a 30-year period to help fund hydropower projects, road and railway construction, and information technology development.

It has often been argued that Western sanctions pushed Myanmar into the hands of the Chinese. That is debatable, but Western policies certainly made it easier for China to implement its designs for Myanmar, causing some in the West to criticise the policy of isolating Myanmar and, as they argued, 'handing it over to China.' These concerns were outlined as early as June 1997 in a *Los Angeles Times* article by Marvin Ott, an American security expert and former Central Intelligence Agency (CIA) analyst. 'Washington can and should remain outspokenly critical of abuses in [Myanmar]. But there are security and other national interests to be served...it is time to think seriously about alternatives,' Ott concluded.[6]

But the turn took some doing. Between 2001 and 2009, the then George W. Bush administration's bipartisan Myanmar policy was not only to maintain sanctions put in place by Congress during the administration of Bill Clinton that had preceded it, but also to impose new punitive measures in an attempt to support Myanmar's democratic forces. Following a renewed mass movement for democracy in late 2007, led by Myanmar's Buddhist monks and therefore called 'the Saffron Revolution', and the regime's disastrous response to a cyclone called Nargis, which devastated the country in May 2008, the Bush administration took a hard line against the regime's leadership. More sanctions were imposed and programmes initiated to support the pro-democracy movement inside the country.

Then came another twist of events. In the early 2000s it was revealed that Myanmar and North Korea had established a strategic partnership – and that prompted Washington to seriously rethink its Myanmar policy. As if the close relationship between China and Myanmar was not bad enough, now Pyongyang was part of the picture. North Korea was reportedly providing Myanmar with tunnelling expertise, heavy weapons, radar and air defence systems, and even missile-related technology. Some leading foreign policy voices, such as then US senator Jim Webb, began arguing that it was high time to shift track and start to engage the Myanmar leadership, which seemed bent on maintaining its grip on power no matter the consequences.

When the Barack Obama administration came into office in January 2009 on a platform of reversing Bush-era foreign policy, many saw an opening for a change in attitudes towards Myanmar as well. Then, in November 2010, elections were held in Myanmar, which formally ended junta rule by Gen. Than Shwe and brought the Thein Sein government into office the following year. It did not amount to more than a cosmetic change as the same people remained in power, but the move was nevertheless seen as an opportunity that the West could use to mend fences with the Myanmar leadership. Myanmar suddenly had a new face and the country also had a new constitution, even if that one had been promulgated after a referendum in May 2008 – as Nargis was sweeping across the country – which was just as phony as the 2010 election.

Despite the fraudulent nature of the referendum and the election, it was the perfect time for the United States and other Western countries to begin the process of détente with the regime in Myanmar, and also for Myanmar's former generals to launch a charm offensive in the West. The United States viewed pulling Myanmar from its uncomfortable Chinese embrace as a key element of this new era – and so did the Myanmar military and its new, quasi-civilian government.

In early December 2011, hardly by coincidence only a few months after Thein Sein had made his speech about Myitsone in the parliament in the new capital Naypyitaw, then US Secretary of State Hillary Clinton paid a high-profile visit to Myanmar, the first such trip by a top-ranking Washington official in more than 50 years. Clinton's visit to Myanmar was followed by one by President Obama in November 2012, who returned two years later as Myanmar finally took its turn as chair of the Association of Southeast Asian Nations, or ASEAN, to which it belonged. In May 2013, Thein Sein became the first Myanmar head of state to visit the United States since the old military dictator Gen. Ne Win was there in 1966.

Relations between Myanmar and the West were improving at a remarkable pace, and became even more cordial after new elections in November 2015. For a change, those were free and fair – and led to a landslide victory for Aung San Suu Kyi's National League for Democracy (NLD). She could not become president, however, because the 2008 constitution stipulated that anyone with close relatives who are foreign citizens cannot assume the posts of president or vice president. Aung San Suu Kyi's two sons are foreign citizens, the older American and the younger British, and that clause in the constitution was most certainly put there to prevent her from becoming Myanmar's president any time in the future. But a new post, that of State Counsellor, was created by the NLD – and that was Aung San Suu Kyi who in that capacity became the de facto head of state.

When Aung San Suu Kyi arrived in Washington in September 2016, US–Myanmar relations had been almost completely normalised. On the occasion of her visit, she and President Obama announced the lifting of all remaining economic sanctions. Myanmar also normalised relations with the European Union, Australia, India and Japan. The turnaround from being an international pariah to becoming the darling of the West was remarkable.

But all was not quite as it seemed. In order to understand the twists and turns in Myanmar politics, it is instructive to look deeper into what was discussed in the inner circles of the military in the early 2000s, when relations with China were still close. Then condemned and isolated by the international community, the ruling military junta announced in August 2003 a seven-step 'Roadmap to Discipline-Flourishing Democracy'. That plan called for the drafting of a new constitution, general elections, and convention of a new parliament that would 'elect state leaders' charged with building 'a modern, developed, and democratic nation'.[7]

The 'roadmap' was made public, but at the same time a confidential 'master plan' that outlined ways and means to deal with both the international community, especially the United States, and domestic opposition was also drawn up. The authors of that plan are not known; however, an internal military document written by Lt. Col. Aung Kyaw Hla, who is identified as a researcher at the country's prestigious Defence Services Academy, was completed and circulated as early as August 2004, less than two months before Lt. Gen. Khin Nyunt, 'China's man', was ousted.[8]

The Myanmar-language document outlines the thinking and strategy behind the master plan. It is, however, unclear whether 'Aung Kyaw Hla' is a particular person, or a codename used by a military think-tank. Anecdotal evidence suggests the latter. Entitled 'A Study of Myanmar-U.S. Relations', the main thesis of the 346-page dossier is that Myanmar's recent reliance on China as a diplomatic ally and economic patron has created a 'national emergency' that threatens the country's independence. Therefore, Myanmar must normalise relations with the West after implementing the roadmap and electing a government so that the regime can deal with the outside world on more acceptable terms.

Aung Kyaw Hla goes on to argue that although human rights are a concern in the West, the United States would be willing to modify its policy to suit 'strategic interests'.

Although the author does not specify those interests, it is clear from the thesis that he is thinking of common ground with the United States vis-à-vis China. The author cites Indonesia under former dictator Suharto and communist-ruled Vietnam as examples of US foreign policy flexibility in weighing strategic interests against democratisation and human rights.

If bilateral relations with the United States were improved, the master plan suggests, Myanmar would also obtain access to badly needed funds from the World Bank, the International Monetary Fund and other global financial institutions. The country could then emerge from 'regionalism', where it depended on the goodwill and trade of its immediate neighbours, including China, and enter a new era of 'globalisation'.

The master plan clearly articulated the problems that must be addressed before Myanmar could lessen its reliance on China and become a trusted partner with the West. The main issue at that time was the detention of pro-democracy icon Aung San Suu Kyi, who Aung Kyaw Hla wrote was a key 'focal point': 'Whenever she is under detention pressure increases, but when she is not, there is less pressure'. While the report implies Suu Kyi's release would improve ties with the West, the plan's ultimate aim – which it spells out clearly – is, in Aung Kyaw Hla's own words, to 'crush' the opposition.[9]

The dossier concluded that the regime could not compete with the media and non-governmental organisations run by Myanmar exiles, but if American politicians and lawmakers were invited to visit the country they could help to sway international opinion in the regime's favour. In the years leading up to the recent policy shifts, many Americans, including some congressmen, did visit Myanmar and often proved less critical of the regime than they previously had been. In the end, it seems that Myanmar's military leaders successfully managed to engage the United States rather than vice versa. As a result, relations with the United States improved exactly along the lines suggested by Aung Kyaw Hla in 2004.

Both China and North Korea were high on the agenda when Clinton visited Myanmar in December 2011. Subsequently, strategic and economic concerns have risen up the bilateral agenda even as human rights and democratisation have been steadily de-emphasised. As a result, the two old adversaries, Myanmar and the United States, increasingly ended up on the same side of the fence in the struggle for power and influence in Southeast Asia.

The developing friendship between Naypyitaw and Washington prompted China to start searching for new ways to shore up their relationship. In 2012, academic journals in China ran several articles analysing what went wrong with Beijing's Myanmar policy and what could and should be done to rectify it.[10] One proposed measure was to launch a public relations campaign in Myanmar aimed at overhauling China's current negative image in the country. Beijing also began reaching out to other elements of Myanmar society – including the NLD and other democrats – utilising the 'government-to-government', 'party-to-party', and 'people-to-people' strategy of the ruling Communist Party of China (CPC). China decided to go beyond having contacts only with a limited circle of military leaders and their business cronies.

Myanmar, on its part, turned not only to the United States but also to its partners in ASEAN, which it chaired in 2014, to further lessen its dependence on China. Even more significantly, when Gen. Min Aung Hlaing, who was appointed commander-in-chief of Myanmar's military in March 2011, went on his first foreign trip in mid-November, he did not go to China – but instead to China's traditional enemy, Vietnam. Myanmar and Vietnam share the same fear of their common, powerful northern neighbour, so it is reasonable to assume that Min Aung Hlaing had much to discuss with his Vietnamese hosts.

While the Myanmar government sought to build deeper relations with other nations in the region, stark domestic challenges continued to hinder meaningful economic or political developments at home. China was well aware of that and used its 'government-to-government' and 'party-to-party' relations to maintain distinct leverage and influence over the Myanmar government as well as the country's many ethnic rebel groups.

Among the many initiatives that Thein Sein took after becoming president was a 'peace process', whereby the government sought a truce with the ethnic rebels. On 15 October 2015, his government signed what was termed a 'Nationwide Ceasefire Agreement' (NCA) with what it claimed was 'eight ethnic armed groups'. As it turned out, only three of those groups had any armed force, and the others were tiny local militias or even ethnic NGOs. Groups representing more than 80 per cent of Myanmar's armed rebels refused to sign it, the UWSA because its leaders said they had already a ceasefire deal with the government, and others because they thought signing an elaborate agreement with the government before any meaningful political talks had been held was the wrong order in which to do things. They wanted talks first, then a political consensus about the country's future, namely whether it should be a federal union, as Myanmar actually was before the military seized power in a coup in 1962, or a centralised state, which it has been ever since.

The NCA was lauded internationally as a significant step towards peace in Myanmar, but only by those who were largely unaware of the country's recent history. There was nothing fundamentally different in Thein Sein's approach than in that of Khin Nyunt in the late 1980s and early 1990s other than that a host of foreign peace-making organisations now became involved. Thein Sein's 'peace process' became a multi-million dollar business, and from it emerged what has been called a 'peace industrial complex'.[11]

Meanwhile, China was outsmarting everybody else, and was able to do so because of its intimate knowledge of Myanmar's ethnic groups – and its ability to play politics on different levels. Although the Chinese government consistently denies that it is interfering in Myanmar's peace process, Beijing's tacit support for the country's largest non-state armed group tells a different story.[12] And China's active interference in Myanmar's ethnic conflicts predates Thein Sein's peace initiatives by more than two decades.

The 1989 ceasefire agreement between the CPB's successor, the UWSA, suited China's new commercial interests; it was also imperative for Beijing to find ways to strengthen the UWSA, and by extension its leverage over the Myanmar government. Thus, the UWSA was able to purchase vast quantities of weapons from China. In the second half of 2012, the UWSA acquired armoured vehicles for the first time. These included an armoured combat vehicle that *IHS Jane's* identified as the

Chinese 4×4 ZFB-05. Furthermore, the UWSA obtained from China huge quantities of small arms and ammunition – and around 100 HN-5 series man-portable air defence systems (MANPADS), a Chinese version of the first-generation Russian Strela-2 called SA-7 Grail.[13] According to the 26 April 2013 *IHS Jane's* report, purchases even included armed transport helicopters: '[The acquisition of helicopters] marks the latest step in a significant upgrade for the UWSA, which emerged as the largest and best-equipped non-state military force in Asia and, arguably, the world.'[14]

The UWSA soon became better armed than the CPB ever was. It can field at least 20,000 well-equipped troops as well as thousands of village militiamen and other supportive forces. Moreover, the top leaders of the UWSA are usually accompanied by Chinese intelligence officers who provide advice and guidance. So what was China up to? Why the arming and continued support of a non-state military force, while, at the same time, having cordial relations with the Myanmar government? Hadn't the CPC abandoned its policy of supporting insurrections in the region?

Beijing's seemingly contradictory foreign policy actually made a lot of sense. There was a carrot – aid and trade – and then a powerful stick. By supporting the UWSA, China was able to put pressure on Myanmar at a time when its relations with the United States were improving. China felt it could not afford to 'lose' Myanmar to the West, and seemed to define Myanmar's foreign relations with other regional actors in zero-sum terms. A strong UWSA provides China with a strategic advantage and is also a bargaining chip in negotiations with Naypyitaw. Significantly, when the President's Office Minister Aung Min visited Monywa in November 2012 to meet local people protesting a controversial Chinese-backed copper mining project at Letpadaung northwest of Mandalay, he openly admitted: 'We are afraid of China…we don't dare to have a row with [them]. If they feel annoyed with the shutdown of their projects and resume their support to the communists, the economy in border areas would backslide'.[15]

By 'the communists' he clearly meant the UWSA and its allies. Among them were the MNDAA, whose weaponry and huge amounts of ammunition had been supplied by the UWSA. The Chinese may be denying giving any material support to the UWSA and indirectly supporting its allies, but what it has received from China is not the kind of equipment that 'falls off the back of a truck', or could be sent to the UWSA by some local officials in Yunnan. The deliveries were almost certainly directed from the highest level of China's intelligence and military authorities in Beijing.

China's hardline approach can also be seen in its attitude towards any other country that wants to have a say in Myanmar's peace process. A Yangon-based US ambassador who visited Kachin State in the north, where heavy fighting has been raging since the Myanmar army went on an offensive in June 2011 – ironically only months after Thein Sein had announced his plans for a peace process – was warned by China 'not to interfere in Myanmar's internal affairs.' Yun Sun, a Chinese scholar whose views often reflect government thinking, wrote an article for the *Asia Pacific Bulletin* in February 2015 headlined: 'The Conflict in Northern Myanmar: Another Anti-China Conspiracy?' The article was published after the Myanmar army's push into Kokang that year, and the arrest of some Chinese illegal loggers in Kachin State. While dismissing such 'conspiracy theories', Yun Sun nevertheless highlighted them, referring to 'China's long-held suspicion that US policy toward Myanmar is part of a grand China containment strategy.'[16] Myanmar, in Beijing's view, is China's turf. Period.

At the same time, Beijing is also playing another 'softer' card by inviting Myanmar politicians and journalists on all-paid 'study trips' to China – and being actively involved in the peace process, initiated by Thein Sein and later pursued along the same tracks by Aung San Suu Kyi when she became State Counsellor in 2016. And here, China's multi-layered foreign policy is obvious. Sun Guoxiang, China's special envoy for Asian affairs at the Foreign Ministry, has repeatedly expressed public support for that process. According to the transcript of a meeting between Sun Guoxiang in February 2017 and representatives from two of Myanmar's ethnic armed ceasefire groups, Sun said: 'China has a unique foreign policy towards Myanmar and respects the sovereignty of Myanmar…we are only doing our duty as a friendly neighbour.'[17]

Sun's cordial tone cuts a sharp contrast with the China-backed UWSA's militant message jointly delivered with six other ethnic groups around the same time the Myanmar government's NCA was concluded. It was a joint salvo, which caught many observers off-guard and raised new questions about China's true position towards the Myanmar government's peace initiative. The seven groups rejected the NCA and called for a more direct, political approach to solving Myanmar's decades-long civil war.[18] The seven-party grouping goes under the elaborate name the Federal Political Negotiation and Consultative Committee (FPNCC) and apart from UWSA includes the KIA, the MNDAA, another former CPB army in eastern Shan State, and armed forces representing the Shans, the Palaungs and the Rakhine. While it would be pushing it a bit far to suggest that any Chinese agency was behind the formation of the FPNCC, the close relationship between the group and China was reflected in a statement it issued congratulating Xi on his re-election as president in March 2018. 'The FPNCC proudly welcomes the strong and positive leadership of the People's Republic of China,' the statement said. 'We value the New Era of Xi Jinping Thought as a promising universal change for our world.' The statement also called on Xi to help solve 'the long-term military and civil conflicts in Myanmar.'[19]

Foreign Ministry envoy Sun Guoxiang is right in stating that China's multi-layered policies towards Myanmar are indeed 'unique' – and, to many outsiders, they often seem contradictory. But under examination, China's foreign policies have their own logic. Envoy Sun's positive message is the first surface layer of China's diplomacy, which is almost always publicly characterised as 'amicable' and 'friendly' towards regional countries with which it engages.

The second layer consists of the International Liaison Department of the Central Committee of the CPC, or the ILD/CPC. The body was originally set up in the 1950s to develop contacts with other communist parties and support revolutionary movements across the globe. These days, however, ILD/CPC representatives are often seen at conferences and hob-knobbing with political parties of all ideological stripes. The ILD/CPC also supports various non-state groups, including armed resistance organizations, like the UWSA, which serve China's long-term strategic and economic interests.

The third layer is the People's Liberation Army (PLA), which maintains links with other militaries across the world. Along with selling weapons to foreign governmental and non-governmental clients, directly or through front companies, it has provided beneficiaries such as the UWSA with a wide variety of weaponry. Some of those armaments are then shared with other ethnic armed groups actively fighting against the Myanmar government.

China may have transformed its economic system from rigid socialism to free-wheeling capitalism, but politically it remains an authoritarian one-party state where the CPC is above the government, with the PLA serving as the armed-wing of the Party. The old policy of maintaining 'government-to-government' as well as 'party-to-party' relations has not changed.

Consequently, China's main man in dealing with Myanmar's many political actors is not Sun but rather Song Tao, head of the ILD/CPC. Song, a senior politician and diplomat, was educated at Monash University in Australia and served as an assistant to the Chinese ambassador to India in the early 2000s before becoming ambassador to Guyana and the Philippines. In October 2015, Song took part in a high-profile visit to North Korea and the following month took over the post as ILD/CPC chief from Wang Jiarui, a CPC veteran who was in charge of maintaining contacts with communist members in countries including North Korea, Cuba and Vietnam. While Song is not a high-profile figure like Sun, he is known to work actively in the background and apparently prefers to engage with Myanmar politicians and top soldiers in Beijing rather than Naypyitaw. But Song did meet with Aung San Suu Kyi in Naypyitaw in August 2016, just weeks before the launch of her own peace process which followed the one initiated by Thein Sein.

The distinction between 'government-to-government' relations maintained by China's foreign ministry and the CPC's 'party-to-party' links with groups such as the UWSA – and given the CPC's position above the government in Beijing and the PLA – explains why China can publicly praise Myanmar's peace process while quietly providing the UWSA with heavy weaponry.[20]

Unlike in Western and Asian democracies, China's foreign ministry is not necessarily the lead actor in shaping policy; rather the CPC is ever-present within those three different levels of engagement. To paint a more comprehensive picture of China's relations with the Myanmar government and ethnic rebel groups, the other two levels of Chinese engagement, dominated by the CPC, must also be examined.

An outreach to Aung San Suu Kyi, pro-democracy activists, and even journalists – including innumerable 'study trips' to China since 2012 – as well as Chinese support for the UWSA all essentially serve the same strategic purpose: put pressure on the military, which really pulls the strings in Naypyitaw, and force it to keep its options open for the future, with the ultimate aim of securing the vital Myanmar Corridor.

There is also a common misperception, especially in the West, that a 'reform programme' is in place in Myanmar, which is eventually going to lead to full-blown democracy. The current constitution provides for what could at best be described as a hybrid system, and any change to any major clause requires 75 per cent approval, followed by a national referendum. With the military appointing a quarter of all members of parliament, it enjoys what amounts to veto power over any changes in the country's power structure.

Among the clauses that cannot be changed without military approval are those stipulating that the military appoints the three most important ministries, namely those of Defence, Home Affairs and Border Affairs. Military control of the Defence and Border Affairs ministries excludes the elected government from military matters as well as issues relating to ethnic insurgencies in border areas. The Home Affairs Ministry controls the police – and the powerful General Administration Department, which staffs all local governments, from the state and region levels down to districts and townships. Elected ministers, or ministers appointed by the elected government, are confined to issues such as health and education, fisheries and agriculture.

When the NLD scored it election victory in 2015, people in Myanmar were enthusiastic, and foreign observers hailed the event as an important step towards democratic rule. But within only a couple of years, it is becoming obvious that Myanmar's first truly elected government since 1960 was a mere fig leaf for continued military rule.

Than Soe Naing, a Myanmar political analyst, told *The Irrawaddy*, a local online publication, in August 2017 that 'according to the very essence of the 2008 Constitution, it is the *Tatmadaw* (military) which will decide the fate of Myanmar's politics.'[21] In the same article, Col. Aung Myint Oo, head of internal and external relations at the National Defence College, stated: 'Considering the reality, it is impossible to remove the military from politics.'

There is a naïve belief among many foreign observers that some kind of 'engagement' with the Myanmar military will make them change their minds. In an article for the *Nikkei Asian Review* on 17 August 2017, William C. Dickey, a former US defence attaché to Myanmar, argues that the US-funded Expanded International Military and Education Training (E-IMET) programme may help the Myanmar military understand issues such as a military justice system that is in accordance with internationally recognized human rights and the principle of control of the military, and 'U.S. engagement with the Myanmar military is necessary to help Myanmar stay on track for democratic reforms.'[22]

That attitude is often dismissed by Myanmar analysts as a 'White Messiah Complex', i.e. all that is needed is for Westerners to invite Myanmar army officers to the West and tell them that they are wrong – and then they will change accordingly. The problem is not that Myanmar military officers are unaware of human rights principles or what civilian control of the military means. There are plenty of papers produced by officers at Myanmar's National Defence College on those subjects. But the Myanmar military has had its own ideology since the late 1950s, the essence of which is that the military has to play a dominant role in political affairs as well as defence – and that deep-rooted belief is not going to change simply because some well-meaning Western instructors tell them otherwise.

Training courses in the West could even be counterproductive as they would only provide Myanmar's military leaders with international recognition and legitimacy, therefore making them more immune to reform. Change may eventually come to Myanmar, but it will have to come from within the country's most powerful institution, the military. It will be home grown, not the result of patronising attitudes of Westerners.

It is also an open question how China would react to such a US-initiated programme of engagement, and an indicator could be how China has come to dominate Myanmar's so-called 'peace process'. While the West, including the European Union, Norway, Switzerland and the United States, have spent millions of dollars on seminars for issues such as women's participation in the peace process, conflict sensitivity and capacity-building, and sponsored study trips to post-conflict Northern Ireland, Colombia and South Africa, China has played its cards more subtly.

This became obvious during peace talks in the capital Naypyitaw in May 2017, when China flew representatives from the seven armed groups in the north – which are opposed to the government's NCA – in a chartered plane from Kunming in southern China. They were led by China's closest ally, the UWSA, and included allied groups from the Kachin and Shan states. China's relations with those seven groups, which by some estimates account for more than 80 per cent of all rebels under arms, puts China in a position that no other foreign power can match.

Even though China has armed the UWSA and, indirectly, some of its allies, it does not want to see a war on its southern frontier. But peace-making is a tool, not a goal for the Chinese. By playing the role of interlocutor China can regain some of the influence it lost when Thein Sein's quasi-civilian government reopened to the West, beginning in 2011. The Chinese have also shown Aung San Suu Kyi and her government that they, not the West, hold the key to peace and prosperity in Myanmar. And while her government recoils from Western criticism for the abusive treatment of the Muslim Rohingya minority on the Bangladesh border, China has chosen a different approach.

The Rohingya crisis became another turning point in Myanmar's relations with the West – this time for the worse. For years, even decades, the Rohingyas have been the target of violence perpetrated by Myanmar's security forces and extremist Buddhist groups, but the latest crisis, which led to an international outcry, began with attacks by Muslim militants on some police and army outposts in the western Rakhine State in October 2016 and August 2017. After the latter wave of insurgent attacks, the Myanmar military retaliated with a massive 'clearing operation'. Hundreds of villages were burnt down, thousands of people killed and over 700,000 Rohingyas fled into Bangladesh.

The international media was quick to blame Aung San Suu Kyi for the carnage. After all, she was the de facto head of state, and should be able to rein in the military. But the Rohingya crisis more than any other serious issue facing Myanmar since it began to open up to the outside world in 2011 unmasked the true nature of the country's power structure. With the military in charge of the defence, home and border affairs ministries – and the military itself being totally autonomous – there was little or nothing the elected government could do.

Even so, many in the West focused their anger on Aung San Suu Kyi, and, if they were aware of her limited powers, they argued that she at the very least should have spoken out against the treatment of the Rohingyas. The US Holocaust Memorial Museum in Washington rescinded its Elie Wiesel Award, which Aung San Suu Kyi had received in 1991. Oxford, the city where Aung San Suu Kyi once lived, stripped her of the Freedom of the City Award it granted her in 1997 for her 'long struggle for democracy'. The Glasgow City Council followed suit and withdrew their offer to honour Aung San Suu Kyi. Her name was removed from the name of a room at Oxford University where she studied in the 1960s and the university removed a portrait of her which was on display at her alma mater, St. Hugh's College.

Unison, one of Britain's largest trade unions, suspended an award given to her while she was under house arrest and there were even calls to revoke the Nobel Peace Prize she was awarded in 1991.[23] That did not happen, but in October 2018, Aung San Suu Kyi became the first person to be stripped of Canadian honorary citizenship, bestowed on her for her struggle for democracy in Myanmar.[24] Then, on 12 November 2018, Amnesty International announced that it had withdrawn its highest honour, the Ambassador of Conscience Award, from Aung San Suu Kyi 'in light of the Myanmar leader's shameful betrayal of the values she once stood for.'[25]

Aung San Suu Kyi, who had been lauded as a civil rights icon on a par with Mahatma Gandhi, Martin Luther King and Nelson Mandela, now became a symbol of repression and, as one UN official had called the carnage in Rakhine State, 'ethnic cleansing'.[26]

The Rohingya crisis provided China with a golden opportunity to improve its till then rather strained relations with Myanmar. When international organisations and institutions were stripping her of awards she had received during her long struggle for democracy, China reached out to her, her government and the Myanmar military, saying that Beijing maintained 'neutrality' on the issue and pledging that it would block any attempt to raise the issue in the United Nations Security Council.

Aung San Suu Kyi may have been opposed to the Myitsone project, but the Chinese surely remembered that she had gone to the site of the Letpadaung copper mine in March 2013 to tell the demonstrators to stop their protests, because those demonstrations, she said, could adversely affect foreign investment flowing into the country. That was the first time Aung San Suu Kyi faced the anger of ordinary people as some of the demonstrators protested loudly against her stand.[27] Some of them even shouted 'does Aung San Suu Kyi stand for the people, or for Wan Bao company?'.[28] (The Letpadaung copper mine is a joint venture between Wan Bao Mining, a subsidiary of NORINCO, or North Industries Group Corporation, a state-owned Chinese company that manufactures military equipment, and the Union of Myanmar Economic Holdings, a military run conglomerate.)

In November 2017, Aung San Suu Kyi was invited to Beijing where she met President Xi. Plans were drawn up to solve the Rohingya refugee issue and to 'normalise' relations between Myanmar and Bangladesh, another country with which China maintains good relations. In the same month, Myanmar's military chief Gen. Min Aung Hlaing also visited Beijing to discuss the Rohingya crisis with Xi. According to a statement issued on Min Aung Hlaing's Facebook page, China stood 'on Myanmar's side…regarding the Rakhine issue.'[29] The statement also said Xi and Min Aung Hlaing discussed ongoing talks with Myanmar's ethnic rebels while China's official news agency *Xinhua* said China was 'willing to play a constructive role…for security and stability in the border areas.'[30]

Such 'friendliness' when other countries have condemned Myanmar comes in handy when China wants to promote its Belt and Road Initiative (BRI) in Myanmar, the most important aspect of which is access to the port at Kyaukpyu. Beijing's bid to regain lost influence through the peace process with the ethnic rebels as well as the Rohingya refugee crisis should be viewed from the perspective of China's broader geopolitical interests. Multi-billion dollar hydroelectric dams – even Myitsone – and mining ventures such as Letpadaung as well as other commercial interests are actually not at the top of China's strategic priorities in Myanmar. Access to the Indian Ocean is.

A contract to build a proper deep-sea port at Kyaukpyu was eventually secured by China's CITIC Group Corporation in 2016. The terms – loans to build the ports and then shares in the ownership – are similar to those concluded for Gwadar in Pakistan, Chittagong in Bangladesh, and Hambantota and Colombo in Sri Lanka. But of all these projects, the port at Kyaukpyu is the most important because the Myanmar Corridor provides China with straightforward and direct access to the Indian Ocean compared with the other, older route, through Pakistan, which climbs some of the highest and most rugged mountains on earth. Kyaukpyu is also near the site of the terminal for China's oil and gas pipelines from the sea to Yunnan.

Since Donald Trump took over as US president in January 2017, China has capitalised on his lack of interest in Myanmar, which was very much on the minds of his predecessor Obama and, especially, Hillary Clinton who saw the country's more open attitude towards the West as one of her success stories as Secretary of State. In May 2017, Chinese warships were even able to hold joint drills with the Myanmar Navy, a significant step forward for China following several years of frosty relations.[31]

At the same time, Myanmar's position on China's Belt and Road Initiative is unclear and no one knows how the country's military and civilian leadership will handle the impact of such a far-reaching project. A delegation led by Aung San Suu Kyi attended a BRI forum in Beijing in May 2016, and the issue was discussed once again when she and Xi met in November 2017. Aung San Suu Kyi welcomed China's proposal to establish an economic corridor through Myanmar but, apart from that, did little more than voicing concern for the environment and proposing employment opportunities for local people.[32] In yet another peculiar twist of events in modern Myanmar history, the staunchly nationalist Myanmar Army may be more opposed to closer cooperation with China than Aung San Suu Kyi. Judging from internal military documents, there is still a strong undercurrent of anti-Chinese sentiment among the officer corps.[33]

So whatever China wishes to achieve in Myanmar, it would have to come gradually and, given the troubled history of bilateral relations, not without apprehension from the Myanmar side. The gas pipeline from Kyaukpyu eventually went into operation in 2013 and, after a two-year delay, the oil pipeline finally followed suit in April 2017. Although the Kyaukpyu port, which was built and is now being expanded by Chinese companies, is designed to allow Chinese ships carrying fuel imports from the Middle East to skirt the congested Malacca Strait, it is not only about oil and gas. The US-based think-tank the Centre for Strategic and International Studies also stated the obvious point that 'building a deep-sea port at Kyaukpyu makes considerable economic and strategic sense for China in its drive to develop its inland provinces. Shipping goods from Europe, the Middle East, Africa and India to Kyaukpyu and then overland to Yunnan could save thousands of miles. It would be far more efficient than sailing all the way through the Strait of Malacca and the South China Sea to ports along China's southern and eastern coasts.'[34]

But even if there now is a basic facility at Kyaukpyu, talks between Myanmar and China about its completion have not been without friction. Initially, when the 2016 agreement was reached, China tried to secure an 85 per cent stake in the port with 15 per cent going to Myanmar. That was soon met with opposition from locals in Rakhine State, who thought it unfair. In October 2017, China agreed to lower its claims to 70 per cent, but a final agreement has yet to be made.[35]

The construction of a railway from Yunnan to Kyaukpyu is another contentious issue. In July 2014 Myanmar let lapse a 2011 Memorandum of Understanding to build such a fast-speed railway connection. The 1,215-kilometre-long Kunming-Kyaukpyu railway would have roughly followed the path of the oil and gas pipelines at an estimated cost of US$20 billion. Under the original MoU, China would have paid for the construction of the railway and then retained management rights. The head of Myanmar's Ministry of Rail Transportation, Myint Wai, said at the time that objections by 'the people and social organisations [of] Myanmar; were reasons for killing the project.[36] The Chinese responded by saying it was 'listening to and must respect the voice of the people of Myanmar.'[37]

But the issue was not dead. In early 2017, the official Chinese news site *Global Times* reported that several members of the National People's Congress, or the Chinese parliament, 'have called for the construction of roads and railways connecting Southwest China's Yunnan Province with the port of Kyaukpyu in Myanmar [because] the section outside of China is a bottleneck in China's strategic plan of opening a trade route to the Indian Ocean.'[38] The same report emphasised that the oil pipeline 'now carries nearly 10 percent of China's oil imports, providing an alternative to the sea route running through the Strait of Malacca.'[39] With improved relations between Naypyitaw and Beijing because of the latter's policy towards the Rohingya crisis, China is in a position to push its infrastructural development plans with greater success than before.

But China, wise from the Myitsone and Letpadaung experiences, also acknowledges that its schemes are fraught with problems. The *Global Times* did not elaborate, but stated that 'the port's construction still faces problems due to political changes in Myanmar and local instability.'[40] It could also have added that one of its preferred business associates in Myanmar, Asia World Company, which was involved in Myitsone and remains a partner in the Kyaukpyu deep-sea port project is headed by one of Myanmar's most controversial tycoons, Htun Myint Naing.

His other name is Steven Law – and he is the son of Lo Hsing-han (Luo Xinghan in Pinyin), a notorious opium and heroin warlord from Kokang. The older Lo built up his drug empire when he was a government-allied militia commander in the early 1970s. But he switched sides in 1973, went underground and linked up with one of the ethnic Shan armies. He was arrested when he sneaked into Thailand in August of that year, and extradited to Myanmar where he was sentenced to death, not for drug trafficking – because for that he had unofficial government permission to trade in narcotics from the Golden Triangle to support his militia – but for 'high treason', a reference to his brief alliance with the Shan rebels. However, the death sentence was never carried out and he was released during a general amnesty in 1980. After that, he built up a new militia force – and the Asia World Company. Lo Hsing-han died in Yangon in July 2013 and his son Steven took over. His alleged drug ties became an issue when he visited Canada in June 2014.[41]

But such considerations are not important to China. Steven Law, an ethnic Chinese, is for them a trustworthy business partner and the development of the Myanmar Corridor is of highest priority. Apart from its involvement in Myitsone and Kyaukpyu, Asia World has also upgraded the road south from the Myanmar border town of Muse opposite Jiegao, and its trucks carry goods across the frontier down to

Mandalay and other central cities and towns. It is still on the Chinese side, however, that most development schemes are taking place.

The construction of a railway from Kunming to the border town of Ruili was in full swing in 2018. New housing estates and shopping centres have sprung up in the area in anticipation of the completion of the railway, and a wide highway leads all the way up to the border at Jiegao. Long tunnels have been blasted through the mountains and concrete bridges built over the ravines along the route from Kunming and Jiegao. Notice boards in Ruili carry maps of the whole region, with lines and arrows showing where roads and railways should be built to Myanmar and beyond.[42]

Most of those links may be still on the drawing board or, like the railway, under construction, but several of those in China have already been completed. The old Burma Road, built during World War II, wound its way in switchback curves over the mountains; the new Myanmar Highway is a straight, four- sometimes six-lane motorway. The still missing link is a similar network of modern connections between Jiegao and Kyaukpyu. And China wants to build roads and railways through Myanmar not only because it wants to facilitate trade. According to the Chinese academic Fan Hongwei, the purpose is also 'to more effectively protect the safety of the oil and gas pipelines.'[43]

It is those strategic goals, not trade routes per se, that worry other countries in the Indian Ocean region. Would 'protecting' the pipelines mean intervention in case of internal turmoil in central Myanmar? Would Chinese warships get access to Kyaukpyu as part of a wider strategy to protect oil supplies by sea to the port and for increasing its influence in the entire Indian Ocean region? Other nations with geostrategic interests in the Indian Ocean seem to think so, and that is causing them to take countermeasures. And the country that is the most concerned is China's regional rival India, which has responded to the Chinese push into Myanmar by strengthening its defences and surveillance capabilities on the Indian islands in the Andaman Sea.

3

INDIA'S ISLANDS

Port Blair on South Andaman Island must be one of the prettiest and tidiest towns in India. Perched on a series of green hills overlooking an azure-blue ocean, and with a population of just over 100,000, it has a laid-back feel to it. There are no traffic jams and hardly any litter even at the bus and taxi station near what is called Aberdeen Market. Indigenous tribes of black-skinned people inhabit the remote interior of the many islands of the Andamans, but Port Blair itself and other major towns here have, over the past century and a half, been settled by Bengali, Tamil, Punjabi, Telugu, Malayali and other migrants from the mainland – and even some Karen from Myanmar – who now all live in relative harmony with each other. It is not without reason a recent academic study of the Andamans was titled 'Mini-India'.[1]

Port Blair is the capital of the Andaman and Nicobar Islands, an Indian Union Territory, but the Nicobars are entirely different from the Andamans. Only 36,000 out of the Union Territory's total population of 380,000 live there. There are hardly any urban areas on the Nicobars and the locals are said to be of Mon-Khmer stock, resemble Southeast Asians, and are not related to the dark-skinned inhabitants of the Andamans. And, apart from personnel from India's armed forces, there are few people from the mainland on the Nicobars. The soldiers belong to the Andaman and Nicobar Command, the Indian military's first and only tri-service command, which was set up in

2001 to safeguard India's strategic interests in the waters east of the Subcontinent – and, more precisely, to keep a watchful eye on China's activities in the same maritime region. Headquartered in Port Blair, it coordinates the activities of the navy, the army and the air force as well as the coast guard in the eastern Indian Ocean.

The distance from the north to the south of the Union Territory is about 750 kilometres, so, including its territorial waters, it covers a significant portion of the part of the Indian Ocean called the Andaman Sea. The distance from the southernmost of the Nicobars to the northern tip of the Indonesian island of Sumatra is a mere 160 kilometres and a 45-kilometre sound separates the northernmost of the Andamans from Myanmar's Coco Islands. The strategic location – and military importance – of the union territory is the reason why tourism remains limited and confined to parts of the Andamans.

There is an Indian Air Force base on Car Nicobar, the main island in the Nicobar chain, and an Indian Navy naval air station at Campbell Bay on the southernmost of the islands. On the Andamans, there are two naval bases, a logistical support base and a naval air station on North Andaman Island. Regular exercises are carried out on the islands involving all three services and, in more recent years, US Navy ships have also paid visits to Port Blair. Idyllic Port Blair has become as crucial to the defence of India as any major military base along its border with China in the Himalayas.

A major concern has always been Myanmar's Coco Islands, and what is – or was – actually happening there. Have the Chinese ever had a presence on the Coco Islands, as the Indian media reported in the 1990s, and, if so, what were they doing on those remote islands? Did they manage a signals intelligence station there to monitor the movements of the Indian Navy in the Indian Ocean or, even more menacingly, India's test range for ballistic missiles and space launch vehicles on its eastern coast, the Indian Space Research Organisation at Sriharikota in Andhra Pradesh, and the Defence Research and Development Organisation at Chandipur-on-Sea in Odisha? Some Indian analysts suggested that the reported construction of a military base on Great Coco, the main island in the Myanmar territory, was linked to China's long-term expansionist designs for the whole Indian Ocean region.

One of the first regional magazines to report on China's new focus on the Indian Ocean was the *Far Eastern Economic Review* as far back as 1993.[2] Apart from the then known delivery of Chinese-made, Hainan-class fast-attack craft to Myanmar, Chinese technicians were also reportedly helping the Myanmar military upgrade their naval facilities near the then capital Yangon and in the southeast of the country. And to build new ones. The Coco Islands were mentioned in those reports, but the magazine also said that 'although China's presence in the Bay of Bengal is currently confined to instructors and technicians, the fact that the new radar equipment about to be installed on the Coco Islands is Chinese-made – and likely to be operated at least in part by Chinese technicians – will enable Beijing's intelligence agencies to monitor this sensitive maritime region.'[3]

The reports nevertheless set off alarm bells in India and elsewhere, leading to wild speculations and misperceptions of what was really happening on the Coco Islands. Indian analyst and commentator on regional issues, Brahma Chellaney, went so far as to say that Chinese 'security agencies already operate electronic-intelligence and maritime-reconnaissance facilities on the two Coco Islands in the Bay of Bengal. India transferred the Coco Islands to Burma [Myanmar] in the 1950s, and Burma then leased the islands to China in 1994.'[4]

The historical record suggests otherwise. The British colonial authorities in Calcutta transferred jurisdiction of the Coco Islands, which at the time had little more than a lighthouse on them, to British Burma, then an Indian province, in 1882. When Myanmar, then known as Burma, was separated from India in 1937 and became a separate Crown Colony, the Coco Islands remained Burmese territory.[5] They were handed over to Subhas Chandra Bose's provisional *Azad Hind* government when Japan occupied the Andamans during World War II and his Indian National Army (INA) combatants, under Japanese auspices, set up their headquarters there. But, in reality, the Andamans and the Nicobars – as well as the Coco Islands – were administered by the Imperial Japanese Navy until the end of World War II. In 1945, following Japan's defeat, the Coco Islands were once again under part of British Burma, and remained a Burmese territory after independence in 1948. In 1953, India sought to lease the lighthouse on Great Coco, but the request was denied by the government in Rangoon (now Yangon).[6]

A military caretaker government, which ruled Burma from 1958 to 1960, established a penal colony on Great Coco in 1959. A handful of former rebels who had been captured and whom the authorities thought should be 're-educated' were sent to the island. But it was not until after General Ne Win and his military seized absolute power in Burma in March 1962 that the Coco Islands gained notoriety. In 1969, Indonesia had turned Buru Island into a penal colony for political prisoners who had been arrested in the wake of general Suharto's takeover a few years earlier and the subsequent massacre of communists and other dissidents. Myanmar decided to model its newly enlarged penal colony on Great Coco after Buru Island, turning it into a hell on earth.

Conditions were harsh and the inmates launched one hunger strike after another, resulting in several deaths. The penal colony was not sustainable, and in December 1971 the government dispatched a ship from Yangon to pick up the surviving inmates. They were transferred back to Insein Jail on the outskirts of the then capital. The Coco Islands were then handed over to the Myanmar navy, which maintained a small garrison there. The camp was subsequently enlarged, as was the airfield on Great Coco. The Coco Islands have since then remained a naval base and out of bounds to civilians.

Despite lurid claims by some Indian analysts and several false alarms about what was happening on the Coco Islands, New Delhi's security planners had good reasons to be concerned about Chinese activities in the area. In August 1994, the Indian coast guard caught three boats 'fishing' close to the site of a major naval base in the Andamans. The trawlers were flying the Myanmar flag, but the crew of 55 was Chinese. There was no fishing gear on board – only radio communication and depth-sounding equipment. The crew was released at the intervention of the Chinese embassy in New Delhi and the incident discreetly buried in the Defence Ministry's file in the Indian capital.[7]

The idea of a new Indian military command on the Andamans was reportedly hatched in 1995 following a closed-door meeting in Washington between India's then prime minister, P.V. Narasimha Rao, and US President Bill Clinton. The plan was finalised when Clinton visited India in 2000, and, as an Indian journalist reported at the time, the new command was to 'have state-of-the-art naval electronic warfare systems that can extend as far as Southeast Asia.'[8] The Andaman and Nicobar Islands were the perfect choice for such a strategically important military command combining the activities of the army, the navy and the air force.

The location of the islands north of Sumatra also meant that Port Blair and towns and villages throughout the Union Territory were badly hit by the 2004 earthquake and tsunami that devastated communities across the entire Indian Ocean. But Port Blair has been rebuilt and life has returned to normal largely thanks to the efforts of the Indian Navy. Cynics would argue that the recovery was carried out with utmost efficiency precisely because the islands are run by the armed forces rather than politicians. India is a vibrant democracy, and no one would want it to be otherwise. But military intervention is often needed to help communities affected by natural disasters.

Now once again idyllic, Port Blair has become as crucial to the defence of India as any major military base in the Himalayas, and it is not difficult to understand why. And, speaking at a round-table conference held on 12 April 2010, organized by the New Delhi-based think-tank the National Maritime Foundation, US Navy Chief Admiral Gary Roughead stated that America's leaders at the highest level have declared that the US and India would be strategic partners for the twenty-first century: 'I'm here to say that the United States Navy in particular is a committed friend to India for the long term.'[9] The aim of this cooperation has never been stated officially, but is nevertheless clear: to counter the rise of China.

The Chinese, on their part, in August 2011 won approval from the Jamaica-based International Seabed Authority – which organises and controls all mineral-related activities in the international seabed area beyond the limits of national jurisdiction – to explore a 10,000-square-kilometre area in the Indian Ocean for 'polymetallic sulphide ore.'[10] *The Times of India* reported at the time: 'The move is bound to draw close scrutiny from India, which is worried about China's military goals in the area.'[11]

This is not the first time the strategic importance of the Andamans and the Nicobars has been recognised, and these islands have a much stormier past than the nearby Myanmar Coco Islands, which were uninhabited when the British arrived there in the nineteenth century.

Indigenous tribes have populated the Andamans for more than 2,000 years, and the long history of the islands has shaped them into the unique place the Andamans and the Nicobars are today.

No outsiders tried to colonise the Andamans until the British East India Company sent Lieutenant Archibald Blair there to survey them in the 1780s. He established a small settlement which was later named after him: Port Blair. The early colonisers encountered the aborigines in the interior of the islands, and, because their skin colour was absolutely black, assumed they were descendants of African slaves the Portuguese had had to abandon there when their ships ran into storms on their way to Macau or some other colony they then had in East Asia.[12]

This was, of course, utterly incorrect. Dark-skinned, so-called 'Negrito' peoples can be found all over the region such as the Semangs of the Malay peninsula and the Aetas of the Philippines. These aboriginal peoples are rapidly dying out – except on the Andamans, where the main tribes are the Great Andamanese, the Jarawas, the Jongils, the Onges and the Sentinelese. Many of them are hunter-gatherers even today and live in protected reserves.

The most isolated are the Sentinelese on North Sentinel Island in the sea to the west of South Andaman Island. They are still vigorously resisting any contacts with outsiders. An Indian naval officer who once tried to land there with gifts in an attempt to establish some kind of rapport with the islanders was met with a barrage of arrows. The most recent victim, an American called John Allen Chau, was killed in November 2018 by arrows fired by the Sentinelese after he had waded ashore on the island in an apparent attempt to convert the tribesmen to Christianity. Indian police used helicopters and a patrol boat to get close to the island, but could not make landfall in order to retrieve Chau's body, or even identify the exact place where he was killed.[13]

Other attempts to land on North Sentinel Island have been equally unsuccessful and no one knows for certain how many people live there today. It could be as few as 40, perhaps as many as 500. The 2001 Census of India records 39 individuals, 21 males and 18 females – but that was based on guesstimates from a safe distance as they could not actually go ashore and meet any of the islanders.[14] Other aboriginal tribes, however, are gradually being brought into the modern world, even if it is a slow and sometimes painful process.

The Mon-Khmer speaking inhabitants of the Nicobars, by contrast, tend their own plantations and vegetable gardens. The first European power to take possession of those islands was the Danes. The Danish East India Company needed a station somewhere between Tranquebar – now called Tharangambadi – then a Danish colony on the coast of southern India, and Siam, where they had strong commercial interests. The Danes occupied the Nicobars in 1755 and, on 1 January 1796, named the islands Frederiksøerna – 'The Frederick Islands' – after their late king, Frederik V.

But the Danes had to abandon the islands time and again because of malaria and other diseases. In the late eighteenth century, Austria, believing that Denmark had given up its claims to the islands, tried to colonise them – the only colony that Austria even tried to establish outside Europe.[15] The Austrians called them the Theresia Islands after their Empress Maria Theresa. The Danes returned, however, and tried to re-establish a presence on the islands. Those efforts were not particularly successful, and in 1868 the colony was sold to Britain. There are no old Danish forts on the islands and the only legacy of Danish rule is that most Nicobarese were converted to Christianity.[16]

The Andamans, meanwhile, had been abandoned by the British after Lieutenant Archibald Blair's initial attempt to colonise them. But after the first Indian War of Independence in 1857, the British again took possession of the islands – to establish a penal colony. Thousands of freedom fighters were sent there to construct prisons and harbour facilities.

The British established their own secluded world on the tiny Ross Island two kilometres off the coast from Port Blair. Old buildings from that time can still be found there, dilapidated, abandoned and overgrown. But once Ross Island, less than a square kilometre in area, had everything the colonials could desire: a secretariat, an officers' club, a hospital, bakery, tennis court, church, bazaar, water treatment plant, ice factory, and printing press.[17]

As India's independence movement grew, so did the prison population on the Andamans. Between 1896 and 1906, a huge, high-security facility was constructed in which freedom fighters from all over India were interned. Called the Cellular Jail because of its shape, the penal colony became better known as *kalapani*, black water, denoting the vast, open sea in the Bay of Bengal between the islands and the mainland, and the horrors of the exile that awaited those who were sent there. And they came from all over India. Prisoners who tried to escape or revolted against the authorities were flogged or hanged. The few who made it outside the walls of the Cellular Jail risked being killed by aborigines who did not like any outsiders, Indian or British didn't matter – and many escapees were found in the surrounding forests, hacked to death or with arrows in their chests or backs.

In the 1930s, several long hunger strikes among the prisoners made the British think twice about the wisdom of deporting people to a remote island. Some would even claim that the Cellular Jail had become a school for the freedom fighters; there, they met new comrades and like-minded people from parts of India other than those from their own home areas or organisations. The last hunger strike, which occurred in 1937, was terminated only after intervention by some of India's most prominent personalities of the time. Mahatma Gandhi sent the prisoners a telegram on behalf of the famous writer and national poet Rabindranath Tagore. The Working Committee of the Indian National Congress advised the prisoners to abandon the hunger strike, assuring them that their grievances would be addressed. Later that year, the first batch of prisoners was transferred to jails on the mainland, and by 1938 many more were gone back to the mainland from across the *kalapani*.[18]

Then, in March 1942, the Japanese army attacked the Andamans and captured them from the British. Ross Island was strafed from the air and some of the buildings were destroyed to make place for Japanese bunkers. The convicts who remained in the Cellular Jail were released. But several of the British officers, and some Indians as well, were beheaded in public to scare the population into submission. With the Japanese came Bose and his INA. On 29 December 1943 the Indian tricolour flew for the first time over 'Free India' as Netaji renamed the Andaman Islands *Shahid Dweep* and the Nicobars, which were also captured by the Japanese, became *Swaraj Dweep*.[19]

In reality, however, 'freedom' meant only that British brutality was followed by Japanese brutality. Locals accused, usually wrongly, of being 'British spies' were stripped and mercilessly caned in public. Others were executed by firing squad or tortured to death. Nearly half the population starved during the Japanese occupation and hundreds of innocent islanders were massacred for no obvious reason at all. Japanese-sponsored 'freedom' just meant another kind of brutal, foreign rule.

The British reoccupied the islands in October 1945. The penal colony was closed down once and for all, and those who so wished could return to the mainland. The Cellular Jail is today a museum to honour all those who were interned or died there. In 1979 it was declared a national monument by the then prime minister of India, Morarji Desai.

After independence, the Andaman and Nicobar Islands were placed under the direct administration of New Delhi and, on 1 November 1956, the whole archipelago was declared a Union Territory. Communications and the infrastructure were improved, people from the mainland were encouraged to settle there, and proper agriculture was introduced as well as a local fishing industry. The old sawmill on Chatham Island, built during colonial days, remains one of the main industries on the Andamans – and in recent years the islands have become a major destination for mainly Indian but also a few foreign tourists.

But the main concern for New Delhi in its easternmost union territory is security. And that concern has only grown stronger as China forges ahead with opening the Myanmar Corridor from Yunnan to the Bay of Bengal. That concern is also why India has turned to the United States for security cooperation. Geopolitical considerations forced India – a close friend of the Soviet Union during the Cold War – to shed its decades-old reluctance to be drawn into America's embrace. In April 2016, India agreed to open some of its naval bases to the United States in exchange for access to weapons technology to help narrow the gap with China.[20] That month, officials also said that Chinese submarines had been sighted in the area on average four times every three months.[21] Since then, India has received US assistance in tracking submarines.

The listening post on the Myanmar Coco Islands may not be as sophisticated as initially thought, and a much bigger worry is posed by the increased presence of Chinese submarines in the sea around the Andaman and Nicobar Islands. It is hardly surprising that China has moved into this particular maritime region as shipping lanes down to the Malacca Straits pass through it. Once around the Malay Peninsula, those lanes lead into the contested South China Sea.

In August 2017, 14 People's Liberation Army Navy (PLAN) ships were spotted by the Indians near the Andamans. They were said to be tasked for 'anti-piracy duties' – one of the reasons also given for acquiring a base in Djibouti – but the ships were accompanied by Chinese submarines. That prompted the Indian Navy to state that it was a rather 'odd' duty for submarines.[22] Admiral Sunil Lanba, the chief of the Indian navy, said in a press conference in New Delhi on 1 December 2017 that PLAN deployments in the Indian Ocean comprise on average six to seven ships on two deployments annually. Conventional boats would be followed by nuclear powered attack submarines, the admiral said and added that 'if there is a future presence of PLAN ships in Pakistan's Gwadar port, whose majority stakes have been acquired by Chinese companies, it will pose a security challenge as well.'[23]

Gwadar in Pakistan and Kyaukpyu in Myanmar – ports located at the end of the Pakistan and Myanmar corridors respectively – have become major concerns in India. But Chinese attempts to secure and defend those two corridors – one to the west of India and the other to the east – are the reason why India feels it is being encircled by China, and therefore has to shore up its defences.

The challenge has been met by a series of joint naval exercises involving India and other nations which share New Delhi's security concerns. Called Exercise Malabar the first three in the series involved India and the United States and were held in the 1990s. They lapsed after Washington imposed military and economic sanctions on India in the wake of its nuclear tests in May 1998, but were revived in 2002 and are now held in the Arabian Sea. A similar exercise in the same waters took place in 2003 followed by more joint US-India exercises off the southwest coast of India in 2004 and 2005. In 2006, a Canadian frigate also joined Exercise Malabar – and then, in 2007, a big step forward in the regional context was taken: over 25 vessels including three aircraft carriers, a nuclear powered submarine, guided missile frigates and destroyers took part in the exercise which involved not only India and the United States but also Australia, Japan and Singapore.[24] And it was held not in the Indian Ocean but off the coast of Okinawa.

Under India's Prime Minister Narendra Modi, who assumed office in May 2014, India has increased investment in the military and, especially, the navy. In addition to the facilities on the Andamans, there is now also a base at Campbell Bay on the largest island in the Nicobar Islands. The aerodromes of both the Andaman and the Nicobar Islands have been expanded and modernised, now taking both advanced hunting planes, transport planes and aircraft that can detect submarines from the air.

Modi is the leader of the Bharatiya Janata Party (BJP) a Hindu nationalist party with a strong anti-Chinese orientation and he has found a soul mate in Japan's Prime Minister Shinzo Abe, who shares his concern about China's expansion. But the India-Japan alliance actually predates Abe's and Modi's respective premierships. Abe, in power from 2006 to 2007 and again since 2012, signed a pact with India for regular military exercises and Japan agreed to sell India two advanced amphibious aircraft a year before Modi became prime minister. A visit to India by then Japanese prime minister Yoshi Mori in August 2000 resulted in a document called 'Indo-Japanese Partnership for the twenty-first century.'[25] In the same year, Japanese aid was also restored after having been suspended since India's 1998 nuclear tests. As Michael J. Green, Japan chair and senior adviser at the Centre for Strategic and International Studies pointed out in 2012, by the 1990s 'conservative Japanese politicians on the right...found common cause with conservative, anti-Chinese Indian political figures.'[26]

Anti-Chinese sentiment is a feature not only of conservative Indian politicians. During a visit to Japan in October 2008 by Modi's predecessor Manmohan Singh, a member of the centrist and some would argue leftist Indian National Congress, documents titled 'Joint Statement on the Advancement of Strategic and Global Partnership between Japan and India' and 'Joint Declaration on Security Cooperation between Japan and India' were signed with Japan's then prime minister, Taro Aso.[27]

The United States remains an important partner for India, but as the Japanese security analyst Satoru Nagao pointed out in a 2013 article, the US is no longer the strong global power it once was. Nagao contends that it falls on India to fill the resulting security vacuum and that Japan would be its willing partner.[28] Increased Indo-Japanese cooperation is also reflected in the volume of bilateral trade between the two countries. From 2000 to 2012, it quadrupled to US$18 billion – which still is much smaller than the US$340 billion Sino-Japanese trade the same year.[29] But the trend is clear: Japan and India are partners in trade as well as regional security, and that relationship has strengthened considerably under Abe and Modi. India is the largest recipient of Japanese aid, while bilateral trade is expected to reach US$50 billion by 2020.

Japan, in accordance with the pacifist constitution the United States forced it to adopt after World War II, should not actually have any military that could once again threaten the Asia-Pacific region. But that attitude towards defeated Japan changed after the Korean War in the early 1950s, when the United States and its allies fought against North Korea supported by China. The US needed a new, powerful military ally in the region – and the response was Japan's 'self-defence forces', which are now one of Asia's strongest and one of the world's best-equipped military units. At the outset, it was stipulated that they would not participate in military activities beyond Japan, but that decision was reversed in the 1990s. It began with Japanese participation in a UN peacekeeping operation in Cambodia in 1992 and was followed by similar interventions in East Timor, Iraq, Nepal and South Sudan. Today, there is no nation – except perhaps China – that challenges Japan's role in, for instance, Exercise Malabar. And the cruelties that the Japanese military committed during its occupation of the Andamans and Nicobars in the 1940s is no longer a topic people wish to talk about today.

Under President Donald Trump, who assumed office in 2017, it is not only the international reputation of the United States which has weakened but also its military commitments abroad – and that despite the US President's seeing eye to eye with both Modi and Abe when it comes to China. It has thus fallen on India to assert its role as a regional superpower, above all in the Indian Ocean, which the Indians have long regarded as their own waters. But for India to do so, it has had to confront a new and more assertive China. As the Indian Vice-Admiral Anup Singh wrote in 2017: 'There is no doubt in anyone's mind now, that China craves a permanent strategic presence in the IOR [Indian Ocean Region]. After all, the various ports and other infrastructure projects she has established in Myanmar, Bangladesh, Sri Lanka, Pakistan, and in a number of East African countries over the past decade, were planned only with the purpose of "enabling" presence in this ocean.'[30]

Singh also believes that China has learned from the experiences of the previous Cold War and added allies in the region by combining long-term strategic plans with loans and financial assistance rather than through direct and open military alliances. And that is the strategy which will secure the Belt and Road Initiative (BRI) and, in particular, the so-called 'Maritime Silk Road' through the Indian Ocean.

India has therefore begun to apply a similar policy, which Prime Minister Modi calls SAGAR, an acronym that stands for 'Security And Growth for All in the Region' and includes helping smaller countries with infrastructure projects as well as combating piracy, smuggling and illegal fishing. The aim is that it will lead to closer economic cooperation between India and its neighbours in the Indian Ocean. But although the Indian economy is expanding rapidly, it lags far behind China's, and SAGAR can hardly compare with the BRI. The emphasis of India's foreign policy will, therefore, be on its navy's military cooperation with like-minded countries, especially Japan and the United States.

And much depends on India. Nagao believes that there are, as he says, three reasons why India is the power that could challenge China's growing influence: 'Firstly, India is located at the northern centre of the Indian Ocean. This means that India can access the Indian Ocean from all sides relatively easily. Secondly, India is the only country among the countries around the Indian Ocean to possess a strong Navy. Thirdly, India has long respected the freedom of navigation in the SLOCs [Sea lines of communication] for all the countries which are near India, in the manner of a responsible maritime power. Thus, if India has the will and enough capabilities, the Indian Ocean will become India's Ocean.'[31]

Nagao is right that India can access the Indian Ocean from its east as well as its west coast. India's smallest union territory, Lakshadweep, is on the western side of the Indian subcontinent. No more than 65,000 people live there, but it is the only one of India's 29 states and 7 union territories besides Jammu and Kashmir where Muslims make up the majority of the population. The archipelago consists of the Minicoy, the Laccadive and the Amindivi Islands and came under British rule in the late eigtheenth century, mainly because the British East India Company wanted to protect the southwestern flank of its growing Indian domains. The islands became a separate union territory in 1956 and received their current name in 1973, which comes from Lakshadwipa, Sanskrit for 'one hundred thousand islands'. There may not be as many islands as that – there are only 10 inhabited islands and another 17 uninhabited ones – but the Union Territory's exclusive economic zone amounts to 400,000 square-kilometres, which makes them strategically important to India. In May 2012, New Delhi decided to build a naval base on the islands to monitor ocean traffic in the western Indian Ocean. This was opened in April 2016.

But the Indian Navy is, of course, not confined to groups of islands off its eastern and western coasts. The 67,228-strong force operates a fleet of one aircraft carrier, one amphibious transport dock, eight landing ships, eleven destroyers, thirteen frigates, one nuclear-powered attack submarine, one ballistic missile submarine, fourteen conventionally-powered attack submarines, twenty-two corvettes, one mine countermeasure vessel, four fleet tankers, and various other auxiliary vessels – a long list of ships that makes India one of the strongest naval powers in the region.[32] As of 2018, India has 67 naval installations along its coasts and on its islands varying from ports with logistic support sites to advanced forward operating bases.

Unlike China, India also has a long history of shipbuilding and navigation. Ancient Indian states and empires traded with the Arab world and Southeast Asia long before Zheng He appeared on the scene, and while his voyages across the Indian Ocean occurred during a very brief period in the fifteenth century and left no lasting impact on the region, the influence of Indian civilization was far more profound. Buddhism and Hinduism spread to South and Southeast Asia, to the states we know today as Sri Lanka, Myanmar, Thailand, Laos and Cambodia – and even to Indonesia, where Buddhism was established before Islam became the predominant religion in the sixteenth century. Pockets of Buddhism still exist in Indonesia and Hinduism has survived on Bali and parts of Lombok. Sanskrit-based writing systems are used even today in Sri Lanka, Myanmar, Thailand, Laos and Cambodia. Classic Javanese also uses a Sanskrit-based system, although the national language, Bahasa Indonesia, is written with Roman script.

The Indians were the main traders, missionaries and explorers in the region for centuries – until the Europeans arrived with their superior firepower. Indian naval power began to decline when they encountered Portuguese mariners and traders in the sixteenth century who came to dominate maritime trade to and from India. Goa on the Malabar Coast was captured by the Portuguese in 1510 and became the first European outpost on the Indian subcontinent. It remained in Portuguese hands until its annexation by India in 1961.

The origin of a 'new' Indian navy can be traced to 1612, when the British East India Company formed a naval arm of ships to challenge the Portuguese, whose influence declined as new colonial masters gained ascendancy over most of Asia. The Indian navy saw action against the French in the eighteenth century, in the First Opium War in China in the 1840s and the Second Anglo-Myanmar war in 1852. When the British Crown took over governance of India from the East India Company following the 1857 uprising, the Indian navy came under more direct centralised and effective command. It participated in World War I as well as World War II, but nearly all its officers were British. It was only after independence in 1947 that Indian officers were promoted to replace British ones. But some of the latter remained even after independence and it was not until the late 1950s that the navy became truly 'Indianised'.

The Indian Navy played a role in the annexation of Goa in 1961 and the Indo-Pakistan wars of 1965 and 1971. The Indian Navy has also intervened in political crises in smaller Indian Ocean nations. In 1983, it planned a mission to avert a coup in Mauritius. But as there was, in the end, no coup, India had no need to intervene. In 1986, however, it moved ships close to Seychelles and did avert a coup there. And, in 1988, it intervened in Maldives to thwart a coup attempt by the People's Liberation Organisation of Tamil Eelam, a group of Tamil militants from Sri Lanka.

Then, in 1999, when India and Pakistan fought a brief war at Kargil in Kashmir, the Indian Navy was deployed in the northern Arabian Sea. Indian Navy aviators flew sorties, and marine commandos fought alongside the Indian army forces at Kargil.[33]

Since then, Indian ships have been involved in numerous relief rescue missions in the Indian Ocean. The largest, not surprisingly, was Operation Gambhir which was carried out following the 2004 tsunami in the Indian Ocean. Indian naval rescue vessels reached affected countries in the region within less then 12 hours after the tsunami struck on the morning of 26 December. Apart from salvaging the Andamans and Nicobars, the mission also led to the decision to enhance the Indian Navy's amphibious force capabilities, including the use of landing platform docks and other vessels, which was done in 2007.[34] By the end of 2019, the Indian Navy expects to have over 150 ships and close to 500 aircraft. India also plans to construct its own aircraft carriers and to expand its fleet of submarines.

When it comes to naval capabilities and experience, India is far ahead of China, which is only now becoming a naval power. But the very fact that China is now challenging India's supremacy in the Indian Ocean, has led to a drive to modernise the Indian Navy – and to cooperate with other countries in the region. Exercise Malabar was the most extensive such joint manoeuvre, but India is also cooperating with France as seen in the agreement between Prime Minister Modi and the French president Emannuel Macron, signed on 11 March 2018, and has made approaches asking whether Australia will allow Indian ships to dock and resupply on the Cocos (Keeling) Islands.

That is still being discussed, but, in May 2018, India secured access to the strategic island of Sabang on the northern tip of Sumatra. India will invest in the port and an economic zone on Sabang, which is located less than 500 kilometres from the entrance to the Malacca Strait.[35] Besides development of its 40-metre deep port, good for all types of vessels, including submarines, Indian naval ships will also be permitted to use those facilities. Luhut Pandjaitan, Indonesia's minister for maritime affairs and a former military officer, said at the time that he was critical of China's Belt and Road Initiative: 'We do not want to be controlled by BRI.'[36] He also questioned China's unilateral claims on the South China Sea, noting that those claims include parts of Indonesia's maritime exclusive economic zone.

And it is not only in the Indian Ocean that India is facing up to China's economic and political expansion. It is also doing so on land – more precisely in countries that form corridors down to the Indian

Ocean: Pakistan and, more importantly, Myanmar. C. Uday Bhaskar, a retired commodore of the Indian Navy, wrote in the September 2010 issue of the Kathmandu-based *Himal* magazine that 'access to and control of the Indian Ocean long remained an abiding strategic concern for the major powers.' Bhaskar goes on to quote Olaf Caroe, governor of the North-West Frontier Province before Partition in 1947, who wrote a book called *Wells of Power* about the extension of the nineteenth-century Great Game into the twentieth century: 'The strategic movements of the Allies in Iraq and Persia in the Second World War were made possible from the Indian base…the importance of the [Persian] Gulf grows greater, not less, as the need for fuel expands, the world contracts and the shadows lengthen from the north. Its stability can be assured only by the close accord between the States which surround this Muslim lake, an accord underwritten by the Great Powers whose interests are engaged.'[37]

Bhaskar adds that almost seven decades after World War II, the enemy, which Caroe referred to as the 'shadow from the north', is no longer the Soviet Union, 'the Russian bear seeking in vain to access the warm-water ports of the Indian Ocean' – but 'the oriental dragon,' namely China. The focus of attention has shifted from west to east in the Indian Ocean. And, of course, between China and the Indian Ocean lies Myanmar – and India and Myanmar share a complicated and delicate history, one marked as much by mistrust as amity.

The role Indians played as intermediaries between the colonial British and the native population precipitated sometimes fierce anti-Indian sentiment. Throughout the 1930s and 1940s, the Myanmar nationalist movement had strong undertones of communal tension. Even today, people of South Asian origin are often looked down on in Myanmar, popularly referred to as *kala*, a Bamar language pejorative meaning 'foreigner' or 'Indian.' Curiously, Caucasians are still called *kala pyu*, which translates from the Bamar language as 'white Indians.'

Still, Myanmar's relations with India were in the main cordial after independence. Myanmar's first prime minister, U Nu, never forgot that without India's massive military and economic aid his government would most probably have collapsed. However, Indo-Myanmar relations chilled after General Ne Win's military coup in March 1962, when his revolutionary council after a few years in power moved to nationalise privately owned businesses and factories, of which an estimated 60 per cent were owned by people of Indian origin. Thousands lost their property and livelihood and during the four-year period spanning 1964 to 1968 some 150,000 citizens of Indian descent left the country.[38]

Many leaders of the formerly democratic Myanmar also fled, among them the deposed Prime Minister U Nu, who went into exile in India. The Indian government put him up in a stately residence in Bhopal, where he remained for well over a decade before returning to Myanmar under a general amnesty in 1980. Bilateral relations between India and Myanmar remained more or less stagnant until Myanmar's 1988 uprising for democracy.

After the uprising was brutally crushed by the Myanmar military, a number of refugees escaped to India. There were not as many as the thousands of pro-democracy activists who escaped to Thailand, but probably about a hundred young Myanmars managed to cross the border into the northeastern Indian state of Manipur, and were later allowed to stay in New Delhi under the protection of the United Nations High Commissioner for Refugees.

In an official statement issued in the wake of the violence, India expressed its support for the 'undaunted resolve of the Burmese [Myanmar] people to achieve their democracy.'[39] The Bamar language service of the state-sponsored radio station All-India Radio, AIR, became even more outspoken in its criticism of Myanmar's new military government, which made it immensely popular with the population at large.

In response, Myanmar's state-run *Working People's Daily* newspaper began publishing outright racist articles and cartoons against AIR and ethnic Indians in general, attempting to revive the anti-*kala* xenophobia of the 1930s. But even then it was clear that India's hard diplomatic stand was not driven by illusions of serving as a regional guardian or promoter of democracy. It was never overlooked that India shares a 1,371-kilometre frontier with Myanmar and that ethnic insurgents fighting against New Delhi had long used under-administered territories in Myanmar as sanctuaries to conduct cross-border raids into India's sensitive northeastern areas. Since the 1960s, Myanmar's only reaction to this situation had been to mount half-hearted and essentially futile military operations against the insurgents, mainly the Nagas.

It was widely believed in New Delhi in the late 1980s and early 1990s that a future democratic government in Myanmar would likely take a more tactful approach. India's sympathy for Myanmar's pro-democracy movement was further strengthened by the fact that its prime minister until December 1989, Rajiv Gandhi, was a personal friend of pro-democracy leader Aung San Suu Kyi.

Their acquaintance dated back to the early 1960s, when her mother, Daw Khin Kyi, served as Myanmar's ambassador to India. Suu Kyi's father, national independence hero Aung San, had also known Rajiv's grandfather, Nehru, personally. But at the time it was also clear that India's support for Myanmar's pro-democracy forces was also guided by an Indian desire to counter its main regional rival China whose influence with Myanmar's internationally isolated generals was growing after 1988.

Around 1993 India began to re-evaluate its strategy due to concerns that its policies had achieved little except to push Myanmar closer to Beijing. The result was a dramatic policy shift aimed at improving relations with Myanmar's generals, as it was also becoming clear that the pro-democracy movement would not achieve power within the foreseeable future. New Delhi's Myanmar policy had also prompted the generals in Yangon to seek military cooperation with Pakistan – which caused even more alarm among India's security planners. In March 1989, a high-powered Myanmar military delegation paid an unpublicised visit to Islamabad, and a deal was signed for the delivery of Pakistani-made machine-guns, mortar bombs and other military hardware. Pakistan also joined China in jointly opposing resolutions condemning Myanmar at the United Nations Human Rights Commission.[40]

At that time, Myanmar's military government had effectively cowed Suu Kyi's National League for Democracy party, once a mighty mass movement, into submission. Nor did the exile community seem to have any impact on political developments inside the country – even as some of them actually stayed in the personal residence in New Delhi of senior Indian politician George Fernandes, who served as defence minister from 1998 through 2004. It was during his time as defence minister that Indian concerns over China's alleged designs for the Coco Islands reached their crescendo. Fernandes was the first to claim, wrongly, that the islands had been part of India until they were donated to Myanmar by Nehru.[41] Fernandes, who once openly branded China as India's 'enemy no 1', was also an ardent supporter of the Tibetan movement in exile as well as Myanmar's pro-democracy students.[42] Some of the latter stayed with Fernandes in his house in New Delhi.

In a curious exposé of Indian covert operations in Myanmar, the Indian media reported in February 1998 that a gang of international gunrunners had been intercepted in a joint operation mounted by the army, the navy, the air force and the coast guard. More than 70 men had been apprehended on 'Longoff Island' in the Andamans and 145 guns seized. Six gunrunners were said to have been killed in a skirmish with the security forces, the reports said. The shipment was headed for Chittagong, *The Times of India* reported, and consisted of automatic rifles, rocket launchers, machine-guns, radio sets and several hundred thousand rounds of ammunition. The guns had been purchased in Cambodia, transported through Thailand, and were meant to be delivered to ethnic rebels in India's northeast.[43]

No one was really surprised, because it had been known for years that Cambodia was awash with all sorts of weapons left over from decades of civil war in that country, and that insurgents in the region were procuring guns from there. At the time, it was also common knowledge that black-market weapons were regularly being transported across the Andaman Sea to the Tamil Tigers in Sri Lanka – or across the Bay of Bengal and on to Bangladesh, where Naga, Manipuri and Assamese rebel groups had sanctuaries and frequently took delivery of guns from Southeast Asia. Gunrunners based in the Thai resort island of Phuket had fleets of small boats and fishing trawlers specifically for that purpose.

But there was something that did not sound quite right in the press reports about this particular incident. 'There is certain information we cannot give owing to the sensitivity of diplomatic relations involved,' Assistant Chief of Navy Staff Operations, Rear Admiral Madanjit Singh, rather cryptically told the *Times of India*. And no one could find 'Longoff Island' on any maps of the area. The action, which was codenamed *Operation Leech*, had in fact occurred on Landfall Island, the northernmost of the Andamans.

And the so-called gunrunners turned out not to be that at all. There were 2 Thai captains and 35 Thai and Cambodian crewmembers on the fishing trawlers that had brought them there. But 36 of those arrested were Rakhine and Karen rebels from Myanmar – who had worked closely with Indian intelligence officers and provided them with information about the activities of northeastern insurgents. In 1995, they had even passed on information that helped Indian security forces capture arms being smuggled by those rebels from Cox's Bazaar in Bangladesh to India in an operation codenamed 'Golden Bird'.[44]

Nandita Haksar, an Indian lawyer who looked into the case, quotes in her book *Rogue Agent* one of the detained Rakhine rebels as saying that they had had meetings in Thailand with a Bamar-speaking, Indian military intelligence colonel called Vijay Singh 'Gary' Grewal long before they set sail for the Andamans. He and other Indian intelligence officers had actually invited them to use Landfall Island, which is uninhabited, as a base for their struggle against the military regime in Yangon.[45] Weapons could be stored there and the rebels could retreat to the island after operations on the Myanmar mainland. In return, the rebels from Myanmar would monitor the illicit arms traffic in the Andaman Sea to make sure ships carrying guns to the Nagas, the Manipuris and the Assamese could be intercepted.

More importantly, the Indians wanted them to spy on a new radar station on the Coco Islands just north of Landfall. And if China gained a toehold in the Indian Ocean, even indirectly through the Myanmar naval base on Great Coco, they would be able to collect intelligence about India's movements in the region. The interception of the three Myanmar 'fishing trawlers' with Chinese crews near the Andamans in 1994 had reinforced those suspicions.

The rationale for supporting certain groups among the Karen and Rakhine rebels was the same as for sending arms and ammunition to the Kachin Independence Army (KIA) in the far north of Myanmar: to prevent arms from reaching the insurgents in the northeast – and to keep on eye on China. Guns were airlifted by helicopter from Dibrugarh to the army base at Vijaynagar right on the Myanmar border, where the KIA had a secret camp. Indian rebels have also had camps in northwestern Myanmar since the Indian Army managed to push ethnic Naga militants across the border into Myanmar. From there, beyond reach of the Indian Army, they launched cross-border raids into India. For years, the Indians tried to persuade the Myanmar Army to drive them out, and, failing that, that the Myanmar and Indian armies should carry out joint or at least coordinated operations against the rebels, which soon also included militants from Assam and Manipur. When there was no response from the Myanmar side, India's security services hoped that the KIA would be more willing to do the job, if they got arms and other supplies from the Indian side.

This policy was the brainchild of Bhibuti Bhusan Nandy, a veteran Indian intelligence officer who served as station chief of the Research and Analysis Wing, RAW, in Bangkok in the 1980s and who later became director of the agency's Special Services as well as additional secretary in New Delhi.[46]

In 1997, however, Nandy had been transferred to the post of director-general of the Indo-Tibetan Border Force and was eventually appointed National Security Adviser to the government of Mauritius. As Nandy was being sidelined, India's Myanmar policy was changing rapidly. In the meantime, the KIA had, to the surprise of many, made peace with the government in Yangon, and the Karen and Rakhine rebels were now insignificant. India now embarked on its diplomatic offensive to wean Myanmar's military government away from its close relationship with China. And cooperation with the Myanmar military, not some rebel groups, was deemed necessary to curtail the activities of the northeastern rebels.[47]

By the time the Rakhine and Karen rebels arrived at Landfall Island, their new 'mentor', Colonel Grewal, was already well connected in Yangon. He had simply lured them into a trap. Six of the rebels were shot on the island before the others were arrested. There was not going to be any Myanmar rebel base on Landfall. In May 1999, the ordinary crew-members were released and repatriated to Thailand. But the Rakhine and the Karens languished in jail first in Port Blair and later in Kolkata. Nandy was upset that contacts he had nurtured carefully over years were ruined, and signed a petition asking for their release, blaming the fiasco on 'a rogue agent.'[48] But it is plausible to assume that Grewal's actions were more in line with India's new Myanmar policy than Nandy's. It was not until June 2011, 13 years after their arrest that they were set free and flown to New Delhi. Myanmar exiles received them as heroes at the airport, cheering and bedecking them with garlands.

By the late 1990s, it was clear that India had a new approach to the 'Chinese problem' in Myanmar. In January 2000, Indian army chief General Ved Prakash Malik paid a two-day visit to Myanmar, which was followed by a reciprocal visit by his Myanmar counterpart, General Maung Aye, to the northeast Indian city of Shillong. The unusual nature of this visit, by a foreign leader to a provincial capital, was accentuated by the arrival of a group of senior Indian officials from the Trade, Energy, Defence, Home and Foreign Affairs ministries to hold talks with the Myanmar general. It was at that time too sensitive to allow a Myanmar general to visit New Delhi, where support for Myanmar's pro-democracy movement was strong among politicians and civil society organisations.

In the aftermath of the meetings in Shillong, India began to provide non-lethal military support to Myanmar troops along their common border. Most of those Myanmar troops' uniforms and some other combat gear now originates from India, as do the leased helicopters Myanmar uses to combat the ethnic insurgents who operate from sanctuaries along the two sides' common border. In November 2000, the Indian government felt confident enough about the improvement in bilateral relations to invite Maung Aye to New Delhi, where he headed a delegation that included several other high-ranking junta members and cabinet ministers. Defence Minister Fernandes, however, pointedly did not meet the Myanmar delegation.[49]

In 2004, junta chief General Than Shwe also visited India, followed in December 2006 by the then third-highest ranking officer in Myanmar's military hierarchy, General Thura Shwe Mann, who toured the National Defence Academy in Khadakvasla, India's premier officer-training school, as well as the Tata Motors plant in Pune, which manufactures vehicles for the Indian military.

In the mid-1990s, AIR's Bamar language service conspicuously ceased broadcasting its anti-junta rhetoric; it is still on air today, but programming consists almost exclusively of Myanmar pop music. A strange kind of 'cultural diplomacy' followed. In the early 2000s, the

Indian right-wing Hindu organization, *Rashtriya Swayamsevak Sangh*, RSS, renewed its presence in Myanmar.[50] The RSS first came to Myanmar in the 1940s to provide social and religious services to the country's ethnic Indian minority, but it lay dormant after the military took over in 1962 and commenced nationalising Indian private companies.

The renewed effort to build up the RSS's Yangon branch was apparently made with the blessings of Maung Aye, a staunch Myanmar nationalist who reportedly frowned on the country's recent economic and military reliance on China. The RSS, which in Myanmar was referred to as the *Sanatan Dharma Swayamsevak Sangh*, appears to have convinced some of the Myanmar generals that Hinduism and Buddhism are indeed 'branches of the same tree' – and that 'the best guard against China is culture,' to quote a Kolkata-based RSS official.[51]

Although the RSS is the parent organisation of the Hindu nationalist Bharatiya Janata Party, which in alliance with several other parties led the Indian coalition government between 1998 and 2004, it is not certain that the Hindu fundamentalists' new mission in Myanmar had the blessings of the Indian government. But cultural ties between the two countries have definitely strengthened in recent years.

So, too, has cross-border trade. Before 1988 there was scant commercial activity along the two countries' shared border, apart from smuggling. In February 2007, Sanjay Budhia, vice president of the Indian Chamber of Commerce and Industries, said in a speech in Kolkata that India and Myanmar 'have set a US$1 billion trade target in 2006-07, up from US$557 million in 2004-05.'[52]

He noted that principal exports from Myanmar to India include 'rice, maize, pulses, beans, sesame seeds, fish and prawns, timber, plywood and raw rubber, base metals and castor seeds.' In return, India exports machinery and industrial equipment, dairy products, textiles, pharmaceutical products and consumer goods. The India–Myanmar trade now rivals that of the booming cross-border trade with China, which has been brisk for almost two decades.

India has also shown a competitive interest in purchasing natural gas from Myanmar and, for a while, in building a 1,200-megawatt hydroelectric power station on the Chindwin River across from India's northeastern region. New Delhi is also actively involved in several infrastructure projects inside Myanmar, including major road construction ventures. The hydroelectric project on the Chindwin had to be scrapped after opposition from environmental protection groups in India, but the desire to buy gas and help Myanmar improve its dilapidated infrastructure remains. The road to Moreh opposite Tamu on the Myanmar border has been upgraded, but it cannot be compared with the wide, dual-carriage-way highway the Chinese have built from Kunming to Ruili and Jiegao.

Today, India sees Myanmar as its 'land bridge' to Southeast Asia and as such a vital part of its new business-driven 'Look East' policy which, under Modi, has become an 'Act East' policy. Already by the turn of the new millennium, India's old policy of covert support for Myanmar rebels and dissidents had been definitely buried. Whatever links India still retains with ethnic rebels in Myanmar is confined to intelligence-gathering.

In January 2007, Indian Foreign Minister Pranab Mukherjee became the first senior leader from a major democracy to visit Myanmar's new capital Naypyitaw, to which the junta moved its administrative offices in November 2005. Even in the midst of the tumultuous anti-government demonstrations led by Buddhist monks in late 2007, senior officials from the Indian state-owned Oil and Natural Gas Corporation, led by Petroleum and Natural Gas Minister Murli Deora, flew to Naypyitaw to sign an agreement to explore for gas in three new blocks in the Bay of Bengal off Myanmar's southwestern Rakhine coast.[53]

India was successfully beginning to wean Myanmar away from its near-total dependence on China for economic and military support by resisting the strong position taken by the US and the European Union against the generals in Naypyitaw. Though still allowing Myanmar dissidents to operate openly in New Delhi, it was becoming clear that India would not risk – to China's benefit – the precious foothold it had achieved in Myanmar since the policy changed in the 1990s. The West-East corridor India wanted to open through Myanmar served a double purpose: to establish direct trade with booming economies in Southeast Asia – and to keep China at bay in Myanmar.

In September 2010, the New Delhi ambassadors of the member countries of the Association of Southeast Asian Nations, ASEAN, were invited to Manipur. They travelled down to Moreh on the Myanmar border. A group of businessmen from Tamu on the other side came across to Moreh to welcome the ambassadors, who 'expressed confidence that trade and commerce between India and ASEAN countries through Moreh would be feasible.'[54]

But for that to materialise, it would be necessary to repair and upgrade not only the pot-holed road that leads from Imphal, the Manipur capital, to Moreh, but the highways to and from Assam as well – not to mention Myanmar's hopelessly inadequate road network and other infrastructure. And before anyone can even think of a highway from India through Myanmar to Bangkok and Singapore, a lasting solution must be found to the ethnic problems and insurgencies in India's northeast.

The problems with cross-border insurgencies also remained and after the attempt to have the KIA drive the rebels out had failed and the Myanmar Army still showed no interest it moving against their bases in the upper Sagaing Region in the northwest, India took matters into their own hands. In June 2015, after Myanmar-based rebels had ambushed an Indian Army convoy in Manipur killing 18 soldiers and injuring at least 11, Indian commandos crossed the border into Myanmar. It is not clear how deep into Myanmar they went, but several rebel camps near the border were attacked and destroyed.

A statement from the presidential office in Naypyitaw, issued the day after the attack took place, asserted that fighting had broken out on the Indian side, denying that any 'outside forces' were using Myanmar as a staging ground for attacks into India.[55] But that was a feeble attempt by the Myanmar government to hide its embarrassment over the fact that there are such bases in the country – and that there was nothing the Myanmar Army could do to prevent the Indian Army from carrying out such a raid.

The reality is also that the Myanmar Army is stretched thin on too many fronts in Kachin and Shan states, where it has for several years been battling Kachin, Shan and other ethnic rebels. It has neither the resources nor the manpower to become engaged in yet another battlefront in the country. Fighting India's wars is not a priority for the Myanmar army; it is not even on its agenda. And if the Myanmar army were to agree to joint operations with India, it would be tantamount to admitting what the Myanmar government has consistently denied – that rebels from India's northeast have bases on the Myanmar side of the border – and such an admission is extremely unlikely to be made.

Taga, the main camp of the Naga, Assamese and Manipuri rebels which the Indian commandos could not reach in June 2015, is located on the Chindwin river, close to the Myanmar Army garrison at Singkaling Hkamti and far from the Indian border, so it is not unconceivable that Myanmar is using them to collect intelligence from the Indian side. Despite Indian efforts to improve relations with Myanmar, the two neighbours are still suspicious of each other. Myanmar has not forgotten India's support for the KIA and other dissidents and, likewise, India does not trust the Myanmar Army because it is turning a blind eye to the presence of Indian rebels on its soil – and for being too close to China.

Several leaders of the Indian rebel groups are also present in Ruili, where the Chinese provide them with shelter. The Chinese may too be using them for intelligence purposes, and as a tit-for-tat for India's allowing the Dalai Lama to have a Tibetan government in exile in McLeodganj in the hills above Dharamshala in northern India. One of India's most wanted men, Paresh Baruah, the commander of the United Liberation Front of Asom (Assam), resides in Ruili and, like other Indian rebel leaders, is able to travel without difficulty from there across the border to northern Myanmar and on to Taga. Several Manipuri groups are also represented in Ruili and travel regularly to Taga for meetings – and such journeys would not be possible without the tacit approval of Chinese as well as Myanmar authorities.[56] Weapons for the Indian rebels come mostly from clandestine arms factories on the Myanmar-China border, or from the black market in China, which many would argue is more grey than black because it is run by well-connected, former Chinese army officers.

Whether India's new 'Act East' policy will be successful depends not only on denying Indian insugents sanctuary in Myanmar and improved infrastructure across its common border. Keeping overall Chinese influence in Myanmar at bay is even more important from a strategic point of view – and that cannot be done in remote mountain areas. The balance of power in the Indian Ocean is far more important and one of India's most crucial lines of defence now goes through the former penal colony that has become the picturesque city of Port Blair. It is from here the Indians – and their allies – are hoping to counterbalance the increasingly important role China is playing in the countries in and around the Indian Ocean.

4

MAURITIUS

Geographically, Mauritius belongs to Africa but the island is located 800 kilometres out in the Indian Ocean from Madagascar and even further from the African mainland. Ethnically, Mauritius also differs significantly from other African countries. About half the population is of Indian origin and there is a sizable minority of people of Chinese descent. The rest is African, Caucasian or a Creole-type mix of several ethnic groups. And the landscape on the island is breathtaking, with its rugged, volcanic mountains surrounding a central high plateau. The island's white-sand beaches and luxury hotels attract more than a million foreign visitors every year, mostly from Europe and North America but increasingly from newly-rich countries in Asia as well.

The relative proximity to the African continent made Mauritius a popular destination also for white South African tourists during the apartheid regime. International boycotts and sanctions prevented them from going to many countries, but Mauritius was not one of them. The 'non-African' African nation of Mauritius even became a transit point for trade between South Africa and countries which should have respected the sanctions but were keen to find a way around them. Thailand, for instance, exported rice to South Africa through Mauritius, and Singapore used the island for the re-export of electronic goods and consumer items. The national carrier *Air Mauritius* connected South Africa with Asia through the island's international airport. It was as uncomplicated as changing planes in Mauritius. As a member of the Organisation of African Unity, Mauritius was, of course, opposed to apartheid. But like many other pocket-sized island nations with a small population and limited natural resources, it had to be imaginative in order to develop its economy. For Mauritius the answer was tourism and transit trade – and it prospered as a result. Per capita income was well above the African average.

The situation changed after South Africa ended apartheid and moved to black majority rule in the early 1990s. South Africans, irrespective of their race, could now travel anywhere in Africa and the world. Other African countries began to develop as well. Mauritius turned to financial services, the tourism industry was further expanded and, because of the island's well-developed infrastructure, it has become an important link for all sorts of trade between countries in Africa and the rest of the world. Modern port facilities in the capital Port Louis, world-class banking services, and the political stability that Mauritius enjoys have given it a clear advantage over its competitors.

As a result, the per capita GDP of Mauritius reached US$10,547 in 2017, up from US$5,679 in 2006, and almost twice that of South Africa, the continent's economic power house. Only the Seychelles with a GDP per capita of US$15,504 has a higher figure – but the Seychelles is a special case where wealth is very unevenly distributed.[1] Mauritius is a modern welfare state with excellent healthcare and education for all. The literacy rate stands at 94.7 per cent for men and 90.7 per cent for women.[2] And, because of a peculiar colonial heritage, French is spoken as well as English, which makes it easy for foreign tourists and businessmen to communicate with the local population and the authorities.

In Port Louis, high-rise buildings tower over old houses made from black, volcanic rock. The island's many hotels, usually located behind palm trees and pristine beaches, are of the highest international standard. In 2017, 1.36 million tourists visited Mauritius, or slightly more than the island's total population of 1.26 million people.[3] Mauritius has become the pearl of the Indian Ocean, a well-developed island with magnificent scenery, the kind of luxury foreign visitors expect to find in the tropics, and financial services which are hard to come by elsewhere in Africa.

In recent years, Mauritius – hardly surprising given its location in the southern Indian Ocean and its role in trade with Africa – has also taken a prominent place in China's strategic thinking. China has invested millions of dollars in a new economic zone and financed the construction of a new terminal at Mauritius' airport.[4] A delegation headed by Xu Jinghu, special representative of the Chinese government on African Affairs, visited Mauritius in April 2017 to 'explore new venues of cooperation'.[5] He met with foreign minister Vishnu Lutchmeenaraidoo, and, according to an official statement issued during the visit, they agreed that 'China can play a crucial role in the Mauritian strategy of setting up Special Economic Zones in targeted countries such as Ghana, Senegal and Madagascar... Chinese investors are encouraged to use the Mauritius financial centre for their African operations.'[6]

Chinese businessmen, and tourists, have become a familiar sight in the streets of Port Louis and the hotels on the beaches. And Chinese money is flowing in for investment and to be deposited in local banks and then used for trade and commerce. Mauritius has become a vital link in President Xi Jinping's Belt and Road Initiative (BRI) – which the Indians perceive as a threat to their interests in the Indian Ocean region. Ties to India have traditionally been strong because of the number of people on the island who are of Indian ancestry.

India's response to China's newly aroused interest in Mauritius came when, in May 2017 – only a month after Xu Jinghu's visit – the island's prime minister Pravind Kumar Jugnauth travelled to New Delhi to meet his Indian counterpart Narendra Modi. Mauritius was granted a US$500 million line of credit to develop the island's infrastructure and an agreement was signed for cooperation on maritime security. Modi said in a speech during the visit that 'the Indian Ocean region is at the top of our policy priorities. Our vision for the Indian Ocean region is rooted in advancing cooperation...[and] our partnership with Mauritius is among the strongest maritime relationships in the world...we will also train and patrol the seas together.'[7]

Srikanth Kondapalli, a professor of Chinese studies at Jawaharlal Nehru University in New Delhi, was quoted by the Indian website *Mint* as saying that 'there must [also] have been some quiet discussions about China and the BRI...India must have pointed out the problems faced by countries like Sri Lanka in terms of debt and Myanmar in terms of ecological problems.'[8] Through the generous loan to Mauritius, India obviously hoped to prevent Chinese state-owned companies from investing in shipping and port projects in Mauritius in the same way as they had done in Pakistan, Sri Lanka and Myanmar.

India's close relations with Mauritius, and the island's ethnic landscape, is a result of its unique history. The island was uninhabited when the first seafaring traders, who were Arabs, arrived about a thousand years ago. They named the island they had found Dina Arobi, or 'abandoned island'. The first European to reach the island is believed to have been the Portuguese navigator Diogo Fernandes Pereira, who arrived there in 1507. He called the island Ilha do Cirne after the name of his ship, *Cirne*, or 'the Swan' in Portuguese. But he and his men did not stay long; they sailed on and discovered another uninhabited, volcanic island which was later named Rodrigues after another Portuguese navigator, Diogo Rodrigues, who arrived there in 1528. That island is now part of the Republic of Mauritius.

The next Europeans to arrive at these islands were Dutch. In 1598, a Dutch ship commanded by Admiral Wybrand Van Warwyck arrived on the main island and named it Mauritius after Prince Maurits Van Nassau, the *stadthouder*, or head of state, of the Dutch Republic. In one of those odd colonial serendipities, the princely head of the *Republiek der Zeven Verenigde Nederlanden* also gave his name to another island on almost the opposite corner of the earth. In 1614, a vessel belonging to a group of Dutch merchants discovered a rugged, windswept and uninhabited island in the sea north of Iceland – and named it Maurits Wylandt, or Mauritius. Perhaps to avoid confusion, the island in the Arctic Ocean was in 1620 renamed Jan Mayen after the Dutch navigator Jan Jacobszoon May van Schellinkhout. No one ever settled there, but whalers from various European countries used it on and off as a base. In 1930, Jan Mayen was made part of Norway, which maintains a meteorological station of the island.

In the beginning, nothing much happened in the "southern" Mauritius either. It was not until the 1630s that the Dutch established a permanent base there consisting of a governor and his men presiding over a small contingent of Dutch convicts and slaves from Madagascar and the East Indies, now Indonesia. Mauritius was tiny compared with

Madagascar – or Java for that matter – but the Dutch were interested in exploiting its forests. Ebony was felled, exported and used to make furniture that was needed in European households in other Dutch colonies in the region, which have now become South Africa, Sri Lanka and Indonesia.

But the poor administration and harsh conditions on Mauritius made the colony unsustainable, forcing the Dutch to abandon it in 1710. There was one thing, however, that the Dutch introduced, which later would form the basis of the island's economy: sugarcane. The Dutch had also brought in pigs, cows and even deer to feed the small but growing population of settlers and slaves. These were needed because the Dutch had killed and eaten all the dodos, a big, flightless bird that was endemic to the island. It was given the name "dodo" because it was considered stupid. They walked right up to humans – and were caught. The birds did not know what humans were, and, in the absence of any other wildlife on the island, they had no natural enemies. The last confirmed sighting of a dodo was in 1662, but the bird has become a national symbol for Mauritius and features on its coins.

The French, already well-established on the nearby island of Réunion as well as on Rodrigues, claimed Mauritius as theirs five years after the Dutch had left. They renamed it Île de France and gradually turned it into a viable colony. The island's infrastructure was improved, a town called Port Louis in honour of King Louis XV was established and made the seat of the government for all French territories in the Indian Ocean with the exception of Madagascar. Sugar, first introduced by the Dutch, became the mainstay of the economy. Slaves were brought from Africa, some artisans arrived from India, and the French planters became relatively wealthy. Between 1767 and 1797, the population reached 59,000 inhabitants, including 6,200 whites, 3,700 free persons of other ethnicity, and 49,100 slaves, mostly from Africa.[9]

Then the French revolution broke out in 1789, and news of the upheavals in Paris and elsewhere reached Île de France a year later. The French planters were not unhappy with the abolition of the monarchy and tried to introduce a more representative political system on the island – but they were fiercely opposed to the new republican government's decision to put an end to slavery in all French colonies. A squadron of French troops which was sent to the island was turned back. In 1803, France's new ruler Napoleon sent a governor to Mauritius to restore order, but the unrest and the weakening of French power in the region made it possible for Britain to intervene. Île de France along with the Seychelles, another French possession, were taken over by the British in 1810 and the 1814 Treaty of Paris formalised British rule over the captured islands. The name of the island reverted to the one the Dutch had given it. It became once again Mauritius, and has remained so since.

English now became the official language, but did not fully replace French and Creole. And those two languages, along with English, are still spoken by the vast majority of the island's inhabitants. Along with language and culture, French-style laws have also been preserved. *Code Napoléon* with its civil laws still exists beside a British-style legal system based on common law. The same applies to Seychelles, which became British at the same time and was part of Mauritius until 1903. No other British possessions have had a similar system with the possible exception of the New Hebrides in the South Pacific. But while the New Hebrides was an Anglo-French 'condominium' and ruled jointly by two foreign powers until it became the independent Republic of Vanuatu in 1980, Mauritius and Seychelles were solely British colonies.

A few British settlers arrived, but the old French plantation owners continued to dominate the economy – and they tried their utmost to defend and preserve slavery, on which their wealth was built. In 1833, a decision was taken in London finally to abolish slavery, and two years later the edict was enforced in Mauritius. The former slave owners were compensated as 70,000 slaves were freed. But the plantation owners still needed labour on the sugarcane fields, and tried to entice many of them to stay on as 'apprentices.' That failed as many former slaves opted instead for other manual work or became fishermen.

The British decided to solve the problem by importing workers from India, which seemed to have an inexhaustible supply of cheap labour. The importation had already begun in the 1820s, but it ramped up in earnest in 1834 as slavery was being abolished. During the years 1834 to 1837 no fewer than 7,000 Indians reached Mauritius.[10] They were called 'indentured labourers' and came mainly from Bhojpur, an impoverished area in northern India which was, for the British, conveniently located within reach of the port at Calcutta (now Kolkata). Others came from Gujarat and Bombay.

In the early years, recruitment and the voyage across the Indian Ocean were in the hands of private interests, and the British-Indian government's only measure of control was to require the recruits to appear before a magistrate to state that they had not been forced to go, and that they were aware of the terms of their contracts. But as many of them were illiterate and had no idea where Mauritius was located on the globe, that procedure was a mere formality. Their contracts, which few of them could read, stipulated that they were to engage in labour in Mauritius for a period of five years and would receive a salary of five Indian rupees per month in addition to rations and clothing.[11]

Due to consistent abuse during the first years, the British government in India passed a law in 1837 to regulate the system. F.W. Birch, a superintendent of the Calcutta Police stated during his examination of an enquiry into the practice in 1838:

> I don't know exactly the precise condition of the coolies in their district, but I believe they are universally poor, and that their conditions is bettered by going to Mauritius. I believe many of them are in a starving condition... I believe that, in the majority of cases, they do not understand anything about it; but they leave home in search of service; at the same time, I believe that if they were told all this, they would care little about it and would still leave home, trusting their nusseeb (fate or fortune).[12]

It was not until 1842 that the entire programme came under governmental supervision When the indentured system formally ended in 1917, more than 450,000 men, women and children had passed through the Aapravasi Ghat, or 'the immigration depot' in Port Louis, a colonial form of Ellis Island in the Indian Ocean. The place is now a UNESCO world heritage site with a museum featuring old photographs of the labourers, the ships they came on, and the plantations where they worked.

As a consequence, Mauritius' economy was booming, but almost solely because of sugar. Annual production increased from 35,580 tonnes in 1837 to 129,210 tonnes in 1860. Port Louis became a busy trading post, new buildings were erected and Mauritius, although still very French in character, played an important role in maintaining

Britain's position as the dominant power in the Indian Ocean region. And it was all built on the hard labour of tens of thousands of workers, male and female, brought in from India.

Conditions on the plantations were harsh and the women often became victims of sexual exploitation by their overseers. The mortality rate was high due to hard work and disease. Because of arbitrary penalties imposed upon them, and other reasons such as theft and productivity being beneath allotted targets, many workers were constantly in debt to the planters.[13] The local plantation owners, the *grands blancs*, did not see the Indian workers to be different from the slaves. They were convinced that the indentured labourers should not have any rights. The workers belonged to their 'owners' just like the slaves.

But even so, some workers were able to save money and send it back to their families in India. It was not much, but enough to encourage more people from the Indian countryside to sign up for a passage to Mauritius. And, as Alessandro Stanziani, a French researcher has pointed out: 'Even though the real conditions of indentured workers were not necessarily better than those of the slaves, who preceded them, the rights which they enjoyed and, above all, the fact that their status was not hereditary constituted essential differences that were to play an increasingly important role in the twentieth century.'[14]

From the colonialists' point of view, the successful shipment of Indian workers to Mauritius marked the beginning of what has been called 'the Great Experiment'. Labour was needed in other British colonies where slavery had also been abolished. The problem was especially acute for local planters in the Caribbean where 750,000 slaves had been emancipated. Mauritius came to serve as the model for a system that sent Indian workers across the world. A total of 238,000 Indians reached British Guiana (now Guyana) in South America during the nineteenth and early twentieth century. Around 145,000 landed in Trinidad in the West Indies and 63,000 were sent to Fiji in the South Pacific. And 150,000 ended up in South Africa, mainly in the Natal colony.[15] Most of the migrants were put to work on sugar plantations but those in South Africa were employed in coal mines, or building railways. Today, Durban in KwaZulu-Natal province is one of the most populous Indian cities outside India.

Elsewhere, people of Indian origin make up 43 per cent of the population in independent Guyana, 37 per cent in Trinidad-Tobago and 30 per cent in Fiji. Other colonial powers such as France, the Netherlands and Spain also followed suit and recruited Indian labour, although not on the same scale as Britain. And smaller numbers of indentured labourers were recruited in China, Madagascar and Southeast Asia. The French imported Indian labourers to Réunion and the Dutch to their South American colony Dutch Guiana, now Suriname, while the Spanish sent Chinese workers to Peru and Cuba. It is estimated that altogether 1.3 million people left their home countries while the system of indentured labour prevailed prior to its eventual abolition in the early twentieth century. And it all began with the arrival of the first batches of Indians in Mauritius in the 1830s.

Theoretically, the workers in Mauritius had the right to return to India once their first five- and then ten-year contracts had expired. But few could afford to pay the fare for return tickets so the vast majority remained on the island. By 1871 more than 68 per cent of the colony's population of 317,000 was Indian of whom 25 per cent were born there. In the 1930s, the percentage of people of Indian descent was more or less the same, but by that time 93 per cent of them were natives. By then, the population had also increased to 393,000. In 1931, the descendants of African slaves and their Creole offspring who had left the plantations and become fishermen or civil servants made up 20 per cent of the population.[16] A number of Chinese had migrated to Mauritius and they formed 2 per cent of the population.

Although the planters saw the importation of indentured labour as a good replacement for slavery, Mauritius was hit by other problems. As the production of sugarcane and sugar beets increased in other countries, Mauritius found it hard to compete. Overproduction in the 1860s also led to lower prices for sugar. Then came the opening of the Suez Canal in 1869. Trade routes shifted away from the southern Indian Ocean. As if the economic decline was not enough, a malaria epidemic in the late 1860s killed more than 40,000 people, hitting the work force, who lived in primitive and unsanitary conditions, the hardest.

But even the Franco-Mauritian plantation owners, who were still called *grands blancs*, or 'the big whites', were affected by the economic downturn. The Polish-British writer Joseph Conrad, when he was still Józef Konrad Korzenlowski and the captain of a ship, stopped over in Port Louis in 1888. He complained of rich merchants forcing unwanted goods on him and was impressed by what he saw:

> The old French families, descendants of the old colonists; all noble, all impoverished and living a narrow domestic life in dull, dignified decay. The men, as a rule, occupy inferior posts in Government offices or in business houses. The girls are almost always pretty ignorant of the world, kind and agreeable and generally bilingual; they prattle innocently in both French and English. The emptiness of their existence passes belief.[17]

Conrad could be accused of being overly condescending in his description of Mauritius' young women, but the British-held island with a French flavour had become a colonial backwater after the sugar crisis and the opening of the Suez Canal. The solution for the plantation owners was to centralise production to make it more efficient and less labour intensive. Many sold smaller holdings, which were bought by Indians who had managed to save up enough money for the deals. For the first time, sugar was produced on small plots of land, and many of those new landowners were Indians. A new Indian middle class began to emerge, which changed the face of Mauritius' economy and politics away from total domination by the *grands blancs*.

With British colonial rule came also British-style education, which further empowered the still small but growing middle class. The emergence of a new, self-conscious identity was boosted by the visit to the island of the Indian independence leader Mohandas Gandhi, better known as Mahatma Gandhi, in 1901. He was then living and working in South Africa, and had heard of the plight of the Indians in Mauritius. In 1907, Gandhi sent an Indian lawyer, Manilal Maganlall, to Mauritius to help the Indians there fight for their rights. Maganlall defended Indian workers in the courts against exploitive employers and also founded the *Hindustan* newspaper. In 1926, the first Indo-Mauritians were elected to the government council.

A Hindu reform movement called 'Arya Samaj' was founded outside of the council to fight for social justice. The Arya Samaj had first come to Mauritius via a group of British Indian Army soldiers based there. It vigorously promoted the teaching of Hindi and the first school to teach in Hindi was opened by the Arya Samaj in 1918. Many Indians were thus able to maintain their ethnic identity, but Creole, French and English, rather than any Indian language, became the lingua francas among them.

The Creole population, meanwhile, formed a political organisation, *Action Libérale*, in 1907. Led by Eugène Laurent, a doctor, it won the 1911 elections in Port Louis, defeating the oligarchs. *Action Libérale* was dissolved shortly afterwards, but Laurent is regarded as one of the pioneers in the struggle for more home rule in Mauritius. A street in Port Louis is named after him. Another Creole doctor, Maurice Curé, founded the Mauritius Labour Party (MLP), or *Parti Travailliste*, in 1936, which attracted not only urban Creole workers but also rural Indian farmers. It was basically a social democrat party, which wanted to protect the rights of the workers in the towns and the plantations, and it soon grew into the most powerful political institution on the island.

A Creole politician, Emmanuel Anquetil, organised the urban working class while Pandit Sahadeo, an Indian, was active in the countryside. Together, they managed to get 30,000 people to take part in Mauritius' first May Day celebrations in 1938. A rally was held on the Champ de Mars, where speakers addressed the huge crowd. Mauritius had come a long way since the first indentured labourers arrived a hundred years before. There were some differences within the Indian community based on caste and religion, but politics seemed to unite them. The Indians were mostly Hindu, but there has also always been a sizable number of Muslims and a few Christians among them.

The Chinese community in Mauritius was much smaller than the Indian and Creole ones, but it was from the very beginning financially strong. Chinese began migrating to Mauritius in the mid-nineteenth century and because of colonial laws that deprived all foreigners of the right to purchase or own land, they were restricted to trade and artisanal work.[18] Most of the Chinese came from today's Fujian and Guangdong provinces on the southern coast of China while others came from the British colonies of Hong Kong, Penang and Singapore. Up until the end of the nineteenth century their numbers never exceeded 3,600. But the Chinese community in Mauritius grew as political turmoil engulfed their home country in the early twentieth century and modern passenger boats made migration easier. In 1931, there were 6,343 people in Mauritius registered as Chinese. By 1952, that number had risen to 10,421. They were still fewer than the other ethnic communities, but they were economically strong because of their involvement in trade and commerce.

After World War I, prosperity returned to Mauritius due to a boom in sugar prices. For the first time, Mauritius' economy also become somewhat diversified with the expansion of its tea gardens and the construction of brick and tile factories as well as a government-run dairy. But the thought of an independent Mauritius remained quite alien until after World War II, when the British began to dissolve their empire. At the same time, influences grew from the Mauritians who had served with the British forces in Africa and the Near East, fighting against German and Italian armies. Some even went to Britain where they became pilots or worked as ground staff for the Royal Air Force.

It was hardly surprising that an increasing number of people in Mauritius wanted at the very least some degree of self-rule. The first general elections were held in August 1948 and were won by the MLP. But suffrage did not become universal until 1959, when the MLP once again emerged victorious from those elections. Its leader, Seewoosagur Ramgoolam, was the son of an indentured labourer who had arrived in Mauritius at the age of 18 in 1896 onboard a ship called *The Hindoostan*. Seewoosagur was born in Mauritius in 1900, went to school there and, in 1921, sailed to Europe. He graduated from University College London and attended classes at the London School of Economics. There was upward social mobility in Mauritian society, of which Seewoosagur Ramgoolam is a shining example.

Back home in Mauritius, Ramgoolam joined the MLP and began campaigning for independence within the Commonwealth. He was not interested in integration with Britain as some kind of overseas county as some of his opponents were proposing. But he was an admirer of Mahatma Gandhi, and wanted to achieve independence without bloodshed. As Mauritius was granted more self-rule, he served as chief minister of the colony from 1961 to 1968, when the colony finally became independent. His title was then changed to prime minister, and by then he had also become Sir Seewoosagur. (He had been knighted in the British Queen's Birthday Honours List in 1965.)

As of 12 March 1968 Mauritius was a dominion where the British monarch was head of state and represented by a Governor-General. But Mauritius was now a sovereign nation, governed by descendants of indentured labourers from India, African slaves and Creole offspring of its ethnically mixed population. Although Mauritius has not been saved from intercommunal violence – in 1964 Indian and Creole communities fought each other in a village called Trois Boutiques, and similar clashes in Port Louis just before independence left at least 25 people dead and hundreds injured before British troops restored order – intermarriage between various ethnic groups have never been uncommon in Mauritius.

But, as it was revealed much later, independence did come at a price. The colony of Mauritius consisted not only of the main island and Rodrigues plus some scattered, smaller islets – but also included the Chagos Archipelago to the north. During secret talks in London, Sir Seewoosagur Ramgoolam had been told in no uncertain terms that independence would be out of the question – unless he agreed to separate the Chagos Archipelago from Mauritius. He did. In November 1965, three years before independence, the British government officially purchased the Chagos Archipelago from Mauritius for three million British pounds. Together with three atolls in Seychelles – Aldabra, Desroches in the Amirantes and Farquhar – it became the British Indian Ocean Territory (BIOT).

The islands that had been separated from Seychelles were returned when it became an independent country in 1976. But the Chagos Archipelago remained British, and between 1967 and 1973, its entire population of between 1,500 and 2,000 people, mostly a Creole-speaking mix of Indians and Africans who had made a living from growing coconuts and collecting guano, was removed and deported to Mauritius and Seychelles. Properties owned by the Seychellois Chagos Agalega Company had been bought by the British state in 1967 for £660,000. The population was gone, all the land was owned by Britain, and the archipelago was placed under direct rule from London.

It seemed like a strange move as Britain was in the process of leaving all its colonies, protectorates and bases 'East of Suez'. But it soon became clearer what the purpose of the creation of BIOT was – when military personnel from the United States arrived on the main atoll of Diego Garcia in March 1971. They came with earth-moving gear, building materials and workers, of whom many were Filipinos, to begin the construction of a giant military base on the atoll. Britain had leased Diego Garcia to the United States military for exactly that purpose. In December 1966 Britain and the United States had signed an agreement that was called 'Availability of Certain Indian Ocean Islands for Defence Purposes' – but it did not specify the types of military uses to which the islands would be put.[19] According to David Vine, an American academic, the agreement had been signed 'under the cover of darkness' without congressional or parliamentary oversight.[20]

It soon became clear what the agreement was all about. Diego Garcia surrounds a lagoon that is 24 kilometres long, 6.4 kilometres wide and nearly ten metres deep. With some dredging and digging, a harbour was constructed. Modern houses connected by paved roads were built on the atoll and a runway long enough for huge military aircraft was taking shape. Diego Garcia began to resemble any US military base elsewhere in the world – but without any potentially troublesome local population nearby.

Diego Garcia's strategic location in the north-central Indian Ocean was not lost on anyone. In case of war or another emergency, it offers access to East Africa, the Middle East, South and Southeast Asia, and oversees vital shipping lanes across the Indian Ocean. And the choice of Diego Garcia was entirely in line with a new US policy for building military bases overseas. Called 'the Strategic Islands Concept', it is the brainchild of Stuart Barber, a civilian working for the US Navy at the Pentagon. His idea was to establish new military bases away from populous mainland areas where they were exposed to local anti-Western opposition. Instead, Barber wrote in a proposal, 'only relatively small, lightly populated islands, separated from major population masses, could be safely held under full control of the West.'[21]

Barber scanned charts of the Indian Ocean to look for a possible location for a new base. In the early 1960s, the old British colony of Aden and the Aden Protectorate had become the Protectorate of South Arabia and the Federation of South Arabia. The two entities merged to become South Yemen in 1967 – and that was proclaimed a Marxist socialist republic in 1970. Well into the late 1950s, Aden had been the second busiest harbour in the world after New York, and was the base from where Britain protected its oil interests in the Persian Gulf. Now it was lost.

Other developments, such as the disastrous Vietnam War, protests against the US bases in Japan, a volatile, anti-Western government in power in Indonesia and India's strategic alliance with the Soviet Union, also convinced him that a strong US presence in the region was needed – and that a new base on an isolated island was the way forward. He looked at Phuket in Thailand, the Australian Cocos (Keeling) Islands, and various smaller islands in Seychelles. Finally, he settled for 'that beautiful atoll of Diego Garcia, right in the middle of the ocean.'[22] The fact that the atoll was British and, as he saw it, almost unpopulated, helped him make up his mind.

Barber also based his small but strategic island concept on previous experiences from the South Pacific, where the US after World War II had turned Kwajalein and Enewetak atolls in the Marshall Islands into formidable military bases devoid of any sizable local population. Enewetak was used for nuclear tests until 1980, and only when those ceased were the old habitants allowed to return. Between 1946 and 1958, the US Navy conducted 68 atomic and hydrogen bomb tests on Bikini, another atoll in the Marshall Islands. At first, the local population continued to live on Bikini but, as many fell sick, probably from radiation, they were removed to other atolls. Kwajalein later became, and still serves as, a missile-testing base. So the idea of using small islands for military purposes was not entirely new, but Barber developed it into a strategic concept, and, in the case of the Chagos Archipelago, he and others thought it best to cleanse the islands of any local population.

The base on Diego Garcia was still under construction when it first saw action. In October 1973, a coalition of Arab states launched a joint surprise attack on Israel, America's main ally in the region. Reconnaissance planes took off from Diego Garcia to assist the Israelis with intelligence. The war ended with a devastating defeat for Egypt and Syria. Israel survived, and the war – and, more importantly, the Islamic revolution in Iran in early 1979, and the Soviet invasion of Afghanistan in December of the same year, prompted the US to expand the base on Diego Garcia, including the completion of a three-kilometre long runway for reconnaissance planes, bombers and in-air refuelling planes. According to Vine, there is also a range of other high-tech and intelligence and communications equipment on the atoll, a satellite navigation monitoring antenna, and docking facilities for submarines. Nuclear weapons are likely stored at the base as well.[23]

The base played an important role in both Gulf Wars, Desert Shield which became Desert Storm in 1990–1991, when US and allied militaries drove Iraqi forces from Kuwait, which they had invaded, and the 2003 US-led invasion of Iraq. All kinds of military equipment was stored at Diego Garcia and naval ships carried supplies to the forces at the Iraqi front. From there B-52 bombers and other military aircraft took off from Diego Garcia and flew sorties over the battlefields. During the US occupation of Iraq after 2003, Diego Garcia served as an important logistics base for the troops there. Diego Garcia has also been used to support combat operations in Afghanistan.

In terms of the number of troops and other personnel – 3,000 to 5,000 soldiers and civilians are deployed there at any given time – Diego Garcia is smaller than America's military outposts in South Korea, on the Japanese island of Okinawa, and in Germany – but its strategic importance is possibly greater.

No outsiders may enter the base, which is a world of its own with houses that resemble those in any American suburb, supermarkets stocked full of food and goods flown in from the United States, hamburger joints, bars and clubs with beer on tap, tennis courts, jogging tracks, and satellite TV with the latest news programmes and shows. In a motion before the British parliament in 2004, Labour politician Alan Meale stated that US Navy recruitment literature described Diego Garcia as 'one of the world's best kept secrets, boasting unbelievable recreational facilities, exquisite natural beauty and outstanding living conditions.'[24]

The notoriety that Diego Garcia earned during President George W. Bush's so-called 'war on terror' included its becoming a 'black site' for the detention and interrogation of terrorist suspects who had been captured in Afghanistan and elsewhere.[25] *Al Jazeera* reported that Diego Garcia had in 2002 and 2003 been used for what was euphemistically called 'extraordinary rendition', or the transfer of detainees without legal process – with the full cooperation of British authorities.[26] Reports of torture of detainees on Diego Garcia also emerged.[27]

The British government at first refused to admit that rendition flights had landed at Diego Garcia for any other reason than to refuel, but, in February 2008, then Foreign Secretary David Miliband told the British parliament that 'contrary to earlier explicit assurances that Diego Garcia had not been used for rendition flights, recent US investigations have now revealed two occasions, both in 2002, when this in fact occurred.'[28] He did not address the issue of torture, but how could he confirm what is happening on a secret base on an off-limits island in the Indian Ocean?

And what happened to the Chagossians, as they are called, the people who were brought from the atolls to Mauritius and Seychelles in the late 1960s and early 1970s? Little is known about the smaller number which ended up in Seychelles other than that they do not want to move to Mauritius, as requested by the Mauritian government, which, despite the 1965 settlement with Britain, still lays claim to the Chagos Archipelago.[29] But those in Mauritius have launched several campaigns for the right to return to their islands. With offspring they now number around 5,000 though, in recent years, 1,000 Chagossians, mostly from the second generation, have left Mauritius and also Seychelles for Britain. In 2002, the British government finally granted them full citizenship because they or their parents were born when the Chagos Archipelago was still a British colony.

The Chagossians have nevertheless filed suits against the British government in the European Court of Human Rights for the right to return to the archipelago. Nothing has happened in that regard, but in March 2006 Britain finally let about a hundred Chagossians travel to the Chagos Archipelago for a ten-day 'humanitarian voyage' to tend to their cemeteries.[30] But they were not allowed to stay overnight on any of the islands. In early May 2015, another group of Chagossians from Mauritius and Britain was also allowed to visit the islands, followed at the end of the month by six Chagossians living in Seychelles.[31] They flew to Bahrain and Dubai from where they were brought to Diego Garcia by a US military transport plane.

The islanders are supposed to have been compensated by the British government but those in Seychelles say they never received anything and those in Mauritius complain that their meagre compensation arrived almost a decade late. In 1972, the British government provided £650,000 to Mauritius to be given to the islanders. But, for reasons that are not entirely clear, the first disbursements were not made until 1977.[32] For years, most Chagossians were living in poorer parts of Port Louis, where many eked out a living as day labourers. It is no wonder they felt homesick. Life on the atolls in the Chagos Archipelago had been simple, but they had been proud of their homes and they had not encountered real misery until they arrived in Mauritius.

Several international human rights organisations have lent support to the Chagossian cause, for the right of the former residents and their children and grandchildren to return, and for adequate compensation for their forced eviction in the late 1960s and early 1970s. More compensation may be given but, despite sympathetic ears in the courts, the possibility of them returning to the Chagos Archipelago and settling there is slim. Those who were born on the islands are getting too old to move back, and the second and third generation, who live in Mauritius, Seychelles or Britain and have never been there, would find it hard to get used to life on remote atolls. And how would they be able to find jobs on those islands? The US base is a possibility but, for security reasons, islanders with opinions about the sovereignty of the atolls would most likely be unwelcome. Nor does the US military want to have any permanent population on Diego Garcia

A more pressing question is Mauritius' claim to BIOT, which has strained relations with the former colonial power. Ties to the British crown were severed on 12 March 1992, exactly 24 years after independence. Mauritius became a republic with a president replacing the British Queen as head of state. But the post of prime minister was retained, and he continued to lead the government. And, over the years that followed the proclamation of the republic, the rhetoric from Port Louis became increasingly anti-colonial.

In a statement to the UN general assembly in 2013, Mauritius' then prime minister Navinchandra Ramgoolam stated that, 'the dismemberment of part of our territory, the Chagos Archipelago – prior to independence – by the then colonial power, the United Kingdom, in clear breach of international law, leaves the process of decolonisation not only of Mauritius, but of Africa, incomplete.'[33] Somewhat ironically, Navinchandra Ramgoolam is the son of

Seewoosagur Ramgoolam, who had, albeit under pressure, agreed to cede the Chagos Archipelago to Britain before independence.

The problems for the United States – and Britain – did not end there. In March 2015, the Permanent Court of Arbitration in The Hague found that Britain's decision to establish a 'marine protected area' around the Chagos Archipelago 'contravened its obligations under the Convention of the Law of the Sea.'[34] In April 2010, the British government had declared that 70 small islands and atolls in BIOT would become a marine protected area – which would prevent people from living there as the terms of reference for the park stated that BIOT, including Diego Garcia, would be reserved for military use. And that appeared to be the real purpose of the decision, according to a 2009 classified telegram from the US embassy in London to Washington, which was made public by WikiLeaks in 2012.[35]

On 22 June 2017, the UN general assembly voted 94 to 15 with 65 abstentions to ask the International Court of Justice in The Hague to issue what is called 'an advisory opinion' on whether Britain had lawfully adhered to the decolonisation process when it separated the Chagos Archipelago from Mauritius in 1965.[36] The action in the UN that was taken against the background of the lease that the US military acquired under the terms of the 1966 agreement with Britain was for 50 years, which expired in 2016 – but then, in November 2016, Britain decided to grant the United States a further 20-year lease on Diego Garcia. The expelled islanders would also get an additional £40 million in compensation over a 10-year period. But no right to return to their islands would be granted.[37]

Thus, the Chagossians, one of the smallest nations in the world, have become a huge international issue involving British courts, the United Nations, the European Court of Human Rights and the Permanent Court of Arbitration – and that was something Barber had probably not envisaged when he floated his Strategic Islands Concept in the 1960s. The Chagossians continue to fight for their rights in a way few would have expected when they were evicted from their islands.

Mark E. Rosen, an American national security lawyer, wrote after the appeal to the United Nations: 'When viewed in isolation, these problems are manageable; but, when out in the larger context of possible Mauritian territorial ambitions, it is clear that the United

States and the UK (United Kingdom) will need to redouble their efforts to deal with the issue of the displaced Chagossians and the economic aspirations of Mauritius. The United States has more to lose in this battle over sovereignty and it would do well to help try and craft a solution that puts it on the right side of this issue because Diego Garcia is irreplaceable real estate.'[38] With a new Chinese base in Djibouti and merchant as well as naval ships and even submarines from China becoming a regular feature in the Indian Ocean, it is inconceivable that the United States would leave Diego Garcia, its by far most important base in the entire region.

The issue has also put India in a dilemma. As prime minister Modi said in 2017, India's partnership with Mauritius is among the strongest in the world. For historical reasons, the two countries have always been close and India has consistently supported Mauritius on the Chagos issue. But India also wants the United States to stay in the Indian Ocean as a counterweight to China's increasing influence in the Indian Ocean region. When the issue was raised in the International Court of Justice in September 2018, India had to say that 'historical facts and related legal positions confirm that sovereignty of the Chagos Archipelago has been and continues to be with Mauritius.'[39]

It will not be easy for India to balance its conflicting interests in the Indian Ocean. Exacerbating India's fears of Chinese penetration of Mauritius, China in 2016 granted the republic US$730 million worth of grants and interest-free loans to construct, apart from the new airport terminal, an Olympic-standard sports complex and swimming pool, and other projects. China and Mauritius have also signed memoranda of understanding for a feasibility study on a joint Mauritius-China Free Trade Agreement to boost investment and bilateral trade. And, as Laura Fatovich from Australia's Future Directions International Institute wrote in June 2017: 'Mauritius claims a high degree of cultural affinity with India but, even so, New Delhi cannot count on enjoying a lasting advantage over Beijing. India's deepening of its relationship with Mauritius, though, can be seen as an extension of its Chinese balancing strategy, and its long-term ambition to be an autonomous global power.'[40]

Mauritius began to diversify its economy in 1970, first with the establishment of an Export Processing Zone (EPZ) and then with a major expansion of its tourism industry. The EPZ with its tax breaks and other incentives, such as founding loopholes in American and European garment quotas, attracted investment mainly from Hong Kong. Textiles and other light-industry items became major exports, and helped Mauritius lessen its traditional dependence on sugar. The businessmen from Hong Kong established at least personal relationships with the local Chinese population in Port Louis' Chinatown, where many speak the same Cantonese dialect.

The tourism industry also took off, and, from the very beginning the emphasis was on the high-end sector of the market. Luxury hotels, not cheap guesthouses, were the model. The remoteness of Mauritius also played a part in keeping backpackers and other budget travellers away. One has to fly there, often over long distances, and that is expensive. In 1970, 27,650 people visited the island, which has increased to more than a million annually today.[41] It began with a limited number of flights from South Africa and Australia, and has since expanded to today's worldwide network including long-haul routes from Europe, North America, the Middle East and South and Southeast Asia.

After the textile industry and tourism came banks, insurance companies and trusts. A modern business centre with information-based technology industries, following the example of India, sprung up in Curepipe, a town on the island's central high plateau. Curepipe also hosts textile factories, a processing plant for diamonds from southern Africa, and several jewellery businesses and shopping centres. The airport, named after Mauritius' first prime minister Sir Seewosagur Ramgoolam, was expanded to become a regional hub.

The immediate development model was Singapore, another island republic which like Mauritius has a well-educated and diverse population – and few natural resources. But Mauritius' main long-term development strategy is focused on becoming a financial centre involving China and India, Asia's two economic powerhouses, and to launch itself as an attractive place for them for doing business with Africa. The question is obvious, though: is the tiny island in the Indian Ocean big enough for both Asian giants? For now, India dominates investment flows to Mauritius, but in 2016, the Bank of China secured a licence to open a branch in Port Louis, which it said will be a 'strategic platform' for its African business operations.[42]

Huawei, China's biggest smartphone maker is also expanding its local presence.[43]

In July 2018, president Xi toured four countries in Africa – Senegal, Rwanda, South Africa and Mauritius – to promote his BRI. He arrived with a 200-strong delegation, and, at the time, the local daily *Mauritius Times* wrote that 'China is one of the countries from which the ancestors of one singularly important component of Mauritius has originated… similarly, successive Chinese regimes have taken great pride in their diaspora in so many parts of the world.'[44]

How enthusiastic the Mauritius Chinese community was over Xi's visit is hard to say, but China has come to the country to stay. India is no longer the only major player. Prime Minister Pravind Kumar Jugnauth said during the visit that China is a 'reliable cooperative partner in the oriental world' and that his country 'respects BRI as it represents the development direction of economic globalisation and open world economy.'[45]

China's most recent project is to build a 'smart city' on the outskirts of Port Louis called Jinfei, a resort offering karaoke, a casino and other forms of entertainment. The first phase of the project will total US$1.5 billion. In 2015, China became the biggest exporter of goods to Mauritius, surpassing India.[46] And it may not only be a question of selling smartphones and promoting karaoke. As the *Nikkei Asian Review* stated in its 24 July 2018 issue: 'There may be geopolitical motives behind China's overtures to Mauritius. To the east is Diego Garcia, a British Indian Ocean Territory and home to the US Navy's largest military base in the Indian Ocean. The French navy has a base on Réunion, just west of Mauritius.'[47]

That assumption is not far-fetched. And that is also the reason why France is strengthening its presence and influence in the Indian Ocean region.

5

THE FRENCH

Réunion is not just French. It is France. Everyone here is a French citizen and the island is part of the European Union. The currency is the Euro, French – and EU – flags flutter over government buildings, the cars all have an 'F' for France on their number plates, and the people vote in French elections. The nine-hour flight from this island in the Indian Ocean to Paris is considered domestic, as Réunion is a French *département* like any other in the country. The island capital, Saint-Denis, has cafés, bistros, patisseries and a grand *Hôtel de Ville*, or city hall.

Only the people may be a bit different from the majority of those in European France, or the *Métropole*, as it is called here. Besides French, they speak Creole, a patois of French and other languages, and Réunion's close to a million inhabitants are of European, Indian, African, Chinese, Vietnamese and Arab descent. Because many are of mixed blood, it is almost impossible to give an ethnic breakdown of the population, but, roughly speaking, a quarter is made up of Europeans, another quarter consists of Indians, and two per cent are either Chinese or Vietnamese. The rest are Africans or Africans mixed with other ethnic groups.

The French, unlike all other former European colonial masters, have done what they can to retain as many of their overseas possessions as possible – and the method has been to turn them into parts of France. That process began as early as the 1940s, when Réunion,

French Guiana, Martinique and Guadeloupe became *départements d'outre-mer*, or overseas departments. Mayotte off the east coast of Africa was awarded the same status in 2011. Other designations are used for French Polynesia and Wallis & Futuna in the Pacific Ocean, Saint-Pierre & Miquelon off the east coast of Canada, and the tiny Caribbean islands of Saint-Barthélemy and Saint-Martin – although the latter is shared with the Dutch.

And then there is Kerguelen. It measures 7,215 square-kilometres and is three times bigger than Réunion with its 2,511 square-kilometres. But as it together with the nearby Crozet Archipelago, the Amsterdam & Saint-Paul Islands and tiny, scattered islands around Madagascar form a *territoire d'outre-mer* – an overseas territory – it does not have the same status as Réunion and Mayotte. The *Terres australes et antarctiques françaises*, or TAAF, the French Southern and Antarctic Lands, as the territory is called, are also uninhabited apart from between 100 and 200 scientists and military personnel who stay there on a rotational basis. Most of them are based on Kerguelen but there are smaller contingents of scientists and soldiers on some of the other islands as well. It is TAAF together with Réunion and Mayotte that gives the French their massive, 2.5 million-square-kilometre Exclusive Economic Zone in the Indian Ocean. And that makes France, despite the distance to Europe, an important regional power.

French rule never comes without a military presence, and none of its Indian Ocean islands is an exception. France maintains 4,500 soldiers and other military personnel in the Indian Ocean region. There are 1,900 regular troops based in Réunion and TAAF, and the French Foreign Legion has a detachment in Mayotte. Another 1,350 soldiers are based in Djibouti and 700 in the United Arab Emirates.[1] Réunion with its bases for the navy and the air force is France's most important foothold in the region, and not to be overlooked is the mysterious island of Kerguelen. Since 1992, the French *Centre National d'Études Spatiales* (CNES) has maintained a satellite and rocket tracking station near Port-aux-Français, the only settlement on that rugged and desolate island in the southern Indian Ocean.

French naval forces took part in the 1991 Gulf War, which followed the Iraqi invasion of Kuwait in 1990. According to an interview with Vice Admiral Philippe Euverte, commander-in-chief of the forces in

French Polynesia, in 1995 Kerguelen served as a logistics base for the operation, indicating that the island is used to store military material. That makes perfect sense given its location and lack of indigenous, or even permanent, population.[2]

French national pride, some would say hubris born out of having once been an important world power and desiring to remain one, has come at a price. Réunion's living standard is not lagging that far behind the *Métropole*. But apart from plants that process sugarcane and tobacco, there is not much local industry. Most consumer goods, and even food, have to be imported and the budget is heavily subsidised by the French government. Between 30 and 40 per cent of the labour force – and as many as 60 per cent among young people – has no work and is dependent on unemployment benefits. The island is spectacular with steep mountains rising up to 3,000 metres above sea level and active as well as dormant volcanoes, but its tourism industry cannot be compared with that of Mauritius.

There are a few beaches, but most of the coastline is rocky, and some well-publicised, fatal shark attacks in recent years, including that of a 13-year-old local surfer in 2015, have kept foreign visitors away. In April 2007, one of its volcanoes erupted and sent tons of lava from the crater down to some coastal communities, which were completely wiped out. Unlike Mauritius, Réunion has no plains, so most people live in Saint-Denis and some smaller towns on the coast. Only a few narrow roads lead through the ravines up to some towns and villages in the mountainous interior of the island.

But Réunion, like Mauritius, was uninhabited when the first European visitors arrived there in the early sixteenth century. While Arab traders were familiar with the island, and may have stopped there to provision with water and food on their way from Madagascar to the islands that now are Indonesia, the 'discovery' of Réunion is attributed to Dom Pedro Mascarenhas, who is said to have arrived here around 1514. Mauritius, Rodrigues, Réunion and some smaller islands in the southern Indian Ocean were named after him and became the Mascarenes. Mascarenhas himself called today's Réunion Santa Apolónia after a Roman Catholic saint.

The Portuguese, however, did little more than name the island and add it to their navigational charts. Then came the French, and they came there to stay. France claimed the island in 1642 and, in 1646, a dozen French army mutineers from Madagascar were deported there as settlers. Although they were repatriated to France after a few years, they could be considered the first of its inhabitants.

In 1649, the island was named Île Bourbon after the royal family who then ruled France and it became a designated French colony. The French East India Company brought settlers to the island, mostly European coffee planters and African slaves who made up the work force. But the numbers were not significant. In 1713, there were only 538 free mostly white men and 633 slaves on Île Bourbon, where they produced some coffee for export.[3] The governor, Bertrand-François Mahé de la Bourdonnais, saw his domain primarily as a base from which France would be able to resurrect its Indian empire, which was being lost to the British, who had succeeded the Portuguese – and the French – as the main colonial power in Asia and other parts of the world.

The French never managed to re-conquer the land they had lost in India, but they managed to keep a few enclaves on the eastern and western coasts of the Subcontinent – and Île Bourbon and Île de France, today's Mauritius. Those islands became plantation colonies rather than bases for conquests. After a crisis in the coffee economy in the late 1700s, the planters began to cultivate nutmeg, cloves, manioc and cotton. But the local population was still poor, and by the 1830s even a third of the white population lived in poverty. The few who prospered became a new elite which here, as in the French colonies in the West Indies, was called *Békés* and dominated the Africans and those of mixed descent.

The French revolution had, incongruous as it may seem, far-reaching consequences for Île Bourbon and Île de France. In 1793 Île Bourbon was renamed Île de la Réunion by a decree from the revolutionary constituent assembly in Paris. The Bourbons had been deposed, so the old name was no longer appropriate. The new name alluded to the union of revolutionaries from Marseilles with the National Guard in Paris. With Napoleon's rise to power the island was given yet another name. In 1801 it became Île Bonaparte.

But the island was far from France and the turmoil that engulfed the country after the 1789 revolution. The breakdown of central authority meant that the elite gained more control of the island's affairs – and one of its first decisions was to oppose the abolition of slavery that the revolutionaries in France had enacted. Paris then sent two officers with 2,000 troops to the island to enforce the ban, but they were met by such resistance from the *Békés* that they were forced to return without accomplishing their mission.

But, as we have seen, the British took advantage of the situation and invaded the island, along with Île de France, in 1810. While the British kept Île de France and the Seychelles, which they had also occupied, Île Bonaparte was returned to France. And the island became once again Île Bourbon and retained that name until the fall of the restored monarchy in 1848, when a new revolution occurred and it got its present name, Île de la Réunion, or simply La Réunion, which it has been called in French ever since.

The restoration of French rule coincided with the loss of Haiti and some other sugar-producing colonies, and that actually rescued the local economy. The production of sugar grew from 21 tonnes in 1815 to 73,000 tonnes in 1860. The population also expanded, from 36,000 inhabitants in 1778 to 110,000 in 1848 as slaves were brought in from Madagascar and the African mainland. Working conditions on the plantations were hard, but some of the slaves managed to escape and hide in the rugged interior of the island. Some of their descendants still inhabit Cilaos, Salazie and Mafate, small towns which even today are accessible only via roads which wind their way through ravines and tunnels before entering a vast open space – the huge crater of an extinct volcano.

In the first years before the final abolition of slavery in 1848, the *Békés* prospered. Saint-Dénis, capital since 1738, became a modern town with stately buildings, parks, warehouses, and one of the ports on the island from where the sugar was exported. But here as in Mauritius, freeing of the slaves meant that another source of labour had to be found to maintain that prosperity, and on Réunion – as in Mauritius – the solution was to import workers from Asia. Within 15 years after 1848, 68,000 labourers arrived, most of them Indians, but there were also a few from China among the work force. Most of the Indians were recruited through the colonies the French still retained in India: Pondicherry (now Puducherry), Karikal (now Karaikal) and

Yanaon (now Yanam) on the eastern, Coromandel, coast, Mahé on the western, Malabar, coast, and Chandernagore (now Chandannagar) on the Hooghly River north of Calcutta (now Kolkata).

All those enclaves, with the exception of Chandernagore, are located in the south, so the Indians who came to Réunion in the nineteenth century are different from the Hindi-speaking people from the Bhojpur region who dominated the work force in Mauritius. The Indians in Réunion are mostly Tamils with some from other south Indian communities. The sugar industry was booming and Réunion was also an important port of call on the sea route from France to French Indochina.

Then came the crisis. A disease ravaged the island's sugar cane plantations only a decade after the abolition of slavery, and there were outbreaks of malaria and cholera. A dramatic fall in sugar prices in the mid-1860s added to the problems and was followed by the opening of the Suez Canal in 1869. Other crops such as vanilla and ylang-ylang were introduced, but Réunion could not escape the fate of becoming a forgotten colony in the Indian Ocean that muddled along with its production of sugar and rum.

Not much happened on the island until World War II broke out and Germany invaded France. In the beginning, Réunion was ruled by the French Vichy-government but, in November 1942, soldiers from Charles de Gaulle's Free French Forces arrived onboard the warship *Léopard* and seized the island. This remote outpost in the Indian Ocean thus became part of Free France, and remained so until the end of the war.

When World War II was over, the French decided to reorganise their colonies along the idea that they should all be united in a global French Union. But the colonies were not treated the same. The oldest ones – Réunion, French Guiana, Martinique and Guadeloupe – became *départements d'outre-mer* in 1946. Those territories had been French since the seventeenth century and had no or negligible indigenous populations, so none of them had any significant independence movement. The people there became 'Frenchmen beyond the seas', in theory no different from the citizens of the *Métropole*.

The subjects in other French possessions in Africa and Asia were, also in theory, citizens of the republic as well, but not with the same rights – and they hardly felt they were French. They demanded the right to rule themselves without interference from Paris. French Indochina became the independent states of Laos, Cambodia, and North and South Vietnam in 1953 and 1954, and then there was no reason why France should also keep its enclaves in India. The French had given up Chandernagore in 1951, and, in 1954, the other four colonies were also merged with India. Chandernagore became part of West Bengal, but the other four were in 1962 constituted as a union territory where French remains an official language along with Tamil, Malayalam and Telugu – and the policemen still wear French-style, flat and circular *kepis*.

France's African colonies became independent in 1960, but maintained close links with France. The only exceptions were Guinea, which went its own way and severed all relations with France in 1958, and Djibouti, which did not achieve independence until 1977. But, in the Indian Ocean, Réunion and TAAF are still French, and will probably remain so for the foreseeable future.

Réunion may be a relatively harmonious mix of various ethnic groups, but the relationship with the *Métropole* has not always been as smooth as it is made out to be in official histories. The dark story of 1,615 children from poor families in Réunion, who were forcibly taken away and relocated to rural areas in the *Métropole* from 1963 to 1982, continues to haunt authorities on Réunion as well as in France proper. Many of the children were abused and discriminated against when they arrived in their new homes far away from their island in the Indian Ocean. The notion was that there were too many people on Réunion, and children from the island would help increase the falling population in the French countryside. Their fate was virtually unknown until one of them, Jean-Jaques Martial, in 2002 filed a suit against the French state for 'kidnapping and deportation of a minor'.[4] The lawsuit was, however, dismissed by French courts and even, in 2011, by the European Court of Human Rights.

And there has been rioting. The first serious riots broke out in 1991, when a popular TV channel, which had been broadcasting illegally since 1986, was shut down. In February 2012, Réunion was wracked by another round of rioting, which lasted for three days and was caused by the rising cost of living – a severe problem in a place where most families have some members who live on social security.[5] But compared to the situation in some Parisian suburbs, ethnic and racial problems in Réunion must be considered relatively minor.

Not even the most extreme politicians on Réunion have asked for full independence from France. In 1959, the island got its own communist party, *Parti Communiste Réunionnais*, but it demanded only more autonomy, not the establishment of a separate People's Republic of Réunion. The party was founded and led by one of the island's most colourful politicians, Paul Vergès, the twin brother of the even more infamous lawyer Jacques Vergès. They were born in Thailand in 1925 to a French diplomat father and a Vietnamese mother and brought up on Réunion. Jacques was only a teenager when he went to Europe to join the anti-German resistance during World War II, and both he and Paul became members of the French Communist Party in 1945.

While in Paris in the 1950s, Jacques befriended Pol Pot and other Cambodian radicals who later became guerrilla fighters in their country and, in 1975, its rulers who carried out a massive genocide on their own population. Jacques became involved in a number of left-wing causes, including support for the armed independence struggle against France in Algeria. As a lawyer, he later defended the Nazi war criminal Klaus Barbie, a Lebanese terrorist called Georges Ibrahim Abdallah – and, in 2008, Khieu Samphan, one of the Khmer Rouge leaders in Cambodia who was facing a UN-supported trial.

One of the many mysteries of his life is that, in 1970, Vergès disappeared from public view. No one knew where the wily lawyer was. Then, in 1978, he reappeared. A rumour was that he had joined the Khmer Rouge, but that has been denied by leaders of that organisation. Other stories had it that he was involved with Palestinian militants, and had gone into hiding in Lebanon or elsewhere in the Middle East. He took whatever happened during those 'missing years' to his grave when he died in 2013.

His brother Paul, though, stayed in Réunion where he led his local communist party. He was elected as a senator in the French parliament in 1996 and again from 2011. For a while, he was also a member of the European Parliament. The old firebrand agitator and activist outlived his brother by three years and died in 2016 at the age of 91. With the passing of the Vergès twins, Réunion has no personalities of the same controversial calibre.

And no such political figures are likely to emerge on Kerguelen, whose only inhabitants are ostensibly engaged in astrophysics, astronomy, geology, biology and zoology. But something is happening on the island that the outside world is not aware of. That became evident when in October 1986 the French navy sank the Australian fishing trawler *Southern Raider*. The action did not attract as much attention as the destruction of Greenpeace's *Rainbow Warrior* in the port of Auckland, New Zealand, the year before. But both cases contributed to the region's perception of French ruthlessness – and there are similarities between the high-profile bombing of the *Rainbow Warrior* and the lesser known sinking of the *Southern Raider*. The *Rainbow Warrior* was on its way to protest a planned nuclear test in Moruroa, French Polynesia, when it was destroyed by commandos sent by France's foreign intelligence services. The *Southern Raider* was sunk when it ventured too close to Kerguelen.[6]

In an interview after the event, *Southern Raider's* skipper John Chadderton said 'they accused us of illegally fishing in French waters, but they interrogated us endlessly about espionage, not fishing.'[7] He and first officer Alistair Annandale were held – and interrogated – for three months on Réunion before they were released.

At the time, is was widely suspected that the French planned to move their nuclear testing site, and their nuclear arsenal, from French Polynesia where a strong popular movement was demanding not only an end to the tests but also independence from France. Kerguelen, of course, has no such troublesome local population. It is an island of glaciers, rocks and mountains where the highest peak, Mount Ross, is 1,850 metres above sea level. Kerguelen is, therefore, ideal for underground storage facilities and, if France so wanted, test sites for nuclear weapons. Or, as one scientist put it, 'the geology of the archipelago is admirably suited to underground explosions.'[8]

It was first proposed that nuclear tests should be carried out on Kerguelen at the end of the Algerian war and the independence of that colony in 1962, when France had to relinquish its test sites in the Sahara. President de Gaulle liked the idea, but the army thought otherwise, preferring the lagoons at Moruroa and Fangataufa in the

Pacific. A major consideration could have been that all nuclear tests in those days were atmospheric. Kerguelen is one of the windiest places on earth, and the winds blow straight to the northeast – towards Australia. In the end, no nuclear tests were carried out on Kerguelen, not in the 1960s and not after France's last test in French Polynesia in 1986.

But there is a satellite and rocket tracking station on Kerguelen, and, from 1968 to 1981, the French maintained a launch site for rockets just east of Port-aux-Français, so the strategic importance of the remote island has never been a complete secret. And what else is hidden in the mountains of Kerguelen will remain a mystery. Because of the windy conditions, there is no airport on Kerguelen. The only link with the outside world is by ship from Réunion and TAAF's chief administrator, who bears the title *préfet*, is also based there, not in Saint-Denis but in the smaller town of Saint-Pierre.

Amsterdam & Saint-Paul, which constitute one of the five districts of TAAF, are much smaller than Kerguelen. There are research stations on both islands as well as on the Crozet Islands, which forms another TAAF district. All those islands are as rocky and inhospitable as Kerguelen, but important enough for France to maintain a presence on along with a semblance of administration to make it an organised entity like any other of its *territoires d'outre-mer.* France claimed the Crozet Islands when they were discovered by Marc-Joseph Marion du Fresne in 1772. Amsterdam had been discovered as early as 1522 by a Spanish explorer and Saint-Paul by the Portuguese in 1559. But they probably considered them useless, and left it to the French to claim them in 1843.

Kerguelen was first sighted by the French navigator Yves-Joseph de Kerguelen-Trémarec in February 1772. The island was claimed for the French crown, but nothing more than that was done about it. No settlement was founded, and it remained totally uninhabited. Captain James Cook visited the island in 1776 during one his voyages across the Indian Ocean, and so did some British, American and Norwegian whalers and sealers. British and German expeditions also reached Kerguelen and its outlying, smaller islands, but, apart from a failed coal-mining venture in the 1870s, France paid little attention to its possessions in the southern Indian Ocean other than claiming them.

It was not until 1893 that France formally annexed Kerguelen, the Crozet Islands, and Amsterdam & Saint-Paul and, in 1924, included those territories as possessions under the French constitution.

Many attempts were made to make use of Kerguelen. Sheep were introduced, but no farmers were willing to settle there. It did not become a French equivalent of the Falkland Islands, where British sheep farmers managed to build up a small but relatively prosperous community. At one stage it was suggested that Kerguelen should become a penal colony, a kind of Antarctic mini-Siberia. But there was no way the island would be able to produce enough food for the prisoners and their wardens. Nothing would grow on the island, whose only edible resource was Kerguelen cabbage, a potassium-rich plant which became essential food for the whalers when they had run out of provisions.

A German ship landed on Kerguelen in 1940, and found it completely deserted. The Germans stayed for a while, stocked up with fresh water and sailed on. The French did not discover that they had been there until after World War II. Eventually, the French found some use for the island. It became a 'scientific colony' in 1950, and, in 1955, TAAF was formed, at first under the administration of Madagascar and Dependencies. It came to be administered from Réunion after Madagascar's independence in 1960.

Even more noteworthy when it comes to maintaining a presence and so motivating a military presence and justifying claims to economic exclusive zones is a chain of even smaller Indian Ocean islands which are also French. Called *Îles Éparses de l'Océan Indien*, or 'the Scattered Islands in the Indian Ocean'. They consist of four small coral islands, an atoll, and a reef in the Indian Ocean. Two of the coral islands, Juan de Nova and Europa, and the Bassas da India atoll lie in the channel between Madagascar and the African mainland and so does the reef, Banc du Geyser. Tromelin, another island, is located in the ocean east of Madagascar and 500 kilometres north of Réunion. The Gloriosa Islands lie northwest of Madagascar. Mauritius claims Tromelin and the Comoros claim the Gloriosa Islands. Madagascar claims all those islands.

'The Scattered Islands' became French in the eighteenth century and were administered from either Mayotte or Réunion, which explains why they have remained French even after Madagascar's independence in 1960. There are no permanent inhabitants on any of the islands, but France maintains meteorological stations, of which some are automated, on all of them except Bassas da India. There are airstrips on all of them except Bassas da India and Banc du Geyser. About 14 French soldiers are based on each of the islands in the Madagascar Strait to show they belong to France and nobody else. The economic importance of those islands is questionable, but they help France to maintain its 2.5-million-square-kilometre exclusive economic zone in the Indian Ocean.

Mayotte north of Madagascar is France's newest *département d'outre-mer* and is as important as Réunion or any of the TAAF islands when it comes to maintaining French power over a large swathe of the Indian Ocean. And if Kerguelen is rugged and desolate, Mayotte is the very opposite. It is a lush, tropical island surrounded by a coral reef. There are 256,000 people living on the island, which geographically is part of the Comoros. Nearly all of the inhabitants on Mayotte are Sunni Muslims, which makes it France's only Muslim-majority *département*. It is also the poorest. But even so Mayotte is much more prosperous than the independent Comoros, nearby Madagascar, and Mozambique and Tanzania on the African mainland. And that has made it a major destination for illegal immigration. Mayotte's GDP per capita stands at US$10,500 while on the Comoros it is only US$1,566.

The other islands in the Comoros were also French until they became an independent republic in 1975. The Comoros still claims Mayotte, but there are historical and geostrategic reasons why the French kept Mayotte and separated it from the other islands. Mayotte was the first of the Comoros islands to come under French colonial rule. In 1841, it was ceded to France by Adrian Souli, the ruler of the island, who came from Madagascar, and the French immediately established a military base on their new possession. The other islands were added to France's colonial empire, and the entire archipelago became French in 1912, first as a province of the larger colony Madagascar and, after World War II, as a separate entity.

The Comoros was poor and actually of little value to the French. The colonial masters introduced sugar, vanilla, coffee and ylang-ylang to uplift the backward economy of the islands, but their main importance was as a way station for ships sailing to India and Southeast Asia. They had one asset the French valued highly: a strategic location in the western Indian Ocean and off the coast of Africa.

When voices were raised for independence in the late 1960s and early 1970s, France realised that it could not retain control over the entire archipelago. But they decided one of the islands – Mayotte – would have to remain French. France did not want to lose such an important foothold in the region. Economic incentives and a long tradition of contacts with France played an important role in persuading the islanders that independence was not something the islanders would desire.

Referendums were held on all four islands of the Comoros, though the votes were counted separately. Three of the islands voted overwhelmingly for independence. Mayotte voted against. Independence had been scheduled for 1978, but, on 6 July 1975, the Comorian parliament decided to proclaim an independent republic. But Mayotte remained with France, and the presence of French troops made it clear to the leaders of the new republic that they should not even think of occupying the breakaway island. The French were keen to keep it well defended.

As a result, Mayotte received substantial subsidies from the French state while the Comoros remained poor. A detachment of the French Foreign Legion, which until 1975 had been based on another of the Comoros, was moved to Mayotte to ensure political stability on what was then designated a *collectivité territoriale*, or 'territorial collectivity', of France, which it remained until it became a *département* in 2011. By contrast, the Comoros went from one economic and political crisis to another, some of them no doubt orchestrated by France.

Coups, coup attempts and political assassinations have become regular features in the political life of the Comoros, a three-island republic with no more than 795,000 inhabitants. An important role has been played by one of most notorious mercenaries in Africa, Robert 'Bob' Denard, a staunch anti-communist Frenchman who served as a colonial police officer in Morocco in the 1950s and then fought against the independence movement in Algeria. He also saw action in the civil wars in the Congo, where he sided with the break-away republic Katanga, in Angola against pro-communist forces, on the side of the Biafra separatists in Nigeria, and in Rhodesia before it became Zimbabwe. Born a Roman Catholic, he converted first to Judaism and then to Islam before reverting to Catholicism. At least at some stage in his career, he worked for the French secret service.

Denard's first intervention in the Comoros occurred when the country's first president, Ahmed Abdallah, was ousted in a coup on 3 August 1975, only 28 days after the proclamation of independence. The new president, Ali Soilih, was a leftist, and therefore not a friend of the old colonial power. France recognised the independence of the Comoros on 31 December 1975, but all active relations, including aid programmes, which amounted to 40 per cent of the national budget, remained suspended.[9]

After France stopped all its aid to the Comoros, the country's treasury was emptied. The government, unable to pay salaries, was forced to dismiss 3,500 civil servants. But Soilih found new allies in Tanzania and North Korea, which provided some limited aid. Economic mismanagement and severe food shortages made people turn against Soilih and there was little resistance when Denard landed with a force of 43 mostly French mercenaries on 12 May 1978. Soilih was deposed and killed two weeks after Denard's coup. The official explanation was that he had 'attempted to escape'.[10]

Ahmed Abdallah returned from exile in Paris and was reinstated as president. For 11 years, from 1978 to 1989, Denard headed Abdallah's 500-strong Presidential Guard. It was during this time Denard converted to Islam, took several wives, and assumed the name Said Mustapha Mahdjoub. Relations with Paris improved, especially as the Comoros provided France with a base to evade international trade sanctions against South Africa because of its policy of apartheid. Denard grew rich from the acquisition of hotels and other real estate, and it was sometimes hard to say who really ruled the country: he or the president.

Opposition against Abdallah and Denard grew as their regime became more oppressive. In February 1982, the Comoros became a one-party state and, two years later, Abdallah won more than 99 per cent of the votes in a presidential election where he was the only candidate. Demonstrators who protested against what now amounted to a dictatorship were beaten and arrested by the Presidential Guard headed by Denard. Most of the guardsmen were indigenous Comorans but they were led by about 30 French and Belgian mercenaries, comrades-in-arms of Denard from his days fighting in Africa's civil wars. The force was widely understood to be funded by South Africa at the rate of US$3 million per year.[11]

But the economy did not improve. The Comoros remained as they had been under Soilih: poor, underdeveloped, and dependent on export earnings from cash crops of unpredictable and generally declining value.[12] As the country was preparing for another round of elections at the end of November 1989, Abdallah was shot dead while asleep in his residence. A disgruntled army officer was blamed for the murder but subsequent evidence pointed at Denard as the culprit. Abdallah had hired another French military consultant who had recommended that the Presidential Guard should be absorbed into the regular army. The confusion was total when Abdallah, fearing a coup, ordered the Presidential Guard to disarm the army.

What happened during those turbulent days has never been made clear, but, on 29 November, Denard and the Presidential Guard seized absolute power in a coup. But that was more than even his old friends in France and South Africa could tolerate. Both countries cut off all aid and decided to isolate Denard. When a demonstration by about a thousand students and workers was violently broken up by Denard's men, the civil service went on strike. Denard finally had to leave the Comoros. He was flown to South Africa with about a dozen of his men and put under house arrest in Pretoria.

Denard remained in South Africa until he was allowed to return to France in February 1993. There, he was arrested, tried – and exonerated of any involvement in the death of Abdallah. Abdallah's family has evidently been persuaded to drop all charges against Denard, so he was acquitted because of lack of evidence.

Back in the Comoros, there was one coup after another. Denard, free from legal problems in France, decided to take advantage of the chaotic situation. He arrived in the Comoros with 33 of his men aboard Zodiac inflatable boats on the night of 27 September 1995 to stage yet another coup, this one entirely for himself. France, which had a new defence agreement with the Comoros, sent an expeditionary force to capture Denard and his mercenaries. He surrendered without a single shot being fired, and was brought back to France.

Denard spent ten months in a Paris jail and then had to face several lawsuits. One of them was for having tried to recruit far-right Italian mercenaries in order to overthrow the country's president who had declared his opposition to Denard's return to the Comoros. Then came another lawsuit related to his 1995 coup attempt. Legal procedures dragged on for years until in June 2006 Denard was given a five-year suspended jail sentence for 'belonging to a gang who conspired to commit crime', but he was absent from the hearings because he was suffering from Alzheimer's disease.[13] Denard died in France on 13 October 2007.

The Comoros has recovered from the days of coups and mercenaries, but relations with France remain strained. The Comoros has not relinquished its claim to Mayotte – and the French have, over the years, strengthened their hold over that island through generous economic subsidies and, in 2011, by integrating it in France as a full-fledged *département*.

But the Comoros have found a new, seemingly more dependable ally: China. Vice President Fouad Mhadji, who is also Health Minister, told a visiting CBS team in November 2014: 'The French were here for 200 years. What did they build? What did they leave us?'[14] Though he was wrong about the French having been there for 200 years, there was no doubt about the anger he felt against the former colonial power. Mohamed Soilih, the director of the Comoros television station, was similarly resentful of France's role in the country's history: 'After 40 years [of independence], China has become the first partner. Before it was France, now it is China.'[15]

China has financed the construction of a new sports stadium and a new airport. It has built a new power plant, clinics, schools, and mosques. Groups of Comoran soldiers have been brought to China for military training and intensive studies in Mandarin. And in December 2015, Chinese President Xi Jinping met his Comoran counterpart Ikililou Dhoinine on the sidelines of a China-Africa summit in Johannesburg, South Africa. Dhoinine expressed his gratitude for China's assistance – and that the Comoros 'is willing to participate in infrastructure cooperation with China under the framework of the Belt and Road Initiative.'[16]

The Chinese, like the French before them, have discovered the strategic value of those otherwise impoverished islands. But despite pleasantries expressed in meetings with Comoran leaders, China's focus is on a much bigger and more important trophy off the eastern coast of Africa: Madagascar. With its 587,041 square-kilometres, the island is slightly larger than metropolitan France, of which it once was a colony. Unlike the other, tiny Indian Ocean nations it is rich in resources. Madagascar has the world's largest reserves of ilmenite, or titanium ore, as well as significant deposits of chromite, coal, iron, cobalt, copper, nickel, sapphires, emeralds and rubies.[17] Madagascar Oil Ltd, an American company, has been drilling for heavy petroleum at the onshore oil field at Tsimiroro since 2010. The reserves there are estimated to have 965 million barrels of petroleum.[18]

Madagascar is also rich in agricultural resources, and fishing and forestry are other important sectors of the economy. The country is the world's leading supplier of vanilla, cloves and ylang-ylang. There are coffee and fruit plantations in the highlands and, even if deforestation is a major problem, there are still many types of hardwood in its lowland jungles. The waters around the island are rich in fish and shrimp.

Of Madagascar's 25 million people 70 per cent have African ancestry while the remaining 30 per cent can trace their ethnic origin to Southeast Asia. Those of Asian descent are believed to be descendants of people who migrated in the seventh and eighth century AD from the archipelago that today makes up Indonesia. Over the centuries, the two cultures and ethnicities have not exactly merged, but developed into what today is called 'Malagasy', a people with a well-defined culture. It is also possible that the emergence of a Malagasy nation is the result of a series of migrations of different peoples over a long time. According to this version of history, migrants from the Indonesian archipelago arrived first and eventually settled in the island's central highlands where they built rice terraces similar to those in Southeast Asia.

The migrants from Southeast Asia were followed by people from the African mainland, either as 'normal' migrants or as slaves. Most of their descendants live primarily but not exclusively in coastal areas. In the eleventh century, Tamil merchants from southern India arrived on the island and brought with them zebus, or long-horned humped cattle, which can still be seen in the highlands. Somehow, these different peoples managed to co-exist and even mix, and became a nation. But despite the existence today of a distinct Malagasy culture, there are 18 or 20 ethnic groups, each with its own territory, though they are remarkably homogenous in terms of language.[19]

In the pre-colonial era – that is, before the French arrived in force in the late nineenth century – there were several kingdoms on the island. But following a century of devastating wars and famine, most of Madagascar was united under Andrianampoinimerina, the king of Imerina, who reigned from 1787 to 1810. The final unification of the island took place in the reign of his son and successor Radama I, who was recognised by the British government as King of Madagascar. His rule lasted until his death in 1828 and, by then, the British were established in South Africa and Mauritius and Radama I had sought to modernise his kingdom along Western lines. A cabinet was established and he encouraged the London Missionary Society to establish schools and churches on the island. The missionaries managed to convert nearly half a million people, and a few youngsters were sent to Britain to further their education.

The missionaries also brought with them a printing press, which resulted in the Marina dialect becoming the official language, written with the Roman alphabet. But this was not entirely a period of enlightenment. Local rulers were engaged in suppressing whatever remained of the old, smaller kingdoms – and acquiring slaves from the African mainland. And it was during this turbulent period in the island's history that French merchants acquired slaves from the mainland as well as Madagascar and sent them on to the plantations in Réunion.

During the late eighteenth and early nineteenth century, Madagascar also gained infamy for being a haven for pirates, and there were even tales of a proto-anarchist colony called Libertatia, which may or may not have existed there as early as the late seventeenth century. According to legend, it was ruled by pirates under the leadership of a captain called James Misson. That may be a myth, but Portuguese, Arab, French and British traders fought against pirates in the waters around the island, leading to increased foreign influence in the kingdom. This was resented by Radama I's wife and successor, Queen Ranavalona I. After she assumed power in 1828, rivals were killed along with Christian converts.

Many Europeans fled the island, but an enterprising few remained. One of them was the French artisan Jean Laborde, who established an agricultural research station near the present capital Antananarivo. He also founded a manufacturing complex where his local workers produced commodities ranging from silk and soap to guns, tools and cement. Madagascar got its first industry, and the overall modernisation of the island was resumed after the death of Queen Ranavalona I in 1861. Her successor King Radama II made a treaty of 'perpetual friendship' with the French, who had been present on the island since their first trading posts were established in the late seventeenth century. But resistance to foreign influence from the indigenous nobility remained, and the king was assassinated after only two years on the throne. The treaty with France was annulled along with the charter for Laborde's company.

Radama II's successors tried to control the situation by playing off the French against the British. Commercial treaties were signed with both countries under King Rainilaiarivony, who also abolished polygamy and slavery. Education was encouraged and even the kings converted to Christianity. But the colonial powers proved to be more interested in gaining control of Madagascar than treating it as an equal partner in trade and commerce. The French were the first to claim the island for themselves. In 1894, they declared a protectorate over the whole island, based on treaties dating back to the 1840s. But Queen Ranavalona III, the ruler of Madagascar, refused to recognise the French proclamation. The French responded by sending an expeditionary force to the island, which occupied Antananarivo in September 1895. The following year, the French declared Madagascar a colony and deported the queen and her prime minister first to Réunion and later to Algeria. The monarchy was abolished and French officials arrived on the island to take over the administration and the civil service.

But Madagascar was different from France's other African colonies. It had a comparatively high rate of literacy and small groups of intellectuals had been educated by European teachers and exposed to Western ideas about liberty and equality. Madagascar was also, after all, a nation, not only a geographic entity drawn up in Berlin in 1884-85, when Africa was divided cartographically between Europe's main colonial powers.

A secret society dedicated to affirming Malagasy culture was formed in 1913. It was brutally suppressed by the colonial authorities, but it forced the French to provide the local elite with their first representative voice in government.[20] Malagasy veterans in both World Wars became engaged in a movement not for independence but to demand French citizenship for all the people on the island. As a result, Madagascar was awarded a new status when France in 1946 adopted a new constitution. It did not become a *département d'outre-mer* like Réunion but a *territoire d'outre-mer* within the French Union. Full French citizenship was accorded to everyone on the island. French colonialism also brought a wide range of other new influences such as French-style education, a judicial system and civil administration based on French models, along with the spread of Christianity, now under the aegis of the Roman Catholic Church.

Despite those changes and reforms, American researcher Helen Chapin Metz explains, 'the political scene in Madagascar remained unstable. Economic and social concerns, including food shortages, black-market scandals, labour conscription, renewed ethnic tension, and the return of soldiers from France, strained an already volatile situation.'[21] Many of the war veterans, who had been shabbily treated while in France, had become radicalised and began to demand full independence. A revolt broke out in 1947, and the French were able to reassert control only after soldiers had been sent to the island to quell the rebellion – and the repression was brutal. Casualties on the Malagasy side were estimated at between 60,000 and 80,000. Twenty of the leaders of the revolt were executed while between 5,000 and 6,000 ended up in prison.

The pressure for reforms continued despite the heavy hand of the French – still a colonial power even if Madagascar was officially a *territoire d'outre-mer.* After France adopted a new constitution in 1958, Madagascar gained the status of a self-governing republic within the French community. But even that did not satisfy the nationalists. A referendum and elections were held and, on 27 April 1959, Philibert Tsiranana, a cattle farmer's son who was educated in France and there become an independence activist, was sworn in as the first president of the republic. The French had to accept the ruling, and Madagascar became a fully independent and sovereign republic on 26 June 1960.

Tsiranana remained Madagascar's president until 1972, and during his time in power, the island experienced political stability and economic growth. He introduced what was called 'Malagasy socialism', a form of social democracy that combined private enterprise, the development of cooperatives, and state intervention in the economy. But once in power he began to manifest authoritarian tendencies. This became evident when a peasant uprising broke out in Toliara, one of the provinces in the republic, in April 1971. The main reason for the revolt was government demands for what the peasants saw as excessive tax collection at a time when local cattle herds were being ravaged by disease. The revolt was brutally suppressed with several hundred dead. Many were also arrested and deported to the island of Nosy-Lava, the site of a maximum security prison off the coast of northwestern Madagascar.

Then, in early 1972, students took to the streets of Antananarivo demanding an end to cultural cooperation agreements with France and replacing educational programmes designed for French schools with curricula emphasising Malagasy culture. Again, the government's response was harsh. Several hundred student leaders and activists were sent to the cells in Nosy-Lava. Economic stagnation compounded Tsiranana's problems, and when workers, public servants, students and peasants began to protest – and the army opened fire on them, killing 40 and injuring 150 people – it was time for him to resign. On 18 May 1972, Tsiranana handed over power to the military under the command of General Gabriel Ramanantsoa, a conservative officer who had served in the French army.

Political stability was soon a thing of the past and one crisis after another beset Madagascar. Ramanantsoa, unable to control the situation, handed power to another army officer, Colonel Richard Ratsimandrava, who was assassinated after only five days in office. It was not until 1975 that a semblance of order was restored. A 'Second Republic' was proclaimed under the leadership of Lieutenant Commander Didier Ratsiraka. He was elected to a seven-year term as president and proclaimed the need for a socialist 'revolution from above'. The country was renamed the Democratic Republic of Madagascar and he sought to radically change society in accordance with principles incorporated in a document called *Charter of the*

Malagasy Socialist Revolution, popularly known as the 'Red Book', or *Boky Mena* in the local language.[22]

Radical leftism was nothing new in Madagascar, but now distinct socialist policies, beyond Tsiranana's modest attempts at social democracy, were implemented by the central government. Madagascar did not technically become a one-party socialist state, given it was ruled by a coalition of six parties called the National Front for the Defence of the Revolution, or *Front National pour la Défense de la Révolution*, FNDR. The French-held sector of the economy was taken over by the state in a programme dubbed 'economic decolonisation'. A US-operated earth satellite tracking station was closed. The French had had to leave their military base at Diego Suarez, renamed Antsiranana after independence, in 1973, a year after Madagascar had established diplomatic relations with the Soviet Union, China and North Korea. The Soviet Union became the primary source of military equipment and Soviet military advisers arrived in Madagascar. Cuba also provided technical assistance, but mostly in the educational field. The new Ratsiraka regime was especially impressed with North Korea whose leader Kim Il Sung had formulated an ideology of self-reliance called *juche*. The North Koreans provided training for Ratsiraka's personal security unit and constructed a presidential bunker at Iavohola 15 kilometres south of Antananarivo.

Since the fall of Tsiranana in 1972, Madagascar had been drifting away from its Western allies and moving closer to the Eastern Bloc. That process was now over. At about the same time, a similar development took place in the Seychelles and, in Ethiopia, emperor Haile Selassie's fall from power in 1974 was followed by the establishment of a military, communist dictatorship in that country. Western powers were also on the way out in other parts of the Indian Ocean region such as South Yemen and several Arab and African states. Those developments help to explain why the British and the Americans decided to build their military base on Diego Garcia. The French were also convinced that they had to stay in the Indian Ocean region.

Madagascar's new socialist policies turned out to be a disaster for the country. The economy went from bad to worse, attempts to introduce centralised government control over agriculture led to food shortages and the economic crisis was exacerbated by mismanagement of the nationalised sectors of industry and manufacturing. In September 1977, Antananarivo was rocked by anti-government demonstrations, and student riots followed in 1978. Ratsiraka had no choice but to turn to the International Monetary Fund, IMF, for help to bail out his government, which teetered on bankruptcy, and to introduce free-market reforms, which did not turn out as expected. Then came in 1989 the fall of the Berlin Wall, the subsequent, rapid collapse of the socialist regimes in Eastern Europe and the dissolution of the Soviet Union in 1991.

The anti-communist torrent reached even distant Madagascar. A general strike was proclaimed in May 1991 and, in August, more than 400,000 people marched on the presidential palace, demanding the resignation of Ratsiraka's government. He agreed to initiate a process of democratisation while holding on to the presidency. A new constitution was adopted in August 1992 followed by elections in November. In the first round of elections, Ratsiraka as head of his new party, the Militant Movement for Malagasy Socialism, or *Mouvement Militant pour le Socialisme Malgache*, secured a mere 29 per cent of the vote while the opposition, an umbrella group of 16 political parties led by Albert Zafy, a French-educated university lecturer, took 46 per cent. Because no party or bloc had an absolute majority, a second round of voting was held in February 1993. Zafy won by a landslide, receiving 67 per cent of the vote. A Third Republic was inaugurated on 27 March with Zafy as the new president.

The optimism that followed the defeat of Ratsiraka's regime and the re-introduction of a more democratic order soon turned into widespread frustrations as Zafy proved unable to solve the country's economic woes. There were also accusations of rampant corruption and no end to Madagascar's perennial problem of the dominant role of the people in the central highlands versus those living in the outlying areas who wanted to manage their own affairs. Like several of his predecessors, Zafy became increasingly authoritarian. When he tried to introduce legislation that would give him more power, he was impeached and forced to resign in 1996. Ratsiraka was voted back into power with promises of decentralisation and economic reforms.

Ratsiraka's second term in office lasted until 2001 when he was defeated by the mayor of Antananarivo, Marc Ravalomanana. After years of political unrest and economic downturn, there seemed to be progress in sight in many different fields. Ravalomanana managed to attract domestic and foreign investment in education, ecotourism and manufacturing. The government built schools and health clinics, and the island's run-down infrastructure saw significant improvements. As a result, Madagascar's GDP grew at an average of seven per cent during the first years of his presidency.

Yet old habits die hard, and even Ravalomanana became authoritarian, corrupt and brutal. Demonstrations against his rule were met with bullets as his presidential guards opened fire on protesters in February 2009: 31 people were killed and at least 200 wounded. The following month he was deposed in a coup. A military-appointed government took over and a Fourth Republic was established in 2010, after a referendum that led to a new constitution being promulgated.

The new president of what was called 'the High Transitional Authority of Madagascar' was the youthful Andry Rajoelina, a former media entrepreneur and mayor of Antananarivo, who was tasked with overseeing the transition towards a new constitutional authority. He was not yet 35 years old when he took over in May 2009 and oversaw the referendum. Rajoelina initiated a range of populist policies such as subsidising petrol, electricity, food staples, and housing for young middle class couples. But the fact that he was not democratically elected led to sanctions and suspension of donor aid. It was also discovered that his administration had sold wood to supplement the national budget, leading to deforestation of what should have been protected areas.[23] Madagascar also saw an increase in crime and its economy was ranked by Forbes as one of the worst in the world.[24]

Elections were eventually held at the end of 2013. Hery Rajaonarimampianina, a former accountant who had served as finance minister under a previous government, became president in January 2014. He remained in power until 7 September 2018, when he was constitutionally required to resign as he would be a candidate for the November election when he may or may not be re-elected. Rajaonarinampianina, whose full name is Hery Martial Rajaonarimampianina Rakotoarimanana has the dubious distinction of being the head of state with the longest name of any nation in the world. More importantly, his rise to power – and the end of the Third and the beginning of the Fourth Republic – coincided with the emergence of China as a global economic power.

Relations had been close since Madagascar severed relations with the Republic of China, or Taiwan, and recognised the People's Republic of China in 1972. But with Deng Xiaoping's return to power in 1977 and 1978, the nature of the relationship gradually turned from revolutionary brotherhood to trade and economic cooperation. Bilateral relations began to blossom under Ravalomanana. Numerous projects involving China were initiated when he was in power. Ravalomanana was a frequent visitor to China, and many Chinese companies arrived in Madagascar to invest and set up businesses. The Chinese firm Maloci opened a cement factory, the Company for External Commerce and Construction, which enjoys the support of the Chinese state and is actually a branch of the state-owned Anhui Fergen Construction Company. That entity was granted contracts to build a new five-star hotel and an international conference centre. Leases and management of certain sugar-producing factories belonging to the national company Siramamy Malagasy were transferred to Complant, a Chinese firm. During one of his many visits to China, Ravalomanana also obtained a commitment from the Chinese Exim Bank for financial backing for the construction of a dam to be carried out by CAMC Engineering, yet another Chinese company.[25]

This increase in Chinese investment in Madagascar was most conspicuous when it came to oil and mining. Sunpec, a Chinese company, was given permission to prospect for oil offshore and several Chinese mining companies explored for iron, titanium oxide, tungsten and even gold. This rapid increase in Chinese involvement in exploiting Madagascar's mineral resources has also precipitated a backlash. In December 2016, local people in the town of Soamahamanina took to the streets to demonstrate against a Chinese company called Jiuxing, which had secured a 40-year gold mining licence on a 7,500 ha piece of land.[26] The Singapore daily *Straits Times* reported that 'across the country, Madagascans have openly expressed their hostility towards the growing presence of China, the country's largest trading partner.'[27] In 2017, the most recent year for which detailed statistics are available, trade between China and Madagascar totalled US$1.25 billion, up from US$297.6 million in 2016 and US$24.4 million in 2011.[28] Of the 2017 total, only US$176.4 million consisted of exports from Madagascar to China.[29]

It is obvious that China is in Madagascar to stay, and the choice of Madagascar as a favourite destination for Chinese investment and businesses is not only because the island is rich in mineral and agricultural resources. Madagascar has Africa's second largest Chinese population. South Africa has by far the largest number of residents of Chinese descent, between 300,000 and 400,000 people. But the Chinese population on Madagascar is estimated at 100,000, twice as many as Angola's 50,000 and far more than the 40,000 in Nigeria and about the same number in Ethiopia.[30]

While many Chinese immigrants in the rest of Africa are new to the continent, that is not the case in South Africa – or Madagascar. The first Chinese in South Africa came during the British colonial period as labourers or to establish various trade and service businesses near the gold and diamond mines around Kimberley and Johannesburg. They were not allowed by law to mine, but they found employment in related fields.[31]

The first Chinese in Madagascar may have been individual traders, but three waves of Chinese migration were registered between 1896 and 1901 to build the road and then the railway linking Antananarivo with Toamasina and the Pangalenes Canal. Most of them came from Mauritius and Réunion, but from 1930 onwards most Chinese came directly from China and mainly from Guangdong in the south.[32] But the numbers were still small, 2,780 in 1936 and 5,573 in 1946. Many of those who arrived at that time had escaped the Japanese invasion of China and were looking for greener pastures abroad. Antananarivo got its own Chinatown, Chinese schools and community halls.

Over the years, more arrived and with diplomatic relations being established in 1972, Madagascar saw a dramatic influx of Chinese migrants. And that has not been without friction. Many 'old Chinese' resent the newcomers. The French researcher Mathieu Pellerin quotes an old-timer as saying that 'the new Chinese come here only to earn money in the short term and then go back to China. For us Madagascar is the land we were born in and shall die in [and] we don't approach things in the same way.'[33] Another 'old' Chinese was quoted as saying that the recent arrivals 'tarnish the general image of the Chinese community.'[34]

But such sentiments are unlikely to change the tide of history. Apart from an influx of Chinese nationals, Antananarivo University has had its own Confucius Institute since 2009. There are another 16 in mainland Africa and, as Pellerin says, 'this strategic pillar of Chinese "soft power" is aimed at propagating Chinese culture through the world and, more prosaically, at providing a source of interpreters accessible to the investors keen to gain a foothold in Madagascar.'[35] The 'new Chinese' have also created what is called the Association of Chinese Traders and Entrepreneurs of Madagascar, which brings together almost 90 Chinese businesses.

Relations between Madagascar and China grew even closer during Rajaonarimampianina's presidency. During a visit to Beijing in March 2017, he signed a Memorandum of Understanding with the Chinese government on jointly advancing the Belt and Road Initiative, and hailed Xi Jinping for his 'wise and visionary strategy.'[36] During the same visit, Xi stated that China 'supports Madagascar in playing its role as a bridge between the Belt and Road and the African continent.'[37] China, Xi said, wants to 'deepen cooperation in agriculture, fisheries, people-to-people exchanges, security, police affairs, justice and law-enforcement.'[38]

All that sounds good in theory, yet despite its mineral and agricultural wealth, Madagascar remains a desperately poor country. According to the International Monetary Fund, GDP per capita is a mere US$1,563 and many people live in abject poverty.[39] Given Madagascar's need for foreign investment and aid, it may be easy prey for China, but given its turbulent history and chronic political instability, it is also a big gamble for anyone who wants to invest or do business there.

Gone are the days of Tsiranana and Madagascar's close relations with France. But that France and other Indian Ocean countries are wary of China's expanding influence in the region became obvious when France's president Emmanuel Macron and India's prime minister Narendra Modi signed their defence agreement in March 2018. France has stepped up its presence in the Indian Ocean as well as the South Pacific, but 'China is not our target,' said Rear Admiral Laurent Lebreton in an interview in August 2018.[40] Then he added that 'the Indo-Pacific is a strategic region for France, depicted as such in the 2013 White Paper on Defence and the 2017 Strategic Defence and Security Review.'[41]

It could not have been said clearer than that. Were it not for China's rise as an Indian Ocean power, why would France increase its presence in that particular region? And why would Macron, when meeting the Australian Prime Minister Malcolm Turnbull in Sydney in May 2018, say that France and Australia – alongside their fellow democracy India – have a responsibility to protect the region from 'hegemony' and stressed the need for preserving 'necessary balances' in the region?[42] This recent change in the balance of power in the Indian Ocean is precisely the reason why France is still holding on to Réunion, Mayotte, Kerguelen and the smaller islands in the region. France may have lost the Comoros and Madagascar, but it is still a major Indian Ocean power and determined to remain so.

6

THE SEYCHELLES

The legendary Irish-British mercenary Michael 'Mad Mike' Hoare, who had fallen in love with the Seychelles, once wrote about the islands:

> Dense mangrove and takamaku trees on the edge of lovely white beaches, with cloves and vanilla high up in the hills surrounding it all crystal clear water. Sounds enchanting, doesn't it? Well, it is – a regular paradise.[1]

That was also how many other foreigners saw the Seychelles, the islands of love where the female variety of a coconut produces a nut called *coco-de-mer* that looks like a woman's sexual organ. On the male tree the flower is shaped like a phallus, and some romantics believe that this was the original Garden of Eden. Even the entry stamp that one gets on arrival at the airport is shaped like that coconut, which is found naturally only in the Seychelles. Some ardent Christians are convinced that the tree on which the nut grows is identical to the Tree of Knowledge in Genesis.

The capital, Victoria, is named after the nineteenth-century British Queen, and with only 27,000 inhabitants it is the smallest capital of any independent nation in the world. Nauru may be smaller yet, but it doesn't really have a capital. And Victoria is rich in colonial architecture. A clock tower, built to resemble the one at London's Vauxhall Bridge – which, in turn, is a smaller version of the famous Big Ben – stands in the centre. The replica of the 'Little Ben', as it is called, was shipped to the Seychelles when the islands were separated from Mauritius to become a colony in its own right in 1903. The street past the clock tower is called Independence Avenue to mark that the Seychelles is an independent republic, which it became in 1976.

The Seychelles may, in the words of Mad Mike, be a 'regular paradise,' but there is an entirely different, darker reality behind its idyllic, picture-book façade. After independence, a group of foreign mercenaries, supported by South Africa and possibly also the US Central Intelligence Agency, CIA, tried to invade the islands and unseat the government in what must have been the most bizarre coup attempt in modern history. When that failed and the mercenaries were defeated, the Seychelles established a close relationship with North Korea.

That was not the end of curious happenings in the islands. In January 2017, shortly before the inauguration of US president Donald Trump, George Nader – a Lebanese-American businessman and lobbyist who serves as an adviser to Mohammed bin Zayed al-Nahyan, the crown prince of the United Arab Emirates – arranged a meeting in the Seychelles which brought together Eric Prince, Trump donor and founder of the private security company Blackwater, with Kirill Dmitriev, who manages a Russian sovereign wealth fund and is thought to be close to Russian president Vladimir Putin.

Before that meeting, Trump's son-in-law Jared Kushner and Trump's now disgraced former security adviser Michael Flynn had met secretly in Trump Tower in New York to set up a secret communications channel between the Trump team and Russia.[2] And it was not by chance that the Seychelles was chosen as venue for a meeting as shady as that. It is a country where many irregular deals have taken place over the years, away from prying eyes and scrutiny by international financial watchdog organisations.

The Seychelles may have the highest per capita income in Africa, but that does not mean that the average citizen is particularly well off. Banks and financial institutions on the islands have become havens for money launderers and tax dodgers, including Russians and other East Europeans, and that has contributed to its high GDP per capita. Many rich foreigners have also settled in the marina with their expensive yachts and in exclusive housing on land for which they have paid fortunes. Luxury hotels and resorts dot the coastlines of Mahé as well as several of the smaller, outlying islands. The gap between the rich and the poor is wide and, as a result of missed opportunities for the many, and resentment at having been cut out of the ostentatious wealth that is visible everywhere, drug addiction is rampant and juvenile delinquency is on the rise.

The Seychelles is also another place where China, India and other regional powers are involved in an intense competition for influence. The islands are strategically well-positioned between the Indian subcontinent and Africa – and to the east lies the British Indian Ocean Territory (BIOT) with the American base at Diego Garcia. It is hardly surprising that not only money launderers, disreputable dealmakers and tourists have long been interested in the Seychelles. In fact, the islands' location in the western Indian Ocean – and therefore close to sea routes between Europe, Africa, Asia and Australia that were established centuries ago – is the reason why they became occupied and inhabited in the first place.

Most of the 95,000 inhabitants are descendants of French immigrants from today's Mauritius and Réunion, and the African slaves they brought with them during the latter part of the eigtheenth century. Like Mauritius and Réunion, the islands were uninhabited before they were 'discovered' by Western colonial powers, but, unlike Mauritius and Réunion, the Seychelles have been saved from frequent name changes. A French sea captain, Nicolas Morphey, arrived there with his ship in 1756 and laid claim to the islands, which he named *Seychelles* after Jean Moreau de Séchelles, the finance minister of the French king Louis XV.

The French were the first to recognise the strategic importance of the islands. The governor of Île de France (Mauritius), Bertrand Mahé de Labourdonnaise realised that if the British ever took charge of the islands they would have an ideal point from which to operate their fleet in that part of the Indian Ocean and, therefore, they had to be occupied. Another reason was that the islands had become a haven for Arab pirates, an ideal refuge in which to repair ships between raids in the waters north of Île de France and Île Bourbon (Réunion).

But it was not until 1770 that a ship carrying settlers from Île de France set sail for the Seychelles. The very first group consisted of 'fifteen white men, seven black slaves, five Indians and one black woman.'[3] More were to follow, and a 'capital' was built near a natural harbour on the main island, which was named Mahé after governor de Labourdonnaise. It is reasonable to assume that living conditions were harsh during those first years. The settlers harvested coconuts and found that various kinds of spices were abundant in the hills on Mahé. But not many chose to go there and by 1794 the Seychelles had fewer than 100 white settlers, and around 500, mainly African, slaves.[4]

By then, the French Revolution had broken out and new, democratic ideas reached even these far-flung islands in the Indian Ocean. The population began to grow with more settlers arriving but, even so, it was impossible for the French to defend the islands against the British, who were taking advantage of the new situation that had emerged with France becoming weakened by revolutionary turmoil. British troops landed in the Seychelles in 1794 and French rule fell apart. Edicts from Paris no longer had any effect, and slavery was not abolished. In 1804 the population comprised over 300 white residents, almost 100 free Africans and more than 3,000 slaves.[5]

Along with Mauritius, the Seychelles became formally British after the 1814 Treaty of Paris and they were administered as one colony. Here as well as in Mauritius proper, the personnel and structure of the French colonial administration were left virtually intact. French and Creole remained the main languages, although English was also introduced in schools and in the administration. The number of Indians among the population was low as very few indentured labourers were brought to the Seychelles. But those who came worked on coconut plantations. A few Chinese also settled in the Seychelles, mostly as shopkeepers and traders.

The abolition of slavery in 1835 had other impacts on migration to the Seychelles. British ships in the Indian Ocean rescued African slaves from Arab ships, and brought them to the Seychelles. In 1866, for example, a single ship, *HMS Lyra*, brought no less than 300 Africans to Victoria, as the main settlement was now called. By 1872, altogether 2,500 slaves had been freed in a similar manner and become residents of the Seychelles.[6]

The Seychelles was also used as a kind of penal colony, but only for high-profile prisoners. In 1877, the Sultan of Perak, a state in British

Malaya, was sent to the Seychelles for his alleged role in the killing of John Woodford Wheeler Birch, the Colonial Secretary of the Straits Settlements, the British colony which was headquartered in Singapore. But it was a mild form of incarceration. The sultan appears to have spent considerable time playing cricket at the local club in Victoria. In 1894, he was allowed to return home. The king of Ashanti, now part of Ghana, was accompanied by 55 followers, including the Queen Mother, 3 wives and 12 chiefs with their slaves when he was sent into exile in the Seychelles in the 1890s. Other deportees included royalty from the Kingdom of Buganda, part of Uganda, a sultan from Somaliland, Egyptians and Palestinians. In 1922, the then Colonial Secretary Winston Churchill suggested that rebels from the Irish Republican Army who had been captured should be sent to the Seychelles. The total number was 5,000. But nothing came of that proposal.[7]

The most famous deportee in more modern times was Archbishop Makarios III of Cyprus. In 1956, the British sent him to the Seychelles because of his role in fomenting communal discord between the Greeks and the Turks in Cyprus. He arrived in the Seychelles along with a number of other Greek Cypriots who were sympathisers of EOKA, or *Ethniki Organosis Kyprion Agoniston*, a nationalist guerrilla organisation that sought to expel the British from Cyprus and unite the island with Greece. Makarios and his men remained in the Seychelles for just over a year, and he had only positive things to say about his time there as he wrote later: 'To get rid of me, the British sent me to the Seychelles and...of course, when I look back at it today, that exile seems anything but tragic. Actually, it wasn't an exile, it was a vacation. I was given a nice house where I was served and respected. The landscape was marvellous, so marvellous that I wanted to see it again, and I went back as a tourist and even bought a small piece of land near the same house, which the owner, unfortunately, didn't want to sell.'[8]

Abdullah Afif Didi, a separatist leader from the Maldives who arrived there in 1963 with his family, stayed longer, but it was not because he was anti-British that he was deported to the Seychelles. From 1959 to 1963, he had been the president of the United Suvadive Republic comprising three of the southernmost atolls in the Maldives – including Addu atoll, which housed an important British military base. The locals declared independence from the Maldives in 1959 because they were unhappy with the central government's imposition of new taxes. Abdullah Afif and his separatist leaders appealed to the British for help, but the response was lukewarm, and even that tacit support vanished in 1961. The British decided to work with the central government of the Maldives, which in any case was a British protectorate. Abdullah Afif approached the Maldivian government several times with requests to be allowed to return home. It was only in 1993, when he was old and in declining health, that he was allowed to travel to the Maldives and visit his relatives. But it was a short visit. He died in the Seychelles on 13 July of that year.

With its rather small population – in the 1930s only around 30,000 people lived on the islands – and limited resources, the Seychelles was truly a colonial backwater. The first two motorcars arrived in 1921, electricity was introduced in 1923, and, as late as 1934, fewer than 60 people visited the islands purely for the purpose of holiday.[9] The only connection with the outside world was by a monthly or bi-monthly British India steamship that plied between Mombasa in Kenya or Durban in South Africa and Bombay (Mumbai) in India, which stopped over at the port in Victoria, or an occasional service to and from Mauritius. The first aircraft to reach the Seychelles was a PBY-2 Twin-Engine Catalina Flying Boat, which landed in the waters off Mahé on 17 June 1939. It was on its way from Port Hedland in Australia via Java, the Cocos (Keeling) Islands, Diego Garcia, and the Seychelles to Mombasa in Kenya. Not a commercial venture, it carried the American zoologist and philanthropist Richard Archbold and Gordon Taylor, a famous Australian aviator acting as navigator on what was the first ever flight of its kind across the Indian Ocean. But there was no regular air traffic until an international airport opened in 1971.

Politically, nothing noteworthy happened until after World War II, when Britain granted suffrage to approximately 2,000 adult male property owners, who elected four members to the Legislative Council, a body that advised the governor.[10] All of them came from a group known as the Seychelles' Taxpayers and Producers Association (STPA), which represented the *grands blancs*, or 'the great whites', who here as in Mauritius were the Francophone plantation owners. But the Seychelles had little to offer other than coconuts and some spices. Nevertheless, STPA was the dominant political force in the Seychelles until the early 1960s, when representatives of the small, urban middle class began to emerge – and several of them came from the Creole community rather than the predominantly white plantocracy.

Until the late 1940s, development of public education was hindered by squabbles over the language of instruction, and the Roman Catholic Church – another powerful institution to which more than 70 per cent of the population belonged – had a virtual monopoly on running schools. The Catholics and also the smaller Anglican Church wanted to favour French, but as public education, although not compulsory, became more widespread in the 1950s, Creole was prioritised, followed by English and then French – and that was a development which empowered those of mixed ethnicity. The *grands blancs* in the STPA were no longer the only social and political force to be reckoned with.

Two men, both of mixed ethnic background, came to dominate this new era in Seychelles politics. One was James Mancham, a pro-Western politician who encouraged free trade and was instrumental in turning the Seychelles into one of the world's most exclusive tourist destinations. The other, France-Albert René, called himself an 'Indian Ocean socialist' and favoured social welfare programmes and a foreign policy that would bring the country closer to the Eastern Bloc. Both were educated in Britain and had backgrounds in the legal profession.

James Mancham was born on 11 August 1939 on Mahé where his father Richard Mancham, who was of mixed Chinese and French ancestry, ran a retail business. James' mother Evelyne was mainly French. After finishing college in the Seychelles, he went by ship to Britain where he studied law at London's Wilson College. He was called to the Bar at Middle Temple, one of the four Inns of Court, in 1961.[11]

It was during his years as a student in London that Mancham became involved in politics. At a reception for the newly appointed British governor of the Seychelles, Sir John Thorpe, Mancham seized the opportunity to call for the repeal of certain laws that protected the almost feudal privileges of the planters, among them one law that made it an offence for an ordinary person in the Seychelles to be in possession of a coconut without a written permit. The speech was reproduced in a local newsletter in the Seychelles, infuriating the planters – and prompting his father to send him a letter in which he wrote: 'I am spending money for you to become a lawyer. Politics is a cheap and dirty occupation. In this day and age, it is best left to opportunists, rogues, and vagabonds.'[12]

Mancham returned to the Seychelles in 1962, and nobody, not even his father, could stop the well-educated young man from getting involved in politics – he meant to challenge the STPA and the old order it represented. Two years after his return home, Mancham founded the Seychelles Democratic Party (SDP), which at first did not seek independence. For a small territory with about the same number of inhabitants as a country town in Britain, that did not seem like a viable option. Mancham's ideal solution for the future of the islands was to be integrated into the British realm, like Hawaii had become a state in the USA in 1959, and Réunion a French department.[13]

But that was not something in which London was interested – and demands for full independence grew stronger after Britain in 1965 removed Île Desroches, the Aldabra Islands and the Farquhar Islands from the Seychelles and grouped them together with Mauritius' Chagos Archipelago to become BIOT. By then, the SDP was not the only political party with a following among ordinary people. In 1963, France-Albert René had formed the Seychelles People's United Party (SPUP), which was allied with radical plantation workers' unions. As a result of popular pressure, the SDP also began clamouring for independence, which was what Britain wanted as well. Why cling on to some forgotten islands in the Indian Ocean, when efforts should be focused on building up a military base in BIOT?

Elections to a new legislative assembly were held in 1970. The SDP got ten seats and the SPUP five. Mancham was sworn in as the first chief minister of the Seychelles while René organised strikes and protests, accusing Mancham of not being a true representative of the people. He had even before the election declared that the SDP was 'the party of those who have, and the SPUP is the party of those who have not.'[14] The battle lines were drawn for the next couple of decades of Seychelles politics.

René was born on 16 November 1935 in the Farquhar Islands more than 600 kilometres south of Mahé. His father was the French administrator and manager of a plantation on the main of the Farquhars. His mother was a local woman from the island. With his income from the plantation, the father was able send his son to a good school in Victoria. At first, young René wanted to become a priest and, when he was 18, was granted a scholarship to study theology in Switzerland. According to historian Tim Ecott, René's political enemies claim that this was a ruse for a relatively poor young man to escape from limited opportunities in the Seychelles for a chance of a better education in Europe.[15] Whatever the truth of the matter, René left Switzerland after a while and travelled to Britain, where he studied at St. Mary's College in Southampton and later at King's College in London before receiving his certification as a lawyer at the Middle Temple in 1958.

He returned to the Seychelles in that year, worked for a while as a lawyer, and then headed back to Britain in 1961, this time to study at the London School of Economics (LSE). In the 1960s, LSE was a hotbed of radical ideas and many of his new left-leaning friends came from the soon-to-be-independent colonies. The SPUP was formed shortly after his return to the Seychelles with a manifesto declaring that one of its main aims was to 'eradicate from society all forms of discrimination, oppression and exploitation, and to establish and maintain the economic and social foundations of a Socialist State through the process of planned development by a strong Central Government in order to stimulate a high degree of economic development in agricultural productivity and industrialisation.'[16]

Needless to say, Mancham's plans for the development of the islands were entirely different. In July 1971, the first jet, a Super VC-10 from BOAC, landed at the newly constructed international airport on Mahé. The construction of the airport was a major achievement which was going to change the Seychelles for ever. It was officially opened by Queen Elizabeth II on 20 March 1972 – and, for the first time in history, the Seychelles was easy to reach from the outside world. Until then, air service had been available only on a restricted basis at a small airstrip built by the US Air Force when it set up a satellite tracking station on Mahé in 1963.

With significantly improved air service, hotels were built, and the islands now had an income on which it could base an independent economy. Coconuts and spices were not much for an independent country to live on. Independence was proclaimed on 29 June 1976 and

Mancham became the first president. For the sake of national unity, René was appointed vice president. The SDP and the SPUP agreed to form a coalition until the next elections, which were scheduled for 1979. As a gesture of goodwill, Britain returned Île Desroches, the Aldabra Islands and the Farquhar Islands to the Seychelles. Only the Chagos Archipelago now remained in BIOT.

Then came the coup. In the first week of June 1977, 60 SPUP supporters who had been trained in Tanzania, took over the police armoury, the radio station, cable and wireless offices, and the airport. A policeman and one of the coup makers died in a shootout during the night of 5 and 6 June. A curfew was imposed, and René was appointed acting president pending the proclamation of a socialist republic. The timing of his takeover of power had been carefully planned, and took place while Mancham was attending the Commonwealth Heads of Government Summit in London.

The news of the coup reached him through a phone call from Adnan Khashoggi, one of the wealthiest men in the world, whose private yacht was anchored off Victoria on the night of the coup. He was one of several international celebrities who had been drawn to the Seychelles when the tourist boom started. Khashoggi reportedly told the deposed president: 'The Seychelles were not like that. They were paradise islands. It was the land of song and laughter, islands in the sun, a place of *joie de vivre* and *plaisir d'amour*, of *laissez-faire*, of *coco-de-mer* and the giant tortoise.'[17]

But the coup was for real. The SPUP merged with some smaller parties and became the Seychelles People's Progressive Front (SPPF), which under a new constitution that was adopted in 1979 became the country's only recognised political party. The first election under the new constitution was held in June that year with René as the only candidate for president. Not surprisingly, he was elected with 98 per cent of the vote.

As promised during previous elections and during his time as both opposition leader and vice president, René proceeded with his programme to stipulate minimum wages, raise salaries for civil servants, and improve housing, health facilities and education. A social welfare system was also introduced and employment opportunities were generated in agriculture and fisheries. Creole was elevated to the status of official language. René's dream of a socialist Seychelles was coming to fruition, and his reforms were no doubt popular.

But there was also another side to his new policies. Prior to the coup, the Seychelles had no armed forces. There was only a police force modelled along British lines. But René believed that a military was needed to help preserve his 'revolution' and advance his socialist policies. Immediately after the 1977 coup, René formed the Seychelles People's Defence Force (SPDF) with the help of instructors sent by his close ally, Tanzania's socialist president Julius Nyerere. The SPDF consisted of 190 soldiers and 10 officers assisted by a 400-strong militia. In addition, René raised an elite force of 30 men as his personal bodyguard. That unit was reportedly trained by a Frenchman who had been one of the infamous French mercenary Robert Denard's henchmen.[18]

Close relations were also established with the Soviet Union, Algeria and Cuba, where young people were sent for military and political training. In 1979, René attended a meeting with the heads of the Non-Aligned Nations in Cuba where he proudly declared: 'Let me first of all state, that I came to Cuba despite and because of the fact that there were so many imperialist manoeuvres to prevent leaders from coming to Cuba for the summit and it gives me great satisfaction to be able to express myself here in Havana only a few miles from the very heart of imperialism…in October 1962, at the time of the so-called missile crisis, I and thousands of others marched through the streets of London chanting, "Kennedy, nom Cuba si". Today, I'm proud to state in Socialist Cuba, "Imperialism, no, Castro, si, Cuba si".'[19]

The United States and other Western nations were concerned. What would happen if the Eastern Bloc gained a strategic foothold in the middle of the Indian Ocean? And the US still had its satellite tracking station on Mahé, which had to be maintained and defended. The answer was to try to dislodge René from power. An outright invasion would have been too provocative, so the answer was to enlist the services of Michael Hoare, who had previously fought for Western interests in the Congo.

Although a gun-for-hire, Hoare was very different from an utter thug like Denard. Born in 1919 in India, he was Irish but from Ireland when it was part of the United Kingdom. At the outbreak of World

War II, he joined the London Irish Rifles and saw action in India and Burma (now Myanmar). He settled in South Africa after the war and in the early 1960s, as an ardent anti-communist, fought for the likewise anti-communist Moise Tshombe, the self-proclaimed president of Katanga, which had broken away from the newly independent Congo, whose first prime minister, Patrice Lumumba, was an ardent Marxist. That attempt at breaking away failed, and Hoare returned to South Africa. By then he had earned the epithet 'Mad Mike', which came from an East German broadcaster who always referred to him as 'the mad bloodhound, Mike Hoare.'[20]

Already in 1979, Hoare had been contacted by South Africa's intelligence service, the Bureau of State Security, or BOSS, which wanted to see René driven from power. At first, Hoare advised against it because any South African involvement in such an undertaking would provoke an international backlash. A better alternative, Hoare argued, would be to approach the Americans whom he though would be interested because of the Seychelles' proximity to Diego Garcia.[21] But at last he relented. According to his own account of the affair, he travelled to London, where he met Mancham to discuss the plan.[22]

It is unclear what transpired from that meeting, but Hoare managed to put a team of mercenaries together who took on themselves the task of staging a coup in the Seychelles. Most of them had a background in South Africa's Special Forces and the Rhodesian Army or had been mercenaries in the Congo. An advance party was sent disguised as tourists, and then, on 25 November 1981, the main force of 44 mercenaries arrived on a Royal Swazi National Airways flight from Manzini in Swaziland masquerading as rugby players belonging to a beer-drinking club called Ye Ancient Order of Frothblowers. The name was taken from a humorous British charitable organisation set up in the 1920s to help disadvantaged children. But the 'new' Frothblowers were anything but charitable. They carried with them in their luggage, hidden under toys they said they were going to give to children in the Seychelles, automatic assault rifles and other military equipment that was needed for the planned coup.

It could have succeeded, had it not been for one of the mercenaries going to the wrong counter at Mahé's international airport. He went to goods to declare, and it was too late when a customs officer insisted on inspecting his bag – and found that it contained a Soviet-made AK-47 assault rifle and ammunition. A firefight broke out between the other mercenaries and the airport's security personnel, killing one of Hoare's men and wounding a Seychelles customs officer.

The ill-fated attempt to overthrow Renés government ended when Hoare and most of his men managed to escape by hi-jacking an Air India plane that had just landed. They forced the hi-jacked Air India plane to fly to South Africa, where they landed at Louis Botha Airport in Durban. Hoare and his fellow mercenaries were taken in a Hercules C130 to Pretoria, where they were put in prison. At first, the South Africans were quite lenient – they were, after all, behind the events – and charged them only with kidnapping. But following international pressure, Hoare was charged with hi-jacking and sentenced to ten years in prison. He was released in 1985 after serving part of his sentence. The others also got prison sentences, but not as harsh as Hoare's. After his release, he settled in Durban in South Africa.[23]

Six of the mercenaries, however, did not make it out and were arrested by the security forces at the airport on Mahé and were later convicted for treason. Four of them were sentenced to death while the other two got long jail terms. But the death sentences were never carried out, and all of them were allowed to leave for South Africa in July 1983. The South African government is said to have paid a US$3 million ransom to secure their release.[24]

Mancham does not acknowledge meeting Hoare in London prior to the coup attempt, but admits that he received a phone call when the mercenaries were apparently on their way to the Seychelles. The anonymous caller said: 'Boss, the movement is on the march.'[25] Who that was is not clear, but it is known than Mancham had met his old friend Khashoggi in New York when a coup was being planned and asked him to help finance it. Khashoggi, whose property in the Seychelles had been confiscated because of his friendship with Mancham, was sympathetic but involved in defending himself in a divorce suit his wife had brought against him in the US and not able to support the plan to oust René.[26]

Another source of money must have been found, and the South African involvement is indisputable. But it is still an open question if the CIA was involved behind the scenes although that is what many suspected. By the time of the Frothblowers' escapades, the US had not only the safety of Diego Garcia to worry about. The Soviets had invaded Afghanistan and the last thing Washington – or Langley – wanted was a pro-Soviet regime in the middle of the Indian Ocean. *The Sunday Tribune*, a Durban newspaper, ran a story a few days after the coup attempt, saying that the plotters had received financial backing from the CIA, which, however, has denied any involvement.[27]

One, unwanted outcome for the Western powers of the ill-fated coup was that René, with Madagascar functioning as a mediator, requested assistance from North Korea to ensure his personal safety and to train his presidential guard.[28] By 1982, North Korean advisors were effectively in charge of the presidential guard as well as the SPDF, now numbering 1,000 soldiers, of whom 750 were in the ground forces and the rest in the air force and the navy.

Maxime Ferrari, the minister of foreign affairs, travelled to Pyongyang to strengthen those ties and later described what he saw: 'The flags of the Democratic People's Republic of Korea and the Seychelles were flying all over the international airport when I landed in Pyongyang...President Kim Il Sung, respectfully referred to as "the Great Leader", was absent from the capital and I was not therefore able to meet him. However, I met then prime minister, Kang Song San, and, of course, the foreign minister, Kim Yong Nam. Most of the discussions dwelt on bilateral cooperation. I was told that a ship bearing five hundred tons of cement was on its way to Seychelles and it was to be a gift from the people of Korea to the people of Seychelles.'[29]

But he was not entirely impressed as he witnessed the personality cult surrounding Kim Il Sung and a people under the total control of their leaders: 'I began to ask myself why president René...had fallen in love with what was happening in this awfully totalitarian country where the dignity of the individual had been tampered with...I remember during the military parade of June 5, 1983, which was celebrated as National Day (the day of the 1977 coup), Seychelles soldiers, who had been trained by North Korean contingents, were shouting slogans like "president René is our Great Leader." I then asked whether Seychelles was on its way to become a similar totalitarian state.'[30]

Ferrari was probably not the only one who was worried about the direction in which René was taking the Seychelles. In August 1982, a rebellion broke out involving disgruntled units from the SPDF – and that was more serious than an invasion attempt by some foreign mercenaries. A group of 88 SPDF officers and soldiers seized the radio station in Victoria, the port and some police stations and took over an army camp on Mahé. The response was resolute – and harsh. Troops loyal to René supported by 400 Tanzanian soldiers crushed the mutiny and recaptured all key installations. The mutineers had to face court martial and the René regime placed the SPDF under firmer control.

There was another coup attempt in 1986, this one led by Ogilvy Berlouis, the minister of defence. This time, René turned to India, which sent the naval ship *INS Vindhyagiri* to Victoria. That was enough to scare the coup makers, who surrendered. Berlouis had been one of the key supporters in the preparations for the 1977 ouster of Mancham and later turned against the regime. At the time of the coup attempt, René was attending a non-aligned conference in Zimbabwe and was able to return home thanks to the loan of a plane from the Indian prime minister Rajiv Gandhi, who was attending the same conference.[31]

Meanwhile, Mancham and thousands of his supporters living in exile continued their campaign for a return to multi-party democracy. They stayed in touch with an underground group on the islands called *Mouvement Pour La Résistence* (MPR), or the Resistance Movement, which consisted mostly of young activists. The MPR leader, Gérard Hoarau, was assassinated in London, where he lived in exile, on 29 November 1985. During Mancham's presidency, he had served as a special assistant to the then government and was arrested and placed under house arrest after the 1977 coup.

Hoarau was released after nine months in custody, and first went into exile in South Africa. But he had his residence permit cancelled and was forced to leave for Britain in 1982 as the South African government was negotiating a secret agreement with René about the release of the Frothblowers then still in jail in the Seychelles. Press reports implicated René's government in the assassination, but it denied any involvement.[32] A number of people were arrested in Britain after the killing, but no one was charged.

The MPR activists still in the Seychelles clandestinely distributed leaflets, accusing René of imposing Marxist ideology on the people against their will.[33] It is impossible to say how effective those young activists were, but the Seychelles' growing role as a tourist destination for the rich and famous may have played a part in eventually persuading René to acquiesce. By the late 1980s and early 1990s, around 100,000 tourists visited the Seychelles annually, and, without the money they brought in, René would not have been able to finance all his social welfare programmes, which he could not afford to scrap. Without those, he would lose his popularity and therefore also his grip on power.

In 1991, René and the ruling SPPF agreed to liberalise the political system. Other parties were allowed to function, and in April 1992, Mancham was allowed to return from exile. A new, democratic constitution was adopted after a referendum, and elections were held in July 1993. It was a victory for René. He received 59.5 per cent of the vote, way ahead of Mancham's 36.6 per cent. René remained as president and won subsequent elections in 1998 and 2001 as well. It was not until February 2004 that he announced that he would step down in favour of his loyal follower, vice president James Michel. But René remained head of the SPPF and as such the power behind the throne.

Mancham never made the political comeback he had probably hoped for. In his capacity as the first president of the Seychelles, he opted instead to become a 'senior statesman' who wrote books and attended international peace and human rights conferences. In 2010, he received the International Jurist Award at the inaugural meeting with the International Conference of Jurists in New Delhi. Mancham died from a stroke on 8 January 2017.

The Seychelles never became a fully fledged socialist state – and the tourism factor was not the only reason why such policies were never implemented. By 1993, the direct contribution of the tourism sector to the GDP of the Seychelles was estimated at 50 per cent and it provided 70 per cent of total foreign-exchange earnings.[34] But the economy had also suffered a setback when the US satellite tracking station – which has been in operation throughout the years of SPPF rule – was closed in 1997. The government lost an annual income estimated at US$8 million from leasing land for the station.[35] By the late 1990s, government spending has risen to 65 per cent of GDP. Large infrastructural projects, among them a US$75 million land reclamation scheme to create space where affordable housing could be built, tore into the budget, and so did the construction of a US$30 million project to build facilities for the Indian Ocean Games.[36] These were not huge amounts of money for most other countries, but for the Seychelles, which in the mid-1990s had only 75,000 inhabitants of whom few were taxpayers, those were outlays the government could ill afford.

In the midst of what appeared to be an impending economic crisis, René and his henchmen discovered that there was money to be made from another capitalist venture. They decided to turn the Seychelles into a financial centre, where foreign businessmen could park money in order to evade paying taxes in their home countries, and set up shell companies to avoid international inspection of their activities and transactions.

This, of course, was not unusual for small island nations wanting to survive, and it is unavoidable that they, in the process, become magnets for dirty money from all over the world. Even Mauritius, which is often held up as a model of a fairly well regulated offshore financial centre, has had its share of shady financial dealings. In a 2012 report on financial crime, the British crime expert Euan Grant, without being specific, points out the United Arab Emirates, Singapore, Hong Kong – and Mauritius – as places where the Russian mafia had 'intimate links.'[37] The Seychelles was also mentioned in passing in his report, but when in the early 2000s it decided to open for business as an offshore financial centre, it quickly became more notorious than any of the other jurisdictions with the possible exception of the United Arab Emirates. The smallness – and the remoteness – of the Seychelles combined with lax law enforcement turned it into a new kind of paradise, this time for fraudsters, money launderers and gangsters.

Mancham had been close to Khashoggi. Among the many moneymen who flocked to the Seychelles in the 1970s and 1980s, René found a companion in the lesser-known but much more disreputable Mario Ricci, an Italian who had come to the Seychelles in the mid-1970s to start a new life. He was born near Lucca in Tuscany in 1929, and had a long history of crime and fraud even before he arrived in the Seychelles. In 1958, he was convicted of fraud in Italy, and then moved to Switzerland where he was convicted of possessing counterfeit currency. Tired of Europe, Ricci lived in Mexico and Haiti before moving to Somalia, where he set up a business exporting grapefruit.[38]

How and when he became a close friend of René's is not clear but, as early as 1978, he managed to persuade the socialist president to allow him to set up a firm called the Seychelles Trust Company, in a joint venture with the Seychelles government. That was the modest beginning of what later was to become a huge industry in the Seychelles. Ricci's company was granted the sole right to incorporate offshore companies and to act as resident agent for foreign companies and foundations registered in the Seychelles.[39] In 1981, the government sold its shares in the Seychelles Trust Company, leaving Ricci in control of the entire operation. That was also the year of the Frothblowers' failed coup attempt, and René was desperate for money and friends. He turned to the North Koreans for protection – and to Ricci to make money.

Ricci became, as the late Stephen Ellis, a historian and expert on corruption in Africa, succinctly put it, 'associated with some distinctly unusual companies in addition to the Seychelles Trust Company. In 1982 he was listed as director of an entity immodestly entitled the International Monetary Funding, or IMF, for short, not to be confused with the International Monetary Fund.'[40] Ricci also used his initials GMR – Giovanni Mario Ricci – to name another company, which according to one of its glossy brochures was 'a conglomerate of companies which operates all over the world' and was 'managed from the operational headquarters in the Republic of Seychelles.'[41]

The 'management', however, consisted of Ricci himself, and members of his and his wife's families. Contacts were established in other tax havens such as Panama, Liechtenstein and Luxembourg. But there was nothing strictly illegal in what he was doing. His companies may have had peculiar names, but they were all properly registered and run in conformity with Seychelles law. By the early 1980s, Ricci had acquired a reputation as someone anyone could approach if they wanted to do business in – and more often from – the Seychelles.

Ricci also managed to obtain diplomatic status when he, in June 1984, was officially accredited as ambassador of the Sovereign Order of the Coptic Catholic Knights of Malta, which turned out to be a commercial company incorporated in New York having nothing to do with the Rome-based charity the Knights of Malta.[42] But through this arrangement, Ricci enjoyed diplomatic status and privileges, including immunity, and he was able to use his diplomatic pouch to receive documents or whatever else he wanted from abroad.

The remarkable Ricci proved his skills as a diplomat through playing all sides in various conflicts involving the Seychelles. The South Africans had been involved in the Frothblowers' fiasco – but Ricci offered the Seychelles to the South Africans as a base for indirect trade with the outside world to circumvent international sanctions. In 1986, GMR was registered to do business in South Africa, which was made possible through a personal relationship that Ricci had established with Craig Williamson, a well-known military intelligence officer.

Ricci's main interest may have been to make money, but for the South Africans it was a question of gaining influence in order to protect their geostrategic interests in the region. Marxist-oriented regimes ruled Madagascar and Tanzania and even South Africa's immediate neighbours Angola and Mozambique. Using the Frothblowers had turned out to be the wrong way to cement those interests so the South Africans also began to play all sides in the drama surrounding the Seychelles.

After the Frothblowers had failed to overthrow René, and Ogilvy Berlouis and his followers in Britain were planning another attempt to get rid of him, contacts were maintained with a diplomat at the South African embassy in London. But, according to Ellis, 'the South African secret services eventually betrayed the coup plot to the Seychelles government in August 1986 and in effect aborted the plan.'[43]

After that coup attempt, South Africa's intelligence agencies, through the Ricci-Williamson partnership, acquired responsibility for government security in the Seychelles. How they got along with the North Koreans also assigned to protect René and his ministers is anybody's guess. But it is plausible to assume that their respective duties were entirely different. The South Africans provided intelligence while the North Koreans were in charge of the presidential security force and therefore, in effect, personal bodyguards.

A South African company called Longreach was put in charge of collecting and providing such intelligence – and Longreach shared its Johannesburg office with Ricci's GMR. After the African National Congress came to power in South Africa in 1994, Williamson had to admit that Longreach was in fact secretly owned by the country's military intelligence services.[44] According to Ellis, 'GMR and Longreach were only two of the hundreds of companies set up or acquired by the South African security establishment in pursuit of the strategy of counter-revolution.'[45] Apart from trying to achieve those strategic goals, some of these companies were 'used to trade in products subject to international sanctions, including oil, but also in less legitimate products such as ivory and rhino horn.'[46]

In another, unrelated, case, in 1995 the Seychelles sold to Cambodia 310 tonnes of munitions seized two years before by the Seychelles Navy from a ship destined for Somalia in violation of a UN-imposed embargo. The navy confiscated 400 tonnes of military equipment, and, rather than handing over the munitions to the UN, sold 90 tonnes of the loot to Zaire and Rwanda, and the rest to Cambodia. The sale included heavy infantry weapons, machine-guns and a variety of Soviet-style 7.62mm and 106mm ammunition. A vessel owned by the Seychelles-based Island Development Company shipped the munitions to Cambodia.[47] At about the same time, a Hong Kong businessman was appointed honorary consul of the Seychelles to Cambodia, but preferred to be based in Hong Kong because it was too dangerous to stay in Phnom Penh. The exact nature of his appointment and duties was never known.[48]

The nature of the Seychelles' role as a 'financial centre', as it is euphemistically called, changed after the democratisation of South Africa and in the wake of the Seychelles' economic problems of the 1990s – and the collapse of the Soviet Union and the Eastern Bloc at about the same time. Ricci began to fade from the scene and eventually settled in Bryanston in Midrand, South Africa. He died on 16 July 2001, but even his death did not put an end to cases in which his name cropped up. In February 2016, he was mentioned in a lawsuit involving manipulations of the rand, the South African currency, and gold smuggling.[49]

The seeds sown by Ricci grew into a booming offshore industry, which took off in the 1990s, and now René's finance minister James Michel emerged as the main player. Michel was also, according to former foreign minister Maxime Ferrari, one of the top leaders who had 'fallen in love' with that 'awfully totalitarian country' North Korea.[50] After succeeding René as president of the Seychelles in 2004, he remained in that post until he retired from politics in 2016 and set up a charity named after himself. The James Michel Foundation focuses on 'the blue economy and climate change.'[51] But it would be surprising if someone as skilled and well-connected as Michel did not maintain his old interest in the Seychelles offshore industry.

In 2012, two strangers from Africa showed up in the Seychelles, where they contacted Zen Offshore, one of many companies on the islands that set up shell companies for foreign clients. Their story was that they represented an individual who served as a contact between the government of Zimbabwe and the region's diamond mines. The representative of Zen Offshore whom they met explained to them how they could have a company registered in the Seychelles and hide behind a complex structure that would make it impossible to identify the actual owners. The company in the Seychelles would be controlled by a company in Dominica in the West Indies which, in turn, would be controlled by a company in Belize in Central America, and so on. 'Anyone trying to discover the real owner would never be able to follow the paper train around the world,' they were told.[52]

What the man from Zen Offshore did not know was that the pair he met were undercover journalists running a hidden-camera sting for a documentary for the Qatar-based TV station Al Jazeera. Their report, which was aired shortly after their visit, 'produced a ripple of scandal in one of the world's most remote offshore havens, a place that's gained a reputation as a magnet for Arab princes, Chinese investors, pirates, fugitives, mercenaries, mobsters – and outlanders who want to hide their money or disguise their business activities… (by creating) elaborate webs that use multiple jurisdictions, multiple front men and multiple layers of ownership.'[53]

The Al Jazeera documentary and a subsequent report compiled by the International Consortium of Investigative Journalists (ICIJ) were based on research into a number of cases involving dirty money and the Seychelles. In 2005, for instance, Radovan Krejčíř, a mob boss from the Czech Republic, arrived in the Seychelles seeking asylum – after jumping out of a bathroom window back in Prague to escape police who were investigating him on murder and money laundering charges.[54]

Krejčíř stayed in the Seychelles for two years, and later claimed that he provided financial support to leading politicians on the islands and, in return, they offered him and his family a new identity.[55] But the Czechs found out who, and where, he was and wanted him extradited. He was not handed over to the Czechs – but left for South Africa on a Seychelles passport under the name 'Egbert Jules Savy.'[56] Although it is not in any way proof of complicity, the Savy family also happens to belong to the Michel's inner circle of local businessmen. In South Africa, Krejčíř was later arrested on kidnapping and assault charges in connection with a US$2 million crystal methamphetamine deal.[57]

There was more on the list of shady deals involving the Seychelles. In 2010, for instance, the government of Kazakhstan issued an arrest warrant for a banking tycoon called Mukhtar Ablyazov, who was accused of having used companies in the Seychelles as part of a scheme that siphoned at least 6 billion dollars from the Almaty-based BTA Bank. Then, in 2011, a subsidiary of the Reserve Bank of Australia admitted that it had channelled millions of dollars in bribes intended for officials in Nigeria through a shell company in the Seychelles linked to a convicted white-collar criminal. In 2012, two businessmen based in Israel pleaded guilty in a US court to operating an illegal Internet pharmacy that laundered much of its profits through the Seychelles.[58]

The Al Jazeera exposé may have placed the Seychelles on the map of investigative journalists and others interested in corporate fraud. But it did not put an end to shenanigans happening on the islands. In December 2012, it was revealed that a North Korean front company, which the UN said was a front for illegal arms shipping, had managed to get passports for its directors from the republic of Kiribati in Micronesia – and from the Seychelles. The Seychelles police said they would 'look into the allegations.'[59]

Then, in early 2013, Marek Trajter, a mobster from Slovakia became a citizen of the Seychelles after cultivating a friendship with one of Michel's closest advisers and making donations to government charities. He was eventually deported after Interpol found out that he was wanted in connection with the murder of another businessman, also associated with the Slovak mafia. Meanwhile Saker el-Materi, the son-in-law of the Tunisian dictator Zine El Abidine Ben Ali, who was deposed in January 2011, fled to the Seychelles after a court in Tunisia sentenced him to 16 years in jail on corruption charges.[60]

The Seychelles' business model was explained by Paul Chow, a Mancham loyalist who now runs an offshore services firm, in the 2014 ICIJ report: ' A lawyer or accountant in the US, Europe or Israel contacts him on behalf of a client and he establishes a company in the Seychelles, with the client as shareholder. He takes a fee for each company he establishes and for taking care of the necessary paperwork that the client needs to open a bank account.'[61] Chow told ICIJ that his profit from that kind of business in 2013 was US$300,000 – an income the average citizen could only dream of. Chow also told the ICIJ: 'The British Virgin Islands...registers 30,000 companies a year. We are about 11,000. We are catching up.'[62] He said the Seychelles is making progress because, unlike Mauritius and other offshore financial centres, it has stood up to pressure from the Organisation of Economic Cooperation and Development and other international financial watchdog outfits.[63]

When Michel stepped down from the presidency in October 2016, he was succeeded by his vice president Danny Faure, a Cuba-educated political scientist. Michel left behind a country that could boast of having the highest GDP per capita in Africa, but that is largely a fictitious figure given the unevenly distributed wealth on the islands, disparities which are reflected in, for instance, the incomes of financial consultants like Paul Chow.[64] Serious social problems lurk behind the islands' paradisiacal façade.

A 2011 study by the Commonwealth Secretariat and the United Nations Research Institute for Social Development identified a number of new problems that traditional social protection schemes such as the closely knit families and elders within local communities have been unable to deal with: 'Alcoholism, welfare dependency, HIV/AIDS and community breakdown are all symptoms of a growing litany of problems facing the government's social policy interventions... poverty in Seychelles has always been a politically highly charged subject – officially it does not exist as there is no official poverty line. Continued resistance to creating one will continue to deprive the government of a core tool in the better targeting of measures to combat poverty.'[65]

There are also 17,000 foreign workers in the Seychelles, a huge figure given the country's total population of 95,000. Most of those employed in construction come from Bangladesh and, to a lesser extent India. Many Indians work as teachers or in the tourism industry, which also employs a significant number of Filipinos. Most of them have skills that the indigenous workers do not have, and generous social welfare programmes have also made it less attractive for locals to look for jobs in the construction or tourism sectors. The Seychelles is not Mauritius, which has managed to solve those problems. Although incidents of social unrest are rare, clashes between demonstrators and police erupted in 2008, when the government banned political and religious organisations from running radio stations. With the gap between rich and poor widening – and resentment growing against foreign workers – social stability is something the Seychelles can no longer take for granted.

And there seems to be no end to monkey business in the Seychelles, as Erik Prince's meeting there in the first week of January 2017 shows. What happened to the secret communications channel that was supposed to have been set up between Trump and Russia is not clear and even government officials in the Seychelles said that they were unaware of the meeting between Prince and Putin's aide Kirill Dmitriev. What they did admit, according to a *Washington Post* report, was that luxury resorts on the islands are ideal for clandestine rendezvous such as that one. Barry Faure, the Seychelles secretary of state for foreign affairs, told the *Post*: 'I wouldn't be surprised at all. The Seychelles is the kind of place where you can have a good time away from the eyes of the media. That's even printed in our tourism marketing. But I guess this time you smelled something.'[66]

A much more serious issue is how the Seychelles has become a frontline state in Indo-Chinese rivalry in the Indian Ocean. And the fact that the Seychelles, unlike for instance Mauritius, has armed forces makes its role in geopolitical power games all the more important. With now only 650 men at arms, the Seychelles military may be small compared with any army in mainland Africa. But when general Wang Guanzhong, a leading member of China's Central Military Commission, visited Victoria in November 2016, enhancing 'defence cooperation' was high on the agenda. The cooperation would include training, the supply of equipment and high-level exchange visits.[67] Wang also met brigadier-general Leopold Payet, the commander-in-chief of the Seychelles' armed forces, to discuss further training of Seychelles soldiers in China. Up until then, around 50 soldiers from the Seychelles had undergone such training. China had also given two light aircraft as well as two naval ships to the Seychelles under a military cooperation agreement signed between the two countries in 2004.[68]

In June 2017, Xu Jinghu, a special representative of the Chinese government, also came to the Seychelles, where she met president Faure and other high-ranking officials. After the visit, China's embassy in the Seychelles posted a message on its website saying that China enjoys 'a traditional friendship' with the Seychelles and that the Seychelles 'appreciates China's long-time contribution to its social and economic development and takes China as a good friend and good brother.' The Seychelles, apparently, 'is ready to work with China to expand mutual beneficial cooperation in Blue Economy, tourism, health, sports and security.'[69]

The Seychelles may be small in area as well as population, but the country's location between Africa, the Arabian peninsula and the Indian subcontinent makes it a vital geographic link in China's Belt and Road Initiative (BRI) stretching from southern China and Myanmar to Africa and through the Suez canal to Europe. But China's overtures towards the Seychelles have not gone unnoticed among other countries with an interest in the Indian Ocean. Among them is India, which in October 2017 dispatched foreign secretary Subrahmanyam Jaishankar on a visit to the Seychelles. It came, hardly by coincidence, shortly after Xu's visit, and he met with president Faure to discuss what was described as 'infrastructural projects' and to scale up relations to a 'more strategic, comprehensive and ambitious partnership between the two countries, an 'engagement required to keep maritime routes between India and the Seychelles.'[70]

India is alarmed not only by growing China-Seychelles defence and economic cooperation, but also by the fast rise in the number of Chinese tourists visiting the islands, up from a mere 500 in 2011 to nearly 15,000 in 2016.[71] Tourists may sound innocent, but a rapid increase in Chinese tourism is seldom only a matter of people wishing to enjoy the sun and beaches. Tourism has in recent years become a 'people power tool'.[72] Tourism is encouraged to countries with which China wants to maintain friendly relations, and discouraged when it wants to punish a nation that is not in Beijing's good books. The latter was in evidence when Chinese and Philippine ships clashed over a disputed shoal in the South China Sea in April 2012 and major Chinese tourism agencies suspended group travel to the Philippines – and, in August 2018, when Palau refused to sever ties with Taiwan, with which the republic in Micronesia maintains diplomatic relations instead of China. Beijing declared Palau 'an illegal destination' – and the number of Chinese tourists fell from 55,000 of a total of 122,000 annually to almost none.[73] On the other hand, China encourages tourism to countries with which it wants to maintain friendly relations, like Thailand and Myanmar and, in the Indian Ocean, Mauritius, the Maldives – and the Seychelles.

In 2011, China also began to look into the possibility of establishing a port in the Seychelles because, Beijing claimed, it wanted to supply naval ships fighting piracy off the coast of Somalia – the same reason that China gives for the need to have a base in Djibouti.[74] The offer actually came from the Seychelles, and Vikram Sood, a former head of India's intelligence agency, the Research and Analysis Wing, told the media he was surprised the Seychelles government, which had traditionally been close to India, had offered naval facilities to China. Sood also said it 'would heighten Indian concerns over China's growing influence' in the region.[75]

Nothing came of that plan, but India clearly felt it had to act on a number of fronts. On 27 January 2018, India and the Seychelles signed an agreement paving the way for the establishment of an Indian naval base and an airstrip on Assumption Island, a small island 1,135 kilometres southwest of Mahé and north of Madagascar. The chief-of-staff of the Indian Navy, admiral Arun Prakash, told *Jane's* that the base was 'a major move forward by India providing it with a more permanent foothold in the Indian Ocean Region.'[76] It was beyond doubt a move to counter not only China's increased influence in the Seychelles but also its presence at its base in Djibouti. India's security interests in the region have also been shown in Mauritius, which does not have regular armed forces but whose coast guards have been supplied with

Indian-made patrol vessels, supposedly to prevent smuggling but also to establish a security partnership between the two countries.

The January 2018 agreement between the Seychelles and India was actually not new. A similar deal had been struck in 2015 during a visit to the Seychelles by India's prime minister Narendra Modi. But that plan never materialised, and even the new deal for a base on Assumption Island soon ran into trouble. In June 2018, the Seychelles government reneged on the agreement, saying it would not present it to the National Assembly for approval because opposition members, who are in the majority, had said they would not ratify it.[77] The Indian media immediately suspected that China was behind the Seychelles' change of attitude towards the planned base.[78]

The cooperation with China has also run into problems however. When a new China-financed parliamentary building was going to be opened in December 2009, the largest opposition party, the Seychelles National Party (SNP) boycotted the ceremony because it felt that such as important building should have been built with the Seychelles' own resources, not by a foreign power. SNP leader Wavel Ramkalawan said that it was utterly inappropriate that a country without democratic institutions would be allowed to build what should be a symbol of Seychelles democracy.[79] He also pointed out that the foundation stone for the building had an inscription only in Chinese and not in the national languages Creole, French and English.[80]

What is often perceived as Chinese lack of sensitivity for feelings in countries where they have established a presence also became apparent when, in February 2018, local truck drivers blocked a street in front of a government building in Victoria. They protested against Sinohydro, a Mauritius-based Chinese company, that was using its own lorries and Chinese drivers for a project to construct a new dam at a reservoir that supplies Victoria and other towns on Mahé with water.[81]

China was not able to establish a naval base on the Seychelles in 2011, and nor was India in 2018. But that will only lead to more intense competition for influence in the Seychelles – and China is definitely on a path where anything, it seems, goes. In May 2015, a delegation led by Li Qun, the Chinese Communist Party chief in Qingdao, a city on the northeastern coast of China, visited Sri Lanka, Mauritius and the Seychelles and talked about an 'ancient marine silk road' that supposedly existed in the past with 'ships coming frequently back and forth between Bangqiao town in Qingdao and South Asia.'[82] Today, he said, as China is taking the BRI further, 'trade and investment will surely experience another boom' in the region.[83]

That, of course, was pure fantasy as China had no merchant fleet after Zheng He's escapades in the fifteenth century. After that and well into modern times, the ships that sailed across the Indian Ocean belonged to various European colonial powers. But regardless of historical inaccuracies presented by Chinese leaders, China is determined to become the most powerful nation in the Indian Ocean. And the implementation of that plan – and India's attempts to counter it – has led to cloak-and-dagger conflicts similar to those in the Seychelles in yet another small island country in the region: the Maldives.

7

THE MALDIVES

The Maldives, like the Seychelles, is a high-end tourist destination usually associated with luxury resorts where guests sip fancy cocktails, relax on white-sand beaches, and swim or dive in the brilliant turquoise waters surrounding the islands. That picture was shattered when, in February 2018, political unrest shook the capital Male, a six-square-kilometre island that is entirely urbanised. Anti-government demonstrators clashed with riot police who fired teargas to disperse the crowds. The crisis culminated in an election on 23 September in which the incumbent president Abdulla Yameen, the architect of the Maldives' close relationship with China, was defeated by opposition candidate, and India's favourite, Ibrahim Mohamed Solih. On 17 November the day Yameen stepped down as the president of the Maldives and Solih was sworn in as his successor, India's prime minister Narendra Modi was the most prominent among the more than 300 foreign dignitaries who attended the ceremony in Male.[1]

Nowhere in the Indian Ocean is the strategic contest between China and India sharper than in the Maldives and, despite the outcome of the latest presidential election, the future of the country remains uncertain. Will the Maldives continue to tilt towards China, a new player in the politics of the islands, or revert to its much older, close relationship with India? The Maldives is a tiny country – only 417,000 people live on its 298 square-kilometres of land – but the 26-atoll archipelago with 1,192 coral islands is located to the immediate southwest of India and covers a huge maritime area stretching 750 kilometres from the north to the south. The widely scattered islands of the Maldives offer strategic vantage points from which to monitor vital shipping lanes in the Indian Ocean and, therefore, the country has come to play a pivotal role in China's Belt and Road Initiative (BRI). But the proximity to India also means that the Maldives more than any other island nation in the Indian Ocean is on the strategic red line that India does not want China to cross.

The conflict between the two political camps spilled over into the streets of Male in February 2018 when Yameen refused to comply with an order by the Maldives Supreme Court for the release of several imprisoned opposition lawmakers, ruling that their trials and sentences were politically motivated. Yameen went even further than turning against the Court. He declared a state of emergency and ordered the arrest of chief justice Abdulla Saeed and judge Ali Hameed – and his estranged half-brother, former president Maumoon Abdul Gayoom, who had sided with the opposition. Thousands of protesters then took to the streets but were dispersed by the police in an action Human Rights Watch characterised as 'an assault on democracy.'[2] More arrests followed, the movement in the streets died down, and Yameen may have thought that he had the situation under control. But, as the election in September clearly showed, that was a serious miscalculation.

For almost exactly 30 years, the Maldives was run by one man, Maumoon Abdul Gayoom. Although he was elected in a reasonably free and fair election in November 1978, once in power he turned into an autocratic ruler who tolerated no dissent. He was both head of government and head of state – and commander-in-chief of the country's armed forces. And Gayoom was re-elected, unopposed, several times, usually receiving at least 95 per cent of the vote. But then, in October 2008, the first presidential election that he allowed to be contested took place. Gayoom won 45.75 per cent of the vote against 54.25 per cent for Mohamed Nasheed, a young, former political prisoner who had become immensely popular especially among the youth. Thanks mainly to tourism, the economy had done well under Gayoom, but many were tired of his repressive policies and widespread corruption within the administration. On 11 November

Nasheed was sworn in as the next president of the Maldives. He was 41 years old and brimming with ideas about how to turn his country into a functioning democracy.

The political and personal differences between the old and new president could not have been greater. Gayoom's father, Sheikh Abdul Gayoom Ibrahim, was a judge in Male who had 8 wives and 25 children. Born in 1937, Gayoom was the eleventh child. He was ten years old when Mohamed Amin Didi, a school principal who later became the first president of the Maldives, sent him and a group of 15 Maldivian boys to Egypt to study. But due to the war with the newly proclaimed state of Israel, the group did not manage to reach Egypt until 1950. In the meantime, they stayed in Sri Lanka, then Ceylon, where they studied first at Buona Vista College in Galle and then at the Royal College in Colombo. Once in Egypt, Gayoom studied Arabic at the Galamuniyaa and Al-Azhar universities. He graduated with honours in 1966, at the top of his class.[3] He also obtained a certificate in English language at the American University in Cairo.

It was during his time in Egypt that Gayoom became involved in politics. In 1966, he and a group of Maldivian students in Cairo sent a letter to Ibrahim Nasir, then prime minister of the Maldives, urging him to reconsider his wish to establish diplomatic relations with Israel. The Maldives, a self-governing sultanate that had also been a British protectorate since 1887, had become a fully independent nation on 26 July 1965. Ibrahim Nasir was not pleased with the protest, and Gayoom lost the financial support he had enjoyed from the Maldivian government and moved to Nigeria, where he became a lecturer in Islamic studies at the Ahmadu Bello University in Zaria, a city in the Muslim-dominated north of the country.

Gayoom returned to the Maldives in 1971 and taught English, arithmetic and Islam at a local school. By then, the more than 800-year-old sultanate had been abolished. On 11 November 1968, the Maldives had become a republic with Ibrahim Nasir as its president. He was not the first president, however, because the Maldives had been a republic for a brief period in 1953 with Mohamed Amin Didi as head of state before the sultanate was revived. But it was Ibrahim Nasir who brought about independence for the Maldives. He also led the Maldives into the United Nations, modernised the fishing industry and took the first steps towards establishing the country as a tourist destination.

But Ibrahim Nasir's style was authoritarian, and Gayoom was one of those who opposed it for its lack of respect for human rights. Gayoom was arrested in 1973, placed under house arrest and then banished to Makunudhoo Island in Haa Dhaalu Atoll, where he remained for five months. After he was pardoned in October 1973, he became an under-secretary in the Telecommunications Department, but was arrested again for criticising Ibrahim Nasir. This time, he was kept in solitary confinement for 50 days in a prison in the capital Male. Once freed, he worked again as a government civil servant and, in 1975, was sent to New York as a member of the Maldives' delegation to the United Nations.

Then, in June 1978, Ibrahim Nasir announced that he would retire and not seek re-election. After several votes in the parliament and then a general election, Gayoom became the president of the Maldives on 10 November. That was the beginning of his 30 years in power. Although tourism had begun on a modest scale under Ibrahim Nasir, it was Gayoom who turned the country into a popular destination not only for the rich and famous but also for more regular visitors. The potential impact tourism could have on the country's Islamic values was solved by turning small, uninhabited islands in the archipelago into resorts. Only hotel staff were allowed to stay there, and the tourists ventured into Male only on brief shopping trips.

In the 1980s, there were three attempts to overthrow Gayoom's regime, the most serious in November 1988 when a group of Tamil Tigers from Sri Lanka supported by a local businessman landed on the islands. They managed to seize the airport on Hulhule Island off Male – the islands are so small so there could be only one thing on each island – and Gayoom had to flee from his residence. India saved him and his government by airlifting a parachute battalion from Agra, more than 2,000 kilometres away. Within hours, the coup-makers had been captured and disarmed. Codenamed *Operation Cactus*, the Indian Navy also took part in the intervention which established India's role as the guardian of Maldivian security.

Gayoom was by no means an Islamist. Bars and discos – though not serving alcohol – were permitted during his time in power. But he had, during his time in Egypt, discovered that Islam was a powerful tool as long as he was able to control it, or as J.J. Robinson, a former editor of the Maldives' only independent English news service, Minivan News, put it in his excellent account of the politics of the islands: 'When the traditional weapons of dictatorship – secret police, custodial torture, exile – began to creak in the face of clamour for reform, he "formalised what had been the status quo since his rule began." The 1997 constitution made the head of state, Gayoom, "the ultimate authority to impart the tenets of Islam." He had – on paper at least – made himself God.'[4]

But that did not help. Gayoom was becoming increasingly unpopular and escaped unharmed from an assassination attempt in January 2008, when a young man for reasons unknown tried to stab him with a knife. Then, in October that year, Gayoom had to give in to the demands of a growing opposition to his rule – and he was defeated by Nasheed in the first election in the Maldives that could be described as truly democratic.

Mohamed Nasheed came from an entirely different background. Born in 1967 to a fairly ordinary middle-class family in Male, he went to school in the Maldives and Sri Lanka. In 1982, he moved to Britain where he studied first at a secondary school in Wiltshire and then at Liverpool Polytechnic, from which he graduated in 1989. Back home in the Maldives in 1990, Nasheed wrote an article for a local political magazine called *Sangu* in which he outlined corruption within the government and claimed that the 1989 general election had been rigged. He was promptly arrested and kept in solitary confinement at the Dhoonidhoo detention centre, which is on an island not far from Male.

On 8 April 1992, Nasheed was sentenced to three years imprisonment for withholding information about a conspiracy to explode a bomb at a meeting with the South Asian Association for Regional Cooperation, or SAARC, in Male. Nasheed denied any knowledge of the bomb plot, and later said he was tortured during his incarceration at Dhoonidhoo. An Amnesty International report on the Maldives listed him as a prisoner of conscience.[5] During his periods spent in jail, Nasheed studied and later wrote three books on Maldivian history, in English as well as Dhivehi, the language of the islands.[6]

Nasheed was released in June 1993, re-arrested in 1994 and 1995 and, in 1996, sentenced to three years in prison for an article he had written about rigged elections in the Maldives. But nothing could stop the young man from opposing the Gayoom regime – and, in 1999, he was elected as a member of the Maldives parliament representing Male. That did not last long, however. He was forced from his seat following a theft charge which was widely condemned at the time as politically motivated.[7] Working outside of the parliament, he, along with other dissidents, tried unsuccessfully to register their political party, the Maldivian Democratic Party (MDP).

The turning point came in September 2003, when Nasheed asked a doctor to see the body of 19-year-old Hassan Evan Naseem, who had died in Maafushi Jail on Kaafu Atoll, before his death certificate was signed. The boy had been arrested for being in possession drugs and, it turned out, had been tortured to death while in custody. That was not actually unusual in the Maldives under Gayoom, but Naseem's mother took the unusual step of displaying her son's bruised and battered body in the centre of Male.[8]

A riot broke out in Maafushi resulting in guards shooting three inmates to death and injuring seventeen. Dissent now spread from the prison to Male, where Gayoom's special operations police cracked down violently on the demonstrators. The Maldives' first ever State of Emergency was declared. Visits from Amnesty International and worldwide media coverage of the carnage followed and, as Robinson points out: 'A world that had heard only about pristine beaches and luxury resorts was introduced to Maldivian politics.'[9]

International pressure forced Gayoom to concede to democratic reforms. The MDP was legalised and Nasheed, who had been in and out of jail since his return to the Maldives, and other political prisoners were released. Nasheed was defeated by Gayoom in the first round of voting in the 2008 presidential election, but a second round was held as no candidate had won an absolute majority. Nasheed got the backing of some of the other candidates who receeived minor percentages in the first round – and Gayoom lost. Nasheed had defeated the man who had had him detained at least 20 times.

People were jubilant. The Maldives had, at last, become a democracy. Nasheed became a favourite of the international media, and a popular

US website dubbed him number nine on a 2010 list of 'Hottest Heads of State.'[10] On 20 October the year before, he had held the world's first underwater cabinet meeting to highlight the Maldives' vulnerability to global warming. The ministers donned scuba diving gear, went into a lagoon six metres below sea level, and signed a letter that was sent to world leaders ahead of a UN climate-change conference, which was going to be held that December in Copenhagen.[11] Most of the islands in the Maldives are only one metre above sea level, and Nasheed's message was that the entire country could disappear into the Indian Ocean unless action was taken to reduce carbon emissions.

There were other, more pressing problems within the government in Male. Several of the politicians who had supported the coalition that ousted Gayoom in 2008 began to distance themselves from the MDP. A main party in the coalition itself, the Islamic Adhaalath Party, cut all ties with the MDP. In the end, the cabinet consisted only of ministers from the MDP. The crisis led to unrest in the streets with the police at first unwilling to disperse anti-government protesters, and even supporting them. When the military also turned against Nasheed, he was forced to step down. On 7 February 2012, he issued a statement saying that, 'I believe if I continue as president of the Maldives, the people of the country would suffer more. I therefore have resigned as the president of the Maldives. I wish the Maldives would have a consolidated democracy. I wish for justice to be established. I wish for the progress and prosperity of the people.'[12]

Nasheed was automatically succeeded by his vice president, Mohammed Waheed Hassan, who was accused of having conspired with the opposition. Whether true or not, Waheed became the most unpopular president the country had ever had. When presidential elections were held in September 2013, he received only five per cent of the vote while Nasheed, also a candidate, received proportionally the most votes, of 46.93 per cent. But he was defeated in the second round with 48.61 per cent against 51.39 per cent for Gayoom's half-brother Abdulla Yameen, or to give him his full name, Abdulla Yameen Abdul Gayoom.

Nasheed was arrested again in February 2015 and ordered to stand trial for his decision while president to arrest Abdulla Mohamed, a judge who was accused of having obstructed police duty by delaying cases involving members of the opposition and barring media from corruption trials. Nasheed was charged under the Anti-Terrorism Act of the Maldives and, on 13 March, the court sentenced him to 13 years imprisonment. Amnesty International said in a statement that, 'this trial has been flawed from start to finish, and the conviction is unsound.'[13]

On 16 January 2016, Nasheed was allowed to leave for Britain to undergo spinal surgery on the condition that he would serve 'the remainder of the sentence upon return to the Maldives after surgery.'[14] Nasheed decided not to return, and, in June, was granted political asylum in Britain. He travelled between Britain and India and settled in Sri Lanka, where he began organising opposition to Yameen's government. His work paid off as Yameen was defeated in the September 2018 election.

Yameen, who was educated in Lebanon and the United States, worked closely with his half-brother Gayoom while he was the president. From 1990 to 2005, Yameen was chairman of the State Trading Organisation (STO), during which time he became associated with one of the biggest corruption scandals in the history of the Maldives.

Grant Thornton, a Singapore-based auditing firm, discovered in 2010 that under a contract with Nasheed's then government Gayoom was receiving a large allocation of oil from the Organisation of Petroleum Exporting Countries (OPEC) channelled through the STO. The Maldives was given a special, cheap allocation of oil because of the group's preferential treatment of Sunni Muslim countries. But the ships carrying the oil from Singapore never went to the Maldives. Instead, the STO was selling on the oil via the black market to international buyers – and one of them was Myanmar's military government. Adding to the controversy was the discovery that several of the companies and personalities the Myanmar junta was using at home and in Singapore to facilitate the trade were sanctioned by the US under a broader scheme to punish Myanmar for its abysmal human-rights record. One of them was Steven Law and his Asia World Company, the son of the former opium warlord Lo Hsing-han and China's main partner for several construction projects in Myanmar.[15]

In 2004, Gayoom and Yameen set up a joint venture between Mocom Corporation in Malaysia and STO called Mocom Trading, which was incorporated in Singapore to sell their allocation from there. According to Grant Thornton, 'STO Singapore and Mocom Singapore each generated sales invoices addressed to Myanmar showing the quantity of barrels delivered and the unit price. The content of the invoices are alike, except for the price per barrel.'[16] The scale of the fraud was in the order of US$800 million, not significantly different from the country's GDP, which at that time was US$1.4 billion.[17]

The fraud was exposed in the Indian magazine *The Week* by investigative journalist Sumon K. Chakrabarti, who described Yameen as 'the kingpin' of the scheme.[18] One of the first acts of Waheed's government when it assumed power in February 2012 was to dissolve the presidential commission which until then had been overseeing Grant Thornton's investigation and terminate the agreement with the firm.[19]

As president, Yameen, who saw New Delhi as the main foreign force standing behind Nasheed and was therefore fiercely anti-Indian, moved the Maldives closer to China. The relationship was not new, but deepened under Yameen to the extent that India perceived it as a threat to its security. The Maldives and China had established diplomatic relations in 1972 and, in October 1984, Gayoom visited Beijing where he signed an agreement on economic and technical cooperation.

In the late 1990s, it was rumoured that Gayoom had concluded a secret defence agreement with China whereby the latter would be given an entire island for a submarine base in return for supplying weapons to the Maldivian army.[20] Nothing came of it but Beijing continued to offer the Maldives blank cheques from the China Development Bank and what it termed 'cultural cooperation' via its Confucius Institutes.

Nothing of note happened until Nasheed was ousted in February 2012. An agreement signed with India's GMR Infrastructure when Nasheed was the president was scrapped without explanation by Waheed in November – and the contract was given to a state-owned Chinese company.[21] Then Yameen took over, and China's relations with the Maldives blossomed. The partnership took a significant step forward when Chinese president Xi Jinping arrived in the Maldives on a state visit in September 2014. The deal to upgrade the Maldives' international airport was finalised and China also undertook to build a two-kilometre bridge linking the airport on Hulhule with Male.

Xi missed no the opportunity to fantasise about the fictitious 'Maritime Silk Road' which China claims existed in the past but never did. Such petty historical details did not prevent Xi from saying that the Maldives, 'was an important stop along the ancient Maritime Silk Road' and, according to official Chinese media, he also welcomed 'Male's active participation in China's 21st Century Maritime Silk Road Initiative.'[22] In December, only two months after Xi's visit, the Maldives signed a Memorandum of Understanding with Beijing in support of the BRI, one of the first countries to do so.

A free-trade agreement between the Maldives and China was signed when Yameen visited Beijing in December 2017. It was Maldives' first and it became the second South Asian country after Pakistan to enter into such an agreement with China. According to a Chinese government statement, China and the Maldives 'would reduce tariffs of over 95 per cent of goods to zero' and the two nations were also 'committed to opening the service market such as finance, healthcare and tourism.'[23] Chinese investors were allowed to operate hotels and resorts, and the Maldives gained a new market for its fish exports.

But the manner in which the agreement was concluded ran into criticism from the MDP and other opposition parties. The MDP said in a press release that 'despite requests the [opposition] MPs were not given access to the document in order to review it before passing. The government allowed for less than an hour for the entire parliamentary process to approve a 1,000-plus page document.'[24]Yameen was simply not interested in what the opposition thought about it. But that had been his leadership style since he became the president in 2013.

The bridge from the airport to Male was completed on 30 August 2018 and inaugurated by Yameen who said at the opening ceremony that it was an 'embodiment of the long relations between the Maldives and China.'[25] It would have been closer to the truth to say that what China had achieved in such a short period of friendship was remarkable. China's investment in infrastructure project to upgrade and maintain airports and ports, in housing estate projects, and in the lease of islands for tourism development, is in the hundreds of millions of dollars. In 2017, 306,000 of a total of 1.39 million tourists came from China, more than from any other country. Number two on the list was Germany with 112,000 visitors followed by Britain's 103,000, 83,000 from India, 62,000 from Russia, and smaller numbers from several other countries.[26] Not only were Chinese visitors more numerous than those from elsewhere, but the December 2017 free-trade agreement also gave businessmen from China an edge over all other foreign investors in the tourism industry.

Among the more controversial Chinese construction projects were plans, announced in early 2018, to build a Joint Ocean Observation Station in Makunudhoo in northwestern Maldives. A correspondent for *The Times of India* wrote at the time that the proposed facility would 'allow the Chinese a vantage point of an important Indian Ocean shipping route…[and] effectively open a Chinese maritime front against India.'[27]

Whether that is the case or if the Chinese are simply interested in keeping a close eye on vital shipping lanes is open to speculation. But the MDP suggested at the time that it could be used for military purposes. China would deny that, and on 25 September 2018 – only two days after the election – Chinese foreign ministry spokesman Geng Shuang lashed out against Nasheed, who from his exile in Sri Lanka had attacked the viability of Chinese projects in the Maldives.[28] Nasheed said many of them lacked transparency and were not conceived or implemented in accordance with 'democratic procedures.'[29] He had earlier accused China of being 'busy buying up the Maldives.'[30] Geng blasted Nasheed for his 'irresponsible remarks,' saying in less than diplomatic terms that China cannot be 'smeared by certain individuals.'[31]

Yameen lost the September 2018 election, but regardless of who will be in power during the coming decade, it will be almost impossible to untangle the web of Chinese contracts that were granted during his tenure even if a successor would want to do so. Some of them are with major Chinese state corporations while others are with smaller ones with Chinese connections or patronage. Nitin Pai of the Takshashila Institution, a Bengaluru-based think-tank, wrote after the election: 'It is unclear if the Maldivian government has the sheer capacity required to renegotiate them all. What Malaysia, Sri Lanka and Pakistan can attempt, the Maldives cannot.'[32]

The semi-official Chinese tabloid *Global Times* stated in a 25 September commentary that 'China doesn't interfere in Maldives' internal affairs and bilateral collaboration serves the national interests of the Indian Ocean nation. That said, whoever takes the presidency, China-Maldives friendly ties will remain.'[33] The editorial added that 'the Yameen government chose to cooperate with China in the interests of Maldives' development and to create tangible benefits for the people.'[34]

But such statements show that China's policy makers have failed to understand the volatile and often unpredictable nature of Maldivian politics. The fact that the old dictator Gayoom had sided with the opposition against his half-brother Yameen is only one example of that. Gayoom was released on bail a week after the September 2018 election, and tweets from his daughter Yumna Maumoon suggest that she had been influential in persuading her father to change sides. 'Hope and pray that all political prisoners will be released soon. The nightmare is finally over Insha Allah. Thank you all who struggled hard for this day.'[35] It is also possible that Gayoom, who was 80 when he was arrested in February 2018, had decided that he did not want to go down in history as a brutal and corrupt dictator but rather as the leader who brought the Maldives into the modern world. And Gayoom began his political career as a defender of human rights and became a victim of repression when Ibrahim Nasir was in power.

The Maldives is even more strategically important than other Indian Ocean states such as Mauritius, the Seychelles and the Comoros, which is why China is not going to let go of its gains in the archipelago. That importance predates today's geopolitical power games by several centuries – and is also the reason why the islands became Muslim. The Maldives lay on the maritime trading routes of early Egyptian, Mesopotamian and Indus Valley civilisations and the first settlers may have been Buddhist and Hindu migrants from today's Sri Lanka and India. Arab traders began visiting the Maldives in the ninth century and had a more lasting impact on life and society on the islands. Many settled on the islands and brought with them African slaves. Over the centuries, a distinct Maldivian nation emerged with influences from the Indian subcontinent, the Arab world and Africa.[36] Islam was introduced by the Arabs and the recorded history of the islands begins in 1153 when the last Buddhist king converted to the new religion, adopting a Muslim title and the name Sultan Muhammed al Adil.[37]

The name of the islands may derive from the Tamil words for garland (*maalai*) and island (*theevu*) or, in Sanskrit, *maladvipa*, which also means 'garland of islands'.[38] There are other theories as well, but most of them refer to islands and garlands, which seems quite appropriate. While Islam came with the Arab traders, *Divehi*, the language spoken on the islands is related to the Singhalese language of Sri Lanka. The writing system, called Thaana, resembles Arabic, but is not the same.

Influences from the Arab and Indian worlds have always been strong but contrary to Chinese claims of a 'maritime silk road' including the Maldives, there is no evidence of early trade with China. Zheng He was aware of the existence of the islands but the description of them, as recorded by Zheng He's interpreter and chronicler Ma Huan, is brief: 'King, chiefs, and people professed the Muslim religion. The people lived of fishing and cultivating coconuts…the inhabitants knew nothing of rice.'[39] The Chinese visitors noted that coconuts, cowrie shells and dried bonito fish were exported 'to foreign countries',[40] but there was no suggestion that any of those goods were destined for China, or that Chinese goods were for sale on the islands. And after that brief stop during one of Zheng He's expeditions, there is no record of any interaction between the Maldives and China until well into modern times.

The first Europeans to establish themselves on the Maldives were the Portuguese, who captured the islands in 1558 and ruled them from their colony at Goa on India's west coast. But Portuguese rule lasted for only 15 years. A local resistance fighter called Muhammed Thakurufaan organised a revolt, and drove them out in 1573, proclaiming himself sultan of the islands. The Maldivians consider him a national hero and his victory over the Portuguese is now commemorated as National Day.

In the mid-seventeenth century, the Dutch arrived on the islands and tried, not very successfully, to establish a presence there. It all came to an end when they were forced out of Ceylon (now Sri Lanka) by the British in 1796. Ceylon became a British colony and the Maldives was included as a protected area, though it was not until 1887 that an agreement was signed and the sultan accepted British influence over external relations and defence. British supremacy remained indirect via Ceylon and the only interference came in 1932, when the Maldives got its first constitution, limiting the absolute powers of the sultans and introducing the post of chief minister. The sultans remained official heads of state except for that brief period in 1953 when the protectorate was a republic under Mohamed Amin Didi.

Britain's policy towards the Maldives was reflected in the first article of its colonial constitution: 'The Maldives is a completely Independent State in regard to her internal affairs and is governed accordingly…the Maldive Islands shall continue under the protection of His Majesty; and His Majesty's Government in the United Kingdom will at all times to the utmost of its power take whatever steps may be necessary to protect the Maldive Islands from hostile attacks.'[41] The only interest the British had in the Maldives was to prevent other powers from capturing the strategically located islands and from there threatening colonial rule in India and Ceylon.

Like with so much else in the region, World War II changed all that. In 1941, the Royal Navy established a base on the island of Gan in Addu, the southernmost of the Maldivian atolls. An airstrip was built along with causeways connecting Gan with other islands in the atoll. Towards the end of the war even a light railway was built on the causeways. Oil tanks were installed beside shore batteries and anti-aircraft guns. The deep-water lagoon at Addu was also ideal for naval refuelling. The best thing about the base was that the Japanese were never aware of its existence.[42] It was hidden on a remote island in the Indian Ocean and, unlike other islands in the region, it was never attacked by Japanese bombers and submarines.

Even after World War II, Gan served as a staging point for aircraft flying between Europe, Singapore, Hong Kong and Australia. The Gan airfield remained an important link in the chain of Indian Ocean bases Britain maintained throughout the 1950s and well into the 1960s. Its importance was underscored when the Royal Air Force (RAF) handed over its bases in Ceylon to that country's own air force in 1957. The base on Addu was taken over by the RAF and designated as RAF Gan.

Two years later, Addu became the centre for the curious breakaway United Suvadive Republic which embarrassed the British, who wanted to maintain their base there without having problems with the Maldivian government. To be on the safe side and avoid any military confrontation between the rebels and a Maldivian naval vessel that had been dispatched to the waters off the atoll, the British sent a regiment to Gan from Singapore and surveillance was increased.[43] A violent conflict was averted, the breakaway republic was dissolved in 1963, and Abdullah Afif Didi, the leader of the rebellion, was sent off by the British to the Seychelles where he died in 1993.

British policy towards the Indian Ocean changed when in July 1967 Prime Minister Harold Wilson announced plans for the withdrawal of Britain's defence role 'East of Suez' by the mid-1970s.[44] But Britain was not going to leave all its commitments 'East of Suez'. Wilson's decision coincided with the creation of the British Indian Ocean Territory and the build-up of the base on Diego Garcia. RAF Gan consequently lost its importance, and the last British forces withdrew from the base in 1976, nine years after the Maldives had become fully independent.

In the 1970s, ships from the Soviet Union, the West's main adversary in the Cold War, began to appear in the Indian Ocean. Friendly regimes in power in the Seychelles and South Yemen helped the Soviets gain a foothold in the region and that was why the RAF negotiated so toughly with the Maldivian government before the base was closed. Britain wanted to ensure they kept the Soviet Navy well away from what could have become an exact counterpart of their base on Diego Garcia.[45]

After the RAF left, the airstrip remained almost unused – until the Nasheed government in 2009 established a public enterprise called Gan Airport Company Limited. In January 2010, it took over management of what had then become Gan International Airport, the second airport in the Maldives after Hulhule. It has been refurbished as a civilian airport owned and managed by Addu International Airport Company and handles mostly Chinese tourists going to nearby resorts. China Southern Airlines flies to Gan from Guangzhou via Colombo, and there is nothing to indicate that the airport will ever again be used for military purposes.

China's only military appearance in the Maldives so far was the arrival at Male in August 2017 of three naval frigates. It was described as a 'friendly visit' by the Maldivian military, which also stated that the Chinese 'will hold special training sessions' with Maldivian soldiers and 'carry out joint sports activities in order to strengthen friendly relations between the militaries of China and the Maldives.'[46] The Chinese also paid a visit to the military base in Girifushi. The exchange came six months or so after Yameen's government had declared its support for China over the disputed islands in the South China Sea.[47]

Indian security analysts reacted to the visit with dismay. Shyam Saran, a former Indian foreign secretary and a China specialist, wrote in the fortnightly news magazine *India Today*: 'The message is loud and clear: China is determined to demonstrate its oft-repeated assertion that the Indian Ocean is not India's ocean.'[48] And when Nasheed urged India to intervene, including sending troops to the Maldives, during the crisis in February 2018, a writer for the *Global Times*, which reflects official Chinese policy, retorted: 'India should exercise restraint... China will not interfere in the internal affairs of the Maldives, but that does not mean that Beijing will sit idly by as New Delhi breaks the principle. If India one-sidedly sends troops to the Maldives, China will take action to stop New Delhi. India should not underestimate China's opposition to unilateral military intervention.'[49]

China's shadow over the Maldives, which has resulted in a bitter rivalry with India, is not the only controversial issue facing the archipelago. More than half the population of the country lives cramped together on Male's six square-kilometres, which makes it one of the most world's most densely populated capitals. GDP per capita was an impressive US$10,535 in 2017, lower than the Seychelles and about the same as Mauritius – but much higher than Sri Lanka's US$4,065 and India's US$1,939.[50] But unemployment is high, especially among young people, drug abuse is rampant and a proliferation of criminal gangs has made it a less secure place than it was until only a few decades ago. Few Maldivians work in the resorts, which are managed by Europeans and Australians and staffed mainly with tens of thousands of poorly paid Bangladeshis.[51] Locals who have made it to the resort islands may have been dismayed by the sight of scantily clad foreign visitors spending amounts of money they could only dream of. It should come as no surprise therefore that the Maldives has become fertile ground for Islamist extremism.

Nasheed, on a visit to London in September 2014, said that up to 200 Maldivians had gone to fight for the Islamic State (IS) in Iraq and Syria – and that from a population of only 417,000.[52] By comparison, a little of over 100 fighters went from India, which has a Muslim population of more than 190 million.[53] Nasheed warned that the situation was deteriorating and claimed that there were links between jihadist groups and the country's military as well as police force.[54] Maldivian society has become much more conservative, he said, because of the influx of Saudi money, paying for Wahhabi imams and mosques, 'and spreading a deeply conservative view of Islam at odds with the islands' traditions.'[55]

The Maldives was not as severely affected by the 2004 Indian Ocean tsunami as Sri Lanka, the Andaman and Nicobar Islands, and, of course, places around the epicentre in northern Sumatra – a total of 130,000 people died in the entire region – but Male was flooded and outlying, low-level atolls were badly affected, with 82 people killed and 24 reported missing, presumed dead. But, ostensibly to help with spiritual and other relief work, Islamic preachers, funded mainly by Saudi Arabia, arrived after the tsunami and began working together with local preachers. Azra Naseem, a Maldivian at the International Institute of Conflict Resolution and Reconstruction in Dublin, explained in an interview with the *Irish Times* what happened: 'It was a turning point in the radicalisation process. Local Islamists were clever in their use of the tragedy to convince Maldivians that the tsunami was punishment from Allah for not practising the "right" Islam – which is the "purist" Islam that Salafis and other fundamentalists want all Muslims to turn to.'[56]

J.J. Robinson noted that 'almost overnight it became accepted that Maldivians needed to travel abroad to learn Islam "properly", and many began accepting free opportunities for "tertiary education" at madrassas in Pakistan and universities in Saudi Arabia. On their return to the islands they would set themselves up as "scholars", wielding dubious certificates and a few words in Arabic to gain respect and convince those around them of their superior religiosity.'[57] Up to the 1990s, few women wore the veil. Today, the Arab-style full veil is a common sight in the Maldives.

In September 2007, a bomb exploded in Male, injuring twelve foreign tourists: eight from China, two from Britain and two from Japan. It soon became clear that Islamic fundamentalists were behind it, and 200 policemen and soldiers were sent to look for evidence on the island of Himandhoo, where the local Dhar-al-khuir mosque had declared itself independent of the government's instructions for religious teachings. They were confronted at the jetty by a small army of islanders armed with batons and knives and wearing red motorcycle helmets.[58] In the ensuing skirmish, a policeman was captured by the islanders and another had his hand severed.

As Robinson explains: 'Shortly afterwards, a video discovered on an Al Qaeda forum was found containing footage taken inside the Dhar-al-khuir mosque moments before it was raided by the police.'[59] According to leaked US diplomatic cables, three Maldivian men were identified as Al Qaeda associates, showing the extent to which the terror group had managed to infiltrate the Maldives. The cable also stated that at least two Al Qaeda-linked operatives had been involved in the bombing, 'in exchange for travel from the islands after the operation and arranged study at a madrassa in Pakistan.'[60]

Islam was becoming a political force to be reckoned with. Soon after Nasheed was elected in 2008, his opponents began portraying him as 'anti-Islamic' and whipped up religious fervour to unseat him. He was accused of being a Western-influenced liberal with no respect for Islamic values. But even Yameen has become a target of the most radical among the Islamic fundamentalists. In 2016, Maldivian jihadists posted a video on a website with pictures of the three most recent presidents, including Yameen, being buried alive and shot up with an AK-47.[61]

It is often forgotten that Islamic *shariah* law, known in Dhivehi as *sariatu*, forms the basic code of law in the Maldives. Islam is the official state religion and article 9 in the country's 2008 constitution stipulates that a non-Muslim cannot become a citizen and citizens are not allowed to practice any religion other than Islam.[62] But strict *shariah* law was never enforced – at least not until recently. In July 2009, an 18-year-old woman fainted as she was flogged 100 times after being found guilty of having had sex with two different men. The young woman, who was pregnant at the time, had her punishment deferred until after the birth of her child. In contrast, *The Independent* reported at the time, the accused men were acquitted, with one of them escaping punishment because he denied the charge.[63] That happened during the presidency of Nasheed, but he apparently felt prevented from speaking out because his fragile coalition depended on support from the Islamist Adhaalath Party – which later cut ties with Nasheed's MDP, a move that caused the collapse of his government.

Another woman, who also stood accused of adultery and had been sentenced to death by stoning in 2015, was more fortunate. The sentence was passed by a court on the remote island of Gemanafushi and then overturned by the Supreme Court in Male. The government intervened in another case, when it overturned a conviction of a 15-year-old rape victim, who was sentenced to 100 lashes for having had pre-marital sex. The girl had been repeatedly raped by her own father, who was later charged with her 29-year-old lover, who was given a ten-year prison sentence.[64] But that happened only after there had been an international outcry against the girl's sentence.

The media also incurred the wrath of the radicals. In 2014, Ahmed Rilwan Abdulla, a prominent Maldivian journalist who wrote about secularism and extremism was abducted. Yameen Rasheed, one of his colleagues, joined a campaign dedicated to finding Abdulla, and was stabbed to death in the stairwell of his apartment building in Male. Rasheed worked as an IT professional and maintained a blog in his spare time where he aimed to report 'the unfiltered truth, the sickening facts, the gruesome details, and – because this is the Maldives – the painfully obvious.'[65]

It is clear that any attempt by India to re-establish its influence in the Maldives would be met with resistance from China and its local proxies – and Islamic radicals. The kind of military intervention that India undertook in 1988 would be impossible today. After Nasheed's call for exactly that in February 2018, a warning came not only from China but also from the Maldives. In a message posted on its website on 13 February, the Maldives defence ministry stated in English as well as Dhivehi that the government 'condemns all such action which constitutes a threat to the nation's independence and national security…such actions…cast doubt upon the excellent relationship India and Maldives have enjoyed for decades.'[66]

India chose instead to invite Yameen to New Delhi in July 2018 – and to sign a defence agreement with the Maldives. Modi said at the occasion that 'India understands its role as a net security provider in the region.'[67] Development of ports, training, supply of equipment and coordinated maritime surveillance were said to be the main elements of the cooperation. But whether it was too little, too late, and if it will result in any substantial cooperation between India and the Maldives, is far from certain. India may have to depend on its new base in Lakshadweep for surveillance of that part of the Indian Ocean.

But even that may not be without problems. The people on Minicoy, the southernmost atoll in Lakshadweep, are culturally and linguistically closely related to the Maldivians and located only 130 kilometres from the northernmost atoll in the Maldives. In July 1982, Abdulla Hameed – a Maldivian minister who is also one of Gayoom's brothers – made a public speech claiming that Minicoy should belong to the Maldives. That precipitated a diplomatic crisis with India, and the government of the Maldives had to make it clear that is does not claim Minicoy. But, as a Maldivian website points out, 'even today many Maldivians privately harbour sentiments such as expressed in the Maldive ministerial speech of 1982.'[68] In fact, Minicoy was never under the Maldivian sultans. The Ali Raja of Cannanore ceded it to British India in 1909 and independent India included it into the new island union territory that was established on 1 November 1956 and named Lakshadweep in 1973.

China's role in the economy and the politics of the Maldives was apparently not discussed. Modi chose instead a more diplomatic approach: 'President Yameen and I are aware of the growing dangers of cross-border terrorism and radicalisation in South Asia. Information exchange between security agencies and training and capacity building of Maldives police and security forces is an important part of our security cooperation.'[69] A Memorandum of Understanding was signed for the conservation and restoration of ancient mosques and other historical monuments in the Maldives as part of what an Indian newspaper termed 'deradicalisation initiatives'.[70]

The Maldives, which had gained a place on the global map of terrorist attacks since the 2007 bombing in Male, also prompted the United States to begin to pay more attention to the country. China's growing influence was another factor for becoming involved in Maldivian affairs. With Male located only 1,275 kilometres from Diego Garcia, developments in the Maldives were becoming a real concern to Washington. US agencies noted in their reports that 'young Maldivians, especially those within the penal system and otherwise marginalised members of society, are at risk of becoming radicalised and some have already joined terrorist groups.'[71]

The Maldives participates in the US State Department's anti-terrorism programmes, mainly for the police to bring their abilities up to international standards. In 2013, then president Barack Obama tried to establish even closer cooperation by getting the Waheed government to sign a Status of Forces Agreement, which would have led to military cooperation between the two countries, possibly including at least a semi-permanent US presence in the Maldives. But the negotiations got derailed when Yameen was elected president in November and decided to move closer to China.[72] US-Maldives relations deteriorated even further before the September 2018 elections after a State Department official said that Washington was concerned about continued 'democratic backsliding' and called for the release of what it called 'falsely accused' political prisoners. Yameen's foreign ministry retorted by accusing the United States of intimidation and 'imposing undue influence' on the election process.[73]

The Maldives did not have any properly organised military until 2006, when Gayoom created the Maldives National Defence Force (MNDF). The old sultans had their personal security forces which took part in royal ceremonies. The central government also had boats, which patrolled the waters around the islands, and a police force. A ministry of defence and national security was set up in 1979, which was the first step towards creating actual armed forces under a centralised command. When that was done in 2006, the president assumed the post as commander-in-chief. The present strength of the MNDF is believed to be around 3,500, consisting of marine corps, coast guards, an air wing, and special forces.[74]

The air wing consists of a Dhruv helicopter donated by India and, in 2006, the Indian Navy gave a Trinkat fast attack craft to the MNDF's coast guard. The force's armoured vehicles are mostly Otokars obtained from Turkey. For such a small country, the Maldives has quite a formidable military. And because it is under the command of the president, it has been used to quell internal dissent, as occurred in February 2018 when soldiers in riot gear surrounded the parliament and arrested two opposition lawmakers.[75]

The Special Forces branch of the MNDF was created in 2009, a specialised group of an unknown number of well-trained elite soldiers. According to the MNDF's website, its men form the 'cream of the crop', are 'generally qualified in parachute jumping', and 'take pride in frequent cross training with foreign elite forces such as the US Special Forces, the US Navy Seals, the British SAS, the National Security Guards of India, and the Army Commandos of Sri Lanka.'[76] How much of that is correct is hard to say, but any details regarding the training of the Special Forces are kept top secret.

China has repeatedly said that it has no plans to establish a military base in the Maldives and called such claims 'totally baseless.'[77] And apart from the arrival of the three frigates in August 2017, China's military has been visible in the Maldives on only one more occasion: in December 2014, China sent 1,000 tonnes of fresh water to the islands by plane and military vessel to help ease a severe water shortage caused by a fire at the country's only water and sewage treatment plant. China's foreign ministry said Beijing had provided emergency aid 'in cash and drinking water' in response to a request by the Maldivian government.[78]

But Nasheed has said China is 'buying up' the Maldives, and that those land acquisitions could, in the long run, have military applications. A constitutional amendment bill, passed on 22 July 2015, allows foreign parties who invest at least US$1 billion to lease land on a freehold basis as long as 70 per cent of the area is reclaimed from the sea. Nasheed has claimed that the new law has led to the leasing out of about 16 islets in the archipelago to Chinese interests, and that they are building ports and other infrastructure there: 'There is land grab going on, that threatens not just the Maldives, but the peace and stability of the entire region. A large emerging power is busy buying up the Maldives, buying up our islands, buying up our key infrastructure, and effectively, buying up our sovereignty.'[79]

China's massive lending to countries such as the Maldives to pay for infrastructural projects is another concern. The Centre for Global Development, a Washington-based think-tank, estimates China's loans to the Maldives at US$1.3 billion, more than a quarter of its current GDP.[80] The two ratings agencies covering the Maldives, Fitch and Moody's, both rate the country as 'sub-investment grade', and the World Bank and the International Monetary Fund see a likelihood of distress if current spending continues – and it will be China that calls the shots in such a situation.[81]

Regardless of who rules the Maldives, China has achieved a dominant role that any future government would find it hard to shake off. And if the Maldives decided to re-establish close links with India at the expense of China, Beijing could easily retaliate with the weapon it has used elsewhere in the world: by 'weaponising' tourism. A tourism boycott of the Maldives like the one China has launched to punish Palau for its relations with Taiwan would be devastating for the Maldivian economy. Tourism accounts for 28 per cent of the Maldives' economy and more than 60 per cent of foreign exchange receipts. And over 90 per cent of the government's revenue comes from duties and tourism-related taxes.[82]

China could also foment political unrest in the Maldives, most likely through proxies and using its patron-client relationship with local politicians such as Yameen. The 'ancient maritime silk road' may be a myth, but it is clear that the strategic importance of the Maldives for Xi's BRI is such that China will do anything to maintain its grip on the Maldives. And that is the bitter reality with which the Maldives has to grapple.

8

AUSTRALIA'S LITTLE DOTS

They are only small dots in the remote, eastern reaches of the Indian Ocean, but the Australian territory of the Cocos (Keeling) Islands boasts a 2,440-metre-long runway on its West Island, underscoring the thinly populated atoll's strategic importance. Some 100 people, mostly Caucasians, live there while another 500 people of Malay origin live on Home Island, the only other inhabited island in the group. And from here it is 2,935 kilometres to Perth. Nearly a thousand kilometres northeast of the Cocos (Keeling) Islands, south of the Indonesian island of Java, lies another Australian external territory, Christmas Island, the home of 1,400 people, of whom 70 per cent are of Chinese ancestry while 20 per cent are Caucasians and 10 per cent Malays.

Small and insignificant as they may be in terms of population and resources – Christmas Island used to have a phosphate mine, but it was closed in 1987, partly reopened in 1991 and then closed again in 2017 – Australia's Indian Ocean territories give the West, including the United States, a strategic advantage in the eastern Indian Ocean. They serve as an outer line of defence for Australia – and in a potential conflict between the West and China, the navies of the United States and its allies could block Chinese oil supplies from the Middle East.

There are currently no military bases on either the Cocos or Christmas Island. But, as Australian defence analyst Ross Babbage wrote in a 1988 study of the territories, in case of an emergency, access to the islands would 'extend Australia's reach into the surrounding region for surveillance, air defence, and maritime and ground strike operations. The islands could, in effect, serve as unsinkable aircraft carriers and resupply ships.'[1] And that explains the long runway on Cocos' West Island – which is lined with huge satellite dishes. There is another signals intelligence station in another part of the island. There are only twice-weekly flights from the Cocos to Perth, but if a conflict breaks out, the airport could accommodate jet fighters, transport planes and even bombers. But, for now, the importance of the Cocos lies mainly in its use as a base for electronic surveillance.

Christmas Island was until recently known as home to Australia's detention centre for illegal immigrants and asylum-seekers. Established in 2001, it housed nearly as many detainees as the permanent population of the island. Most of them came from the Middle East and Sri Lanka, and the ships that had carried them were intercepted in the sea south of Java. The policy was not to allow them to enter the Australian mainland before their cases had been processed. In that way, it would serve as a deterrent as Australia immigration authorities suspected most of them were economic migrants, not political refugees. Similar detention centres were set up on Nauru in the Pacific Ocean and Manus, an island off the coast of Papua New Guinea. Those camps remain, but the closely guarded facility on Christmas Island was closed in 2017 following several hunger strikes and fights between the detainees and the Australian staff.

Since the phosphate mine as well as the detention centre have shut, there is little activity on Christmas Island. Tourism has never been encouraged on those islands either. There is hardly any accommodation for visitors and few places to eat and drink. Australia's defence authorities want it that way. The Cocos and Christmas Island are not as secretive and off-limits to visitors as France's Kerguelen, but Australia's presence in its Indian Ocean territories is motivated by similar strategic considerations. And, although few are willing to say it openly, the main concern is China's expansion into the Indian Ocean.

The importance of the Cocos and Christmas Island – both of them originally British possessions – became apparent during the World Wars of the twentieth century. One of the first naval battles of World War I was fought in 1914 near the Cocos between the British and the

Germans, resulting in the sinking of the German cruiser *SMS Emden* by Britain's *HMAS Sydney*. Guns from *Emden* were later put on display in Sydney and Canberra. Japan invaded Christmas Island and bombarded the Cocos during World War II.

Today, naturally, neither Germany nor Japan poses a threat to Australia, but China's involvement in upgrading ports in Myanmar, Sri Lanka and Pakistan has tilted the balance of power in the Indian Ocean. It is hardly surprising that Australia has upgraded its signals intelligence facilities on the Cocos – and shares the information with the United States. Together with the US base on Diego Garcia, France's presence in the southern Indian Ocean, and India's upgrading its bases on the Andamans and Nicobars, a pattern is beginning to emerge, but the battle lines are far from clear with no one wanting to be seen as being openly anti-Chinese.

Both the Cocos and Christmas Islands were originally uninhabited. The Cocos were first sighted by a European when Captain William Keeling of the British East India Company sailed past them, but probably never went ashore, in 1609. He saw the coconut trees on the horseshoe-shaped coral atolls so it was natural that he named them the Cocos Islands. But to distinguish them from similarly named islands – those now belonging to Myanmar and another group of islands off the coast of Costa Rica – the name of the British navigator who 'discovered' them, was added. Thus, they got their rather curious double-name: the Cocos (Keeling) Islands. Christmas Island was given its name by Captain William Mynors, also of the British East India Company, who arrived there on Christmas Day, 25 December 1643.

The British Empire annexed the Cocos in 1857 and Christmas Island in 1888. They were placed under the administration of the Straits Settlements, a British crown colony that consisted of Singapore, Malacca, Penang and the island of Labuan off the northwestern coast of Borneo. By the mid-1950s, with impending independence for the Straits Settlements – and Malaya – the British, recognising the strategic importance of the islands, began making preparations to transfer them to Australia – not unlike the separation of the Chagos Archipelago from Mauritius a decade later.

In 1955, the Cocos were transferred to Australian control while Christmas Island became Australian in 1957 after the British government had paid Singapore £2.9 million in compensation, a price based on the estimated value of the phosphate Singapore would lose because of the transfer. The negotiations preceding the transfer were criticised by local Singapore politicians. Among them was the future leader Lee Kuan Yew, who stated in the Singapore House of Assembly in June 1957: 'To give away all the appurtenances of Singapore before we take over is a downright swindle. A few years ago they gave away Cocos Islands, now it's Christmas Island.'[2] But Christmas Island became Australian and Singapore, unlike Mauritius which wants to renegotiate the deal with the Chagos Archipelago, has never raised the issue of sovereignty. The first Australian administrator arrived in 1958 and the islanders became Australian citizens.

The Cocos, though, were still ruled in a feudal manner by the Clunies-Ross family, planters originating from the Shetland Islands. The first in a dynasty which was to become known as 'the Kings of the Cocos' was John Clunies-Ross, who had come to the seas of Southeast Asia as a third mate and harpooner on a whaling ship called the *Baroness Longueville*.[3] When the ship returned to Britain, Clunies-Ross decided to remain on various islands in what then was the Dutch East Indies and today constitutes Indonesia. In 1825, he intended to first inspect Christmas Island as a possible trading site, but strong monsoon winds brought him south and he arrived at the Cocos in early December. He decided that those uninhabited islands were more suitable because there was no natural harbour on Christmas Island while West Island in the Cocos had a well-sheltered lagoon where ships could be anchored.

Clunies-Ross was not the only one who laid eyes on the Cocos in the 1820s. Alexander Hare, the son of a London watchmaker who had settled in Malacca with a harem of local women, sailed on the same ship as Clunies-Ross to the Cocos in 1826 and also decided to set up a base there. Later, when Clunies-Ross was away in London, Hare moved to West Island with his men and about 90 slaves he had brought from Java. Clunies-Ross arrived in 1827 with a group of convicts brought in from Java as indentured labour. More coconut trees were planted, and the Cocos became an important supplier of copra and coconut oil, which was shipped mostly to Batavia (now Jakarta). Goats, chickens and other domestic animals were brought in from Java, enabling the community to become self-sustaining. Food also came from gardens on the islands and there was plenty of fish in the surrounding seas. Clunies-Ross helped the Cocos Islanders build wooden fishing boats, which understandably but somewhat incongruously resembled those used in the Shetlands.

But the Cocos were not big enough for two such enterprises, and, as Hare mistreated his workers, many of them escaped and began working for the more humane Clunies-Ross. Hare was forced out of the Cocos, and Clunies-Ross became their sole ruler. He moved to Home Island and tried, in vain, to persuade the British or the Dutch to annex the islands so they would be placed under some higher authority that would provide protection from other interested parties. That did not happen, but in 1839, the British ship the *Beagle* anchored there; onboard was Charles Darwin. Darwin made copious notes on the flora and fauna of the islands and it was here that he first made a thorough study of coral atolls and found out how they had been created by submarine volcanic action.[4] Darwin also wrote that Clunies-Ross' Malay workers 'are now nominally in a state of freedom, and certainly are so far as regards their personal treatment; but in most other they are considered as slaves.'[5]

John Clunies-Ross died in the Cocos in 1854 and his son John George Clunies-Ross took over. He was married to a Malay woman, which marked the beginning of the ethnically mixed family who for more than a century to come ruled the islands. It was during his 'reign' that the British eventually annexed the Cocos. In 1857, a British ship, *HMS Juno*, commanded by Captain R.N. Freemantle, arrived there. The Union Jack was hoisted, the guns of *Juno* fired a royal salute and Clunies-Ross the Second was proclaimed 'Governor of the Settlement during Her Majesty's Pleasure.'[6]

But Freemantle may have claimed the islands for the British crown by mistake. He thought he had arrived at the now Myanmar Coco Islands north of the Andamans.[7] What was done was done though, and the Cocos (Keeling) Islands were placed under the jurisdiction of the Straits Settlements. But there was little or no interference from Singapore, and Clunies-Ross the Second, who died in 1872, was succeeded by his son, George Clunies-Ross. In 1885, the first inspector from the Straits Settlements arrived and, probably believing that the Cocos were too small and too remote to be governed effectively from

Singapore, granted the Clunies-Ross family the right to run the islands 'in perpetuity.'[8]

The population of the islands was at that time probably around 500, or slightly fewer than today. Not many, but they needed timber to build boats and houses, and good soil for their gardens, so they ventured to the then uninhabited Christmas Island where one John Murray, a Canadian of Scottish descent, found phosphate in the ground. Murray pressed for the British annexation of Christmas Island to secure this potentially valuable mineral resource. That happened in 1888 when Christmas Island also came under the jurisdiction of the Straits Settlements and Murray, together with George Clunies-Ross founded the Christmas Island Phosphate Company. But personal disputes arose between the two because Clunies-Ross preferred to stay with his Malay workforce on the coconut plantations on the Cocos, so made Murray the sole manager of the company. Clunies-Ross was interested only in getting his share of the profits from the mine.[9]

The labour force on the Cocos was entirely Malay and Sunni Muslim. Several male members of the Clunies-Ross family married Malay women, but never converted to Islam. They remained devoted to their Christian faith and continued to live on Home Island, where they had built a stately mansion called Oceania House. They were supreme rulers of the islands, but there is nothing to indicate that they physically maltreated their workers. The 'Kings of the Cocos' looked after them and their families quite well. Every boy who reached the age of 14 came on the family's payroll and was offered employment on the plantations while the girls, when they turned 13, could find work in gardening, sewing sails, and sweeping and repairing roads.[10]

The rule of the Clunies-Ross family was perhaps benign, but as the islands were brought into the modern world after the two World Wars, their system of governance was becoming unacceptable. Everyone on the Cocos was dependent on jobs and schooling provided by the Clunies-Ross, and the workers were paid in a local currency called the Cocos Rupee. It consisted of notes made of sheepskin with the denomination printed on them and, since many of the workers were illiterate, the different shapes and sizes of the notes enabled their values to be recognised.[11] Later, those sheepskin notes were replaced by plastic tokens. But the catch was that the Cocos Rupee, whether made from sheepskin or plastic, could be used only in stores run and owned by the Clunies-Ross family.

The Cocos acquired their strategic significance during World War II when the first airstrip was built on West Island. Because the Japanese had occupied Christmas Island, the Cocos played an important role in the defence of not only the islands but also Australia. There were 3,000 soldiers sent to the islands, and planes took off from West Island to support the re-conquest of Singapore and Malaya. A telegraph station was also established on West Island. But, once the war was over, the British closed down the Cocos as an active-service station and evacuated all the military personnel from the atolls. While the evacuation was going on, the Cocos passed from a military to a civil control under a newly appointed administrator, a development that marked the beginning of the end of the rule of the Clunies-Ross family.

But the strategic importance of the islands increased in the 1950s as both Qantas and South African Airways from 1952 to 1967 used the airstrip on West Island as a refuelling stop on routes from Australia to South Africa. World War II was over but new conflicts erupted in the region, especially in British Malaya, where a communist insurgency broke out in the late 1940s. The Cocos regained their strategic significance. Some military personnel returned to the islands, and aircraft fuel depots were built for civilian as well as military use.

It was clear that the British government could not let Singapore keep the islands when that colony became self-governing in 1959. The handover to the Australians in 1955 was also timely, as Indonesian airspace was closed to them when Indonesia was ruled by Sukarno, a fiercely anti-Western autocrat. The West Island airstrip grew busy with not only Australian but also British and New Zealand planes stopping over to refuel because they had to fly around Indonesia on their way to Singapore. British aircraft carriers, then still plying the Indian Ocean, picked up provisions on the island, food and other necessities which had been flown in from mainland Australia. In 1966, the runway on West Island was extended to accommodate jets and other bigger aircraft.

By the 1970s, the Cocos had become an embarrassment to Australia. A visit by the UN's Committee of 24 – a special unit set up to oversee the transition of former colonies to full independence – in

1974 highlighted the lack of the islanders' awareness of their political rights and criticised their heavy dependence on the Clunies-Ross family.[12] Four years later, the Australian government forced the last of the Kings of the Cocos, John Cecil Clunies-Ross, into an agreement under which the islands were purchased for 6.25 million Australian dollars (US$5.89 million at that time's exchange rate).[13]

But he and his family continued to live undisturbed in their Oceania House until July 1983, when Australian Territories minister Tom Uren announced that the remaining five hectares, including Oceania House, would be compulsorily acquired with 'the intention that the Clunies-Ross leave the islands forever.'[14] Uren got support from the newly created Cocos Islands Council, and because independence was not a realistic option for such a small territory, it chose in a UN-supervised referendum held on 6 April 1984 to become an integral part of Australia. Of 259 valid votes cast, 229 voted for integration, 21 for free association and 9 for independence.[15] The game was over for the Clunies-Ross family. They had lost their 'coral kingdom'.[16] Oceania House is still there, but empty. No one has lived there since the Clunies-Ross family departed for the Australian mainland.

The Cocos now got their own police force consisting of five local constables entrusted with the duty of looking after the airport on West Island. In August 1986, a company of 126 Australian soldiers parachuted onto the Cocos in a long distance deployment test of airborne forces. It was the first military manoeuvre of its kind involving the Cocos after Australia had assumed full responsibility for the islands.

Christmas Island has an entirely different historical trajectory because of its phosphate mine, the management of which required a much closer relationship with Singapore than the more remote Cocos with its coconut plantations ever had. Hundreds of workers, mostly Chinese, were recruited from Singapore from where large quantities of its phosphate were also re-exported to Australia and Europe. Murray remained in charge of the operations until he died in a motorcycle accident in 1914. Apart from being a businessman he was also a botanist and was exploring the forest-clad interior of the island when he fell off his motorcycle.

Other managers took over and a settlement called Flying Fish Cove sprung up in a bay where ships could anchor. It was not a proper harbour, and the phosphate had to be brought to the freighters on smaller vessels. In the same year as Murray died, a railway was built to transport the phosphate from the mine to the shore. Stores were opened in Flying Fish Cove, which soon also had a Chinese temple and a Malay mosque. A police force consisting mostly of Sikhs from India was brought in to maintain law and order.

Eager to lay their hands on the mine and also to control a strategically important island south of Java, the Japanese moved on Christmas Island in early 1942. On 21 January, a Japanese submarine torpedoed and sank the Norwegian freighter *Eidsvold*, which had anchored in the bay outside Flying Fish Cove to load phosphate. There was panic on the island, and 50 British officials and engineers along with some from the Asian work force left for Perth in February, the only possible refuge because Singapore had fallen to the Japanese that same month. The Sikh policemen who remained had heard of Subhas Chandra Bose's Indian National Army – and rose in mutiny against the British. Five officers were killed and their bodies thrown into the sea. About 20 other Europeans were locked up in the small prison that the British had built on the island.[17] With no resistance left, the Japanese occupied Christmas Island unopposed on 31 March. The Japanese cruiser squadron that invaded the island landed a force comprising 450 infantry soldiers, 200 field engineers, and 200 artillery personnel equipped with four 120mm field guns and four 80mm anti-aircraft guns.[18]

The mine was in Japanese hands, but British warships that circled around the island made it nearly impossible to bring the phosphate out and food in. Survival became a problem and, in November 1943, more than half the population was moved to prisoner of war camps near Surabaya in the Japanese-occupied Dutch East Indies. Only 500 Chinese and Malays, 15 administrators from Japan and a contingent of Japanese soldiers remained on the island,

Japanese attempts to use Christmas Island as a base to occupy the Cocos proved more difficult than anticipated. The weakness of the occupying force on Christmas Island was one factor, a failed mutiny on the Cocos another. A bombardment from a Japanese submarine caused little damage, and the British were quick to act when a group of soldiers from Ceylon, who had been sent to the Cocos to defend the islands, mutinied. A firefight broke out, a Ceylonese soldier was killed and a British officer wounded. Seven of the mutineers were sentenced to death during a hastily arranged trial on the Cocos. Three were executed while the other four had their sentences commuted to life in prison. Those who were hanged were the only soldiers the British executed for mutiny during World War II.[19]

As the war was nearing its end, the Japanese soldiers on Christmas Island were becoming increasingly demoralised. The British reoccupied the island in October 1945 without meeting any real resistance. The Japanese were apprehended and sent to Singapore and then back to Japan. Eight of the Sikh policemen who had joined the Japanese were found in a camp in Java and were sentenced to life imprisonment. Peace was restored on Christmas Island, many of the workers returned from the camp near Surabaya – and the mine was once again turning out phosphate for export.

The Australian takeover in 1957 had no profound impact on Christmas Island or how the mine was being run. Nothing changed in the lives of the islanders until 1987, when the phosphate was almost depleted and local salaries had risen to the same levels as in mainland Australia. The mine was no longer profitable, and was closed. Attempts to reopen it were not successful, and Christmas Island had to look for another source of income. The island, with its rocky shoreline, is not suitable for beach tourism but another solution to attract outside visitors was found in 1993. A casino was opened on the island. Direct flights from Jakarta were introduced to attract gamblers but the 1997 Asian financial crisis affected Indonesia more than other countries in the region. Few, even the rich, had enough money to spend and the casino was closed down in 1998. The detention centre for illegal migrants gave the island some income, but even that is now gone. This leaves Christmas Island with an uncertain future.

Australia is not going to give it up though, because its strategic value remains regardless of difficulties for the local economy. It has been suggested that the airport on Christmas Island should be expanded and turned into an air base. Christmas Island was also once the intended location of a major spaceport with a launch facility to be operated by the Asia Pacific Space Centre. The plan did not materialise, probably because it was difficult to find enough money for it. But, as defence analyst Carlo Kopp puts it, 'the location is suitable for launches in both equatorial and polar orbits.'[20]

Australia's threat perception has long, at least officially, focused on possible aggression by Indonesia. The proximity to Indonesia, and the old leader Sukarno referring to northern Australia as 'Irian Selatan' or 'South Irian' when he was in power in the 1950s and early 1960s, certainly strengthen the argument that a possible invasion would come from the immediate north.[21] But even the most paranoid Australian defence analysts would at least in private agree that it would be extremely far-fetched to assume that Indonesia ever intended to invade Australia and that even if it did entertain such thoughts, it would not possess the military means to do so.

The Australian Department of Defence's 2016 Defence White Paper outlines three strategic interests that would guide the country's foreign and military policies, the first being the military alliance with the United States, the second the need to establish partnerships with the militaries in Papua New Guinea, East Timor and other Pacific island nations, and the third – a stable Indo-Pacific region and the need to address the increased military power of China.[22] The white paper states that 'the growth in the capability of China's military forces is the most significant example of regional military modernisation'[23] and goes on to say – perhaps so as not to appear too provocative – that 'other countries are also undertaking extensive modernisation programmes.'[24]

The dilemma of Australia's security planners is that the country's alliance with the United States has been the cornerstone of its defence strategy since the end of World War II – at the same time as China in more recent times has become its largest trading partner. In 1951, the Australia, New Zealand and United States Security Treaty (ANZUS) was formed consisting of those three countries. Australia was also a founding member of the Southeast Asia Treaty Organisation (SEATO) – which brought Australia together with the United States, Britain, New Zealand, the Philippines, Thailand and Pakistan – in 1954.

SEATO was dissolved in 1977, but ANZUS has survived although New Zealand has become a less than enthusiastic participant because of its anti-nuclear policy which has led to disputes with the United States. ANZUS today is basically a US-Australia military alliance. In the past, it was, like SEATO, a pact aimed at containing the spread of communism in the region. Today, it is China's expanding influence in the region that is the main concern.

Throughout the 1960s and well into the 1970s, it was China's policy to export world revolution, and the much-maligned domino theory – if one country fell to communism, others would fall like domino bricks lined up on a board – actually had some validity. China's support for the Communist Party of Burma (CPB) was part of that policy masterminded by Kang Sheng, Chinese security and intelligence chief and the official who maintained contacts with communist parties and other revolutionary organisations in the region and the world. He wanted to see Chinese influence spread through the region, all the way down to Australia.[25]

Once the CPB had taken over Myanmar, the next in line of the Maoist parties in the region was the Communist Party of Thailand (CPT), and then the Communist Party of Malaya (CPM) and the Communist Party of North Kalimantan (CPNK; the Malaysian communists considered Malaysia a colonial creation, so there was one communist party on the Malay Peninsula and another in Sarawak and Sabah on Borneo). Further down Southeast Asia was Partai Komunis Indonesia (PKI), the powerful communist party in Indonesia. And, eventually on Kang Sheng's list of the region's parties that he thought would emerge victorious: the Communist Party of Australia (Marxist-Leninist) (CPA[ML]).

Set up in 1964 and led by Ted Hill, an Australian barrister, who had broken with the main, pro-Soviet Communist Party of Australia, the CPA(ML) with its militant, Maoist stance did gain some support among radical students in Australia, and even from the Builders Labourers Federation in Sydney and the Tramways Union in Melbourne. But it was ludicrous to believe that Hill's tiny communist party would ever manage to stage a Maoist revolution in Australia, or that even any of the other, stronger communist parties in the region would win. That though was Kang Sheng's plan. He believed in the ultimate invincibility of the power of the Chinese Communist Party and the Maoist ideology it represented.[26]

Kang was not alone in that belief. Chinese premier Zhou Enlai declared in an internal Chinese Communist Party document dated

December 1971 that 'the general strategy of our nation for the present is: to promote war and further revolution.'[27] Vietnam was of course where the fiercest battles were being fought, but there China had to vie for influence with its then archenemy, the Soviet Union. The CPB, CPT, CPM, CPNK, PKI and CPA(ML) were all truly Maoist parties loyal to Beijing.

The domino that could fall was, from America's and Australia's more realistic point of view, Vietnam. A total of 60,000 Australians – ground troops, air force and navy personnel – served alongside the US Army in Vietnam between 1962 and 1972. There were 521 Australian soldiers who died in the war while 3,000 returned home wounded.[28] But Australia's participation in the war proved unpopular at home and anti-war demonstrations were held in all the major cities. Many protestors declared their support for the South Vietnamese guerrilla forces, *Front National pour la Libération du Sud Việt Nam*, or FNL, which was supported by the North, China and the Soviet Union.

While Australian soldiers went to fight in Vietnam, American GIs came to Australia for rest and recreation from the war. A red-light district full of seedy bars, strip joints, brothels and nightclubs sprung up in Kings Cross in Sydney, which made Australian participation in the Vietnam War even less popular among ordinary citizens. Heroin from Southeast Asia's Golden Triangle, where the borders of Myanmar, Thailand and Laos intersect, was brought to Sydney and the drug trade flourished in Kings Cross.

The Australian soldiers began to return home in November 1970 when the so-called 'Vietnamisation' of the war began. But it was only when Gough Whitlam of the Australian Labor Party (ALP) took office in December 1972 that all the soldiers were recalled. Whitlam also decided to establish diplomatic relations with the Democratic Republic of Vietnam, or North Vietnam, as well as China, thus ending his predecessors' policy of isolation and hostility towards both Beijing and Hanoi. On 24 June 1973 China and Australia signed their first trade agreement, and, in November, Whitlam became the first Australian prime minister to visit China. He was received with great fanfare, cheering crowds, rows of Chinese leaders and an hour-long meeting with the ageing Chairman Mao Zedong. Many felt that China and Australia were starting afresh.[29]

Whitlam was re-elected in 1974 – but was forced to resign in November 1975 under controversial circumstances. He had lost a majority in the Senate, and that made it possible for the opposition to win a vote in parliament, which, in turn, prompted Australia's governor-general John Kerr, the representative of the Queen, to dismiss his government. The opposition leader Malcolm Fraser was appointed interim prime minister awaiting new elections, which were held in December. Fraser's Liberal-Country Party Coalition won.

It is highly unusual for the governor-general, who holds a largely ceremonial post, to intervene in politics. But it was widely suspected – and reported – that the US Central Intelligence Agency (CIA) was behind the manoeuvres.[30] Rumours at the time had it that Whitlam intended to close the American bases in Australia, including possibly the vital signals intelligence station at Pine Gap near Alice Springs in the desert of central Australia. Construction of the station began in 1966 and it was completed in 1970. From there, the US in collaboration with Australia could monitor everything from the firing of ballistic missiles to local phone calls in the region.[31]

By 1975, the Vietnam war was over and the communists had won. In the end, no dominoes fell outside of Indochina, but Australia and the United States still had to be vigilant. Advanced signals intelligence facilities were at various points in time built at Shoal Bay on the coast of Australia's Northern Territory and at Geraldton north of Perth in Western Australia. Additional signals intelligence facilities are located near the capital Canberra. Documents leaked to the media by former US intelligence analyst Edward Snowden confirmed Australia's involvement in sharing intelligence information with the United States.[32] The Cocos could have been added to the list as its monitoring capabilities cover a large swathe of the Indian Ocean.

While regional terrorist networks, especially those based in Indonesia, are among the entities that are being monitored, there is no doubt that an increasingly assertive China is the main perceived threat and target for US-Australia defence cooperation even if it is only number three on the list of priorities in the 2016 defence white paper. And here money speaks. China-Australia trade was worth US$129 billion in 2017, an increase of 16 per cent compared to 2016.[33] China imports from Australia huge quantities of iron ore and other minerals, which are needed in its fast expanding industries, as well as wines and agricultural products such as soya beans. Australia would find it hard to maintain its high living standard without the income its business with China generates. A 2015 free-trade agreement with China strengthened that relationship and a subsequent Australian government report stated that 'China is Australia's number one export market, our largest source of international students, our most valuable tourism market, a major source of foreign direct investment and our largest agricultural goods market.'[34]

What Kang Sheng and his revolutionary allies failed to achieve on the battlefield in the Maoist era, the new China's economic czars have done through trade and economic expansion. They, too, believe in the invincibility of Chinese power, but along the lines charted by Deng Xiaoping and his 'capitalist roaders', as they were branded during the Cultural Revolution of the 1960s. The Myanmar corridor down to the Indian Ocean, once meant to export revolution and, in the Deng era, to strengthen China's economic and strategic influence, is now a fact – and Australia has become so economically dependent on China that maintaining a friction-free relationship with Beijing is of paramount importance when the government in Canberra formulates its foreign policy.

Australia's dilemma is reflected in two schools of thought. One has been articulated by Hugh White, a professor of strategic studies at the Australian National University, who in his book *The China Choice: Why America Should Share Power* and several essays argues that Australia does not have to choose between the United States, its traditional security patron, and China, its biggest trade partner, because there is a real danger that the Australians could find themselves drawn in a major war if they had to choose sides in the conflict between those two superpowers.[35]

The best solution for everybody concerned, White argues, would be if the United States gave up its claim to sole leadership and reach a compromise with China by which the two countries would share power in the Indo-Pacific region and become strategic partners rather than rivals.[36] White also believes that there are grounds for hope that the United States can reach a deal with China that Beijing would be willing to stick to.[37] Among the more controversial suggestions by White on how that would be accomplished would be for the Unites States 'to accept the legitimacy of the present system of government in China, including the monopoly of power of the CCP (the Chinese Communist Party).'[38]

Other security analysts argue that such a policy of appeasement has little chance of success because China is not interested in seeking a compromise with the United States. It wants control and domination. John Garnaut, who used to work for the *Sydney Morning Herald* and now is a security consultant, quotes in one of his essays on relations between China and Australia, Bilahari Kausikan, a former Singapore top diplomat as saying that, 'China does not just want you to comply with its wishes. Far more fundamentally, it wants you to think in such a way that you will of your own volition do what it wants to without being told. It's a form of psychological manipulation.'[39]

If Kausikan is right, that leaves little room for any kind of compromise and makes the idea of power sharing between the United States and China at best little more than wishful thinking and, at worst, a policy that resembles British prime minister Neville Chamberlain's failed policy of appeasement towards Germany in the 1930s. Germany never honoured the 1938 Munich Agreement with Britain. China has already shown that it does not respect any international agreements other than those it likes. All other agreements are treated as 'unequal treaties' and, therefore, invalid. In June 2017, for instance, Chinese foreign ministry spokesman Lu Kang surprised the residents of Hong Kong – and the world – by saying, 'now that Hong Kong has returned to the motherland for twenty years the Sino-British Joint Declaration, as a historical document, no longer has any realistic meaning.'[40]

The Sino-British Joint Declaration was signed on 19 December 1984 in Beijing by China's then premier Zhao Ziyang and Britain's prime minister at the time, Margaret Thatcher. Under the principle 'one country, two systems' Hong Kong would remain autonomous and nothing would change for 50 years after the Chinese takeover of sovereignty on 1 July 1997.[41] But on what was the twentieth anniversary of the Chinese takeover of Hong Kong, Lu also said that the Joint Declaration 'does not have any binding power on how the Chinese central government administers Hong Kong. Britain has no sovereignty, no governing power and no supervising power over Hong Kong. I hope relevant parties will take note of this reality.'[42]

The debate in Australia about China's growing influence comes against the backdrop of allegations of Chinese meddling in Australian universities and news stories about ethnically Chinese businessmen with ties to the government in Beijing giving generously to election campaigns.[43] In 2015, the Australian Security Intelligence Organisation (ASIO) even warned the major political parties that two of Australia's most generous donors had 'strong connections to the Chinese Communist Party' and that their 'donations might come with strings attached.'[44]

In December 2017, ALP lawmaker Sam Dastyari quit the Australian Senate after press reports about his connections with Huang Xiangmo, a donor with links to Beijing.[45] In 2016, Dastyari defended China's policy on the South China Sea at a gathering while he was flanked by Huang – and that is not the policy of Dastyari's party, the ALP.[46] In December 2017, it was revealed that Huang, an Australian-Chinese billionaire who is the chairman of the Yuhu Group of companies, had met ALP leader Bill Shorten who also reportedly wanted to secure donations.[47]

Huang gave money not only to the ALP but also to its main rival the Liberal Party of Australia (LPA). Because of the controversy and the ASIO warning, in March 2018 Huang told both the ALP and the LPA to hand back the altogether 2 million Australian dollars he had given in various donations, 'and I will happily donate them to charity.'[48] His challenge came after Western Australian MP Andrew Hastie had handed back all the money he had received in donations from Huang since 2012. When concerns over Chinese meddling in Australian politics were raised in the media and among politicians, the party-run Chinese tabloid *Global Times* said in an editorial that, 'Australia calls itself a civilised country. While it is economically dependent on China, it shows little gratitude.'[49] Garnaut argues that China's quest for international influence follows a pattern which he calls 'United Fronts' and is under the Liaison Department of the Chinese Communist Party, in effect an intelligence organisation.[50] According to Garnaut:

> United Front work is a methodology and strategic framework for exploiting the internal divisions of adversaries. The strategy involved forming tactical alliances with secondary adversaries in order to isolate,

> 'struggle against' and crush a designated primary enemy. Historically, the Party's leading agents were trained in the Soviet Union, and its institutional and ideological structures were grafted directly from the Comintern. Those structures were infused with a distinctly Chinese tradition of statecraft and they evolved to meet different challenges. The most important institutional difference between the Chinese Communist Party and its Soviet ancestor was the CCP's massive expansion of its 'united front' system during the protracted anti-Japanese and civil wars of the 1930s and 1940s. What began as a Leninist tactic was bureaucratised in China as a central United Front Work Department and an outward-facing analogue, the Chinese People's Political Consultative Conference. The point is that United Front work was instrumental in defending and extending the interests of the Party today.[51]

Evidently, although it is a policy dating back to Maoist days, it is a much more effective way to gain influence in Australia than supporting Hill's CPA(ML). And letting Australian politicians benefit from the largesse of allied donors is not the only way. Chen Yonglin, a Chinese diplomat who defected to Australia in 2005, believes that China has more than 1,000 agents operating in the country.[52] That makes perfect sense given China's vast economic interests in Australia. The agents concentrate on collecting commercial, technological and military data, and identifying zero-day cyber attack vulnerabilities. According to *The Sydney Morning Herald*, 'Australian defence-related programmes that China has hacked into include the F-35 joint strike fighter, the P-8 Poseidon electronic surveillance aircraft, and joint direct attack munitions (kits that allow bombs to be guided). Chinese hackers have also penetrated federal government departments and agencies, apparently to collect data and gain a better understanding of our operating systems.'[53]

The 1.3 million ethnic Chinese community in Australia is another target for Chinese intelligence services. That includes monitoring the activities of Chinese dissidents and Tibetans living in Australia. At the same time, some Chinese students are pressured to report on fellow Chinese students. Students from China who are on Chinese government scholarships are especially vulnerable because they are expected to 'show their gratitude' by informing on their fellow students and ethnic Chinese they may meet in Australia. They may also be told to find out more about certain Australian politicians. In July 2018, Australia decided to bar foreign university students from interning in MP's offices following concerns about alleged Chinese espionage and interference in domestic affairs.[54] In 2018, there were more than 500,000 foreign students at Australian educational institutions and 30 per cent of them came from China.[55]

Even more rattling for Australia's security establishment, in July 2017 it was disclosed that the police were seeking to charge Roger Uren, a former high-ranking intelligence official, with breaching spy agency laws after ASIO discovered a cache of classified files during a raid on his home in late 2015.[56] The documents contained details of what Western agencies knew about the operations of Chinese intelligence. The raid was prompted by allegations that Uren's wife, Sheri Yan, a well-known face on the Australia-China social scene, was a Chinese agent. She was accused of having introduced an alleged Chinese spy to her Australian contacts. As a result of these introductions, the alleged spy, Colonel Liu Chaoying, had several meetings with a wealthy Melbourne businessman with political connections.[57]

It was suspected that Uren had obtained the secret documents ASIO found when he, prior to 2001, served with the prime minister's intelligence analysis agency, the Office of National Assessments. The ASIO agents who raided Uren's home in Canberra were working closely with the US Federal Bureau of Investigation, who had arrested and charged Sheri Yan in New York in October 2015 with bribing the former president of the UN General Assembly, John Ashe. Yan pleaded guilty to being involved in the transfer of US$200,000 allegedly made by a company owned by Chau Chak Wing, who had also donated funds to Australian politicians.[58] Yan was sent to jail but her husband has staunchly denied that he, or his wife, ever spied for China. Chau Chak Wing was not charged with any wrongdoing, and sued a journalist for defamation. Uren asserted that he and his wife believed the money paid to Ashe was a speaking fee, not a bribe.[59]

Whether Australia wishes to admit it or not, the country has become so involed in regional power plays that it will be impossible to stay neutral in the way Hugh White advocates. The importance of continued cooperation between the United States and Australia is highlighted in most documents by the Australian Department of Defence and the

Australian Army. In November 2011, then US president Barack Obama announced that 2,500 US troops would be based in the northern city of Darwin. This was part of his policy to strengthen the United States presence in Pacific Asia. Obama then assured Beijing that it was not a counterweight to its growing influence in the region, but it did not convince the Chinese.[60] The official *Xinhua* news agency published a statement saying 'China has always opposed any moves that complicate the disputes with involvement of external forces, insisting bilateral dialogue is the best option.'[61]

Australia's reputation in the region suffered a severe setback when then US president George Bush in 2003 characterised the country as America's 'deputy sheriff' in the region – and Australia's prime minister John Howard's response was evasive and ambiguous when confronted by the media about that new designation in regional power politics.[62] Bush's remark came in the wake of an Australia-led intervention in East Timor that restored order after people there had voted in a UN-supervised referendum for independence from Indonesia and pro-Indonesian militias had gone on a rampage in the territory. The Malaysian politician Mahathir Mohamad shot back, saying that 'Australia has to choose whether it's an Asian country or a western country. If you take the position of being a deputy sheriff of America, you cannot very well be accepted by the countries of this region.'[63]

Not to be seen as being only an ally of the United States, Australia has also initiated defence cooperation with India. But this is about more than simply improving Australia's image in the region. Both Australia and India share common security interests. Putting strategic cooperation between Australia and India in an historical perspective, an Indian participant at a conference in New Delhi in February 2013 reminded the Australians about the aforementioned *SMS Emden*'s raids in the waters around India, Southeast Asia and Australia which ended with its sinking near the Cocos.[64] That was possible only because of an intelligence network in the region that stretched from the Andaman Islands, where the British then had a base, to Sydney.

Today, a hundred years later, Australia is a sovereign nation, albeit a member of the Commonwealth with Queen Elizabeth as the country's head of state, and the military of independent India commands the bases on the Andaman Islands – plus advanced electronic equipment for monitoring the eastern part of the Indian Ocean. The sinking of the Kaiser's ship is history, but now there are other challenges in the region, the Indian participant pointed out.[65] India and Australia must therefore strengthen cooperation in the same spirit as that which prevailed in 1914.

Whether the Australian participants at the conference were impressed is difficult to determine, but military cooperation on all levels between India and Australia has increased in recent years. India is identified in the Australian Department of Defence's 2016 Defence White Paper as an important partner in the region – which does not rule out the old alliance with the United States. That alliance will remain while cooperation with India will increase. According to the White Paper, India plays a major role in the region and 'in addition to having a stronger role in the Indo-Pacific region, India is also likely to become a more active and influential global power, supported by its economic growth. India could be the world's third largest economy before 2030.'[66] The White Paper also highlighted the fact that development in the Indian Ocean is an important aspect of Australia's security policy planning. The Indian Navy's use of the Cocos to refuel and collect supplies, which has been suggested, should be seen in that context.

But Australia's relationship with India is not without its problems. India can openly challenge China, but Australia cannot. Although Australia is concerned about China's ever-increasing role in the Indian Ocean, Canberra simply cannot afford to be seen as hostile to China. Australia has therefore participated in some but not all Exercise Malabar exercises and instead preferred to hold bilateral naval drills with India, the United States and sometimes Japan – and those have often been done under cover of being exercises to combat pirates or to assist in rescue work in the event of natural disasters. Australia also collaborates militarily with Singapore and Vietnam, so despite the subterfuge it cannot have escaped anyone's attention that China is its main concern. Vietnam and China are historical enemies and Singapore is China's rival when it comes to gaining influence in overseas Chinese communities. And Australian then foreign minister Julie Bishop received a sharp rebuke from her Chinese counterpart, Wang Yi, after she in 2013 condemned Beijing's declaration of an air defence identification zone in the East China Sea.[67] Wang said he believed Australia's stance could 'jeopardise relations between the two nations.'[68] Bishop further angered the Chinese when in a speech at a conference in Singapore in mid-March 2017 she said that China's lack of democracy was a constraint on the country reaching its full economic potential.[69] During a visit to Australia in late March 2017, China's premier Li Keqiang warned Australia not to take sides in the South China Sea dispute and other regional conflicts 'as happened during the Cold War.'[70] He went on to assert[71] that Beijing pursued an 'independent foreign policy of peace' based on 'national development paths suited to our traditions.'[72]

Australia's dance on the tightrope in the conflict – or to cite Hugh White: 'our aim is to convince Washington that we are supporting it against China, and to convince Beijing that we are not'[73] – is in the long run untenable. Its politicians and academics, who are trying to appear neutral in the conflict, will sooner or later have to face up to reality. But that will not be easy with a new president in the White House who seems to be less committed to the region than his predecessors. Donald Trump's first phone call soon after his inauguration in January 2017 to then Australian prime minister Malcolm Turnbull was outright abusive. Turnbull told Trump that Obama had promised to take 1,250 of the illegal immigrants Australia holds on Nauru and Manus – and Trump shot back that the deal was 'dumb' and 'stupid.'[74] At the end of the call, Trump told Turnbull: 'I have been making these calls all day and this is the most unpleasant call all day. Putin was a pleasant call. This is ridiculous.'[75]

Both Trump and Turnbull tried to smooth over the discord, but the damage was done and it was clear that Trump does not possess the necessary qualities as a statesman – and that his commitment to America's traditional allies in the Indo-Pacific region is shaky, to say the least. But America's defence planners may be cleverer than that, realising that China's influence in the region cannot be contained without a partnership that includes as many as possible of the other concerned countries. And whether Trump is abusive or not, Australia's role is pivotal in that context and the facts speak for themselves.

Australia plans to spend US$140 billion on military hardware over the next decade, the largest build-up of its military capabilities in peacetime in the country's history.[76] 'I make zero apologies for wanting to ensure the nation's security and to protect our servicemen and women,' Christopher Pyne, Australia's defence industry minister said in August 2018. 'We live in a more unsettled region than we have seen in several decades...one of the developments in our region in the last few years is the militarisation of islands in the South China Sea by the People's Republic of China.'[77] Beijing's push to modernise its armed forces and its move into the Indian Ocean has prompted a response from other countries in the region, and set off an arms race of which we have probably seen only the beginning. And despite Canberra's reluctance to declare openly where it stands and, for some, its attempt to appear neutral, Australia's security planners appear to be fully aware of the consequences of China's increasing influence in the Indian Ocean. A war may not be necessary, but a Neville Chamberlain-style approach may not work either.

And here, Australia's Indian Ocean islands will play an important role in protecting the country's interests. The 2016 Defence White Paper states that 'infrastructural work' on 'the Cocos (Keeling) Islands will be needed to ensure airfields and associated facilities to support the new fleet of P-8A maritime surveillance and response aircraft.'[78] Infrastructural work is also being undertaken on Christmas Island, and, as a 2017 Australian government document states, 'the strategic location of Australia's Indian Ocean Territories provides agencies, particularly the Australian Departments of Defence and Immigration and Border Protection, with a unique staging point for the protection of Australian Government interests in the region.'[79]

According to the same document, defence capabilities and assets in the Indian Ocean territories include 'manned and unmanned maritime surveillance and response aircraft, offshore patrol vessels, destroyers, frigates, support vessels, small patrol boats, watercraft, and naval combat helicopters...and the Indian Ocean territories are well placed as critical assets in the theatre of anti-submarine warfare.'[80]

Apart from Christmas Island and the Cocos, Australia has also a third external territory in the Indian Ocean, the Heard and McDonald Islands, not far from Kerguelen. Originally claimed by Britain in 1910, they became Australian in 1947, are uninhabited, covered in ice – and located 4,099 kilometres southwest of Perth. Scientists visit the

Heard and McDonald Islands occasionally though there is nothing to indicate that they are playing any role in Australia's defence plans. But the strategic importance of Christmas Island and the Cocos should not be underestimated. Those old bailiwicks of phosphate miners and the 'Kings of the Cocos' could, as Ross Babbage wrote three decades ago, sooner or later come to serve as unsinkable aircraft carriers and resupply ships.

9

THE FUTURE

It has long been assumed that an armed conflict involving global as well as regional superpowers would begin around the Spratly Islands in the South China Sea, through which vital oil supplies pass from the Middle East to East Asia's booming economies, and where several countries have overlapping territorial claims, China has built artificial islands inside disputed maritime areas, and China as well as the United States have sent warships as a show of strength to each other. When the Permanent Court of Arbitration in The Hague in July 2016 ruled in favour of a complaint brought to it by the Philippines, concluding that China has no 'historical right' to the territory it claims in the South China Sea including most of the Spratly Islands, China was infuriated. China rejected the ruling, but a new international dimension was added to the dispute.

This is why the South China Sea is one of the world's most closely watched regions. Nothing happens there without spy satellites from various countries zooming in on the action, whether it be the movements of warships, new Chinese construction projects, or any unusual developments that could affect the balance of power in the area. And although the US and others have protested against China's policy of turning underwater shoals and reefs – because that is what the Spratly Islands consist of – into actual islands with harbours and airfields, little has been done, or is likely to be done, about it. In many ways, China has won the battle for the Spratlys because no one really wants a conflict in the South China Sea, which would have immediate and disastrous consequences. All that the United States, and the countries that have territorial claims in the area – which apart from China include the Philippines, Vietnam, Malaysia, Brunei and Taiwan – can do is protest. And, on a practical level, the US and its allies can send ships and aircraft to ensure that freedom of navigation through the South China Sea prevails.

It is far more likely that something would go fundamentally wrong in the Indian Ocean where, despite attempts at forging alliances, the situation is much less clear when it comes to regional defence commitments. Widespread corruption in the Maldives and the Comoros, and the Seychelles' reliance on so-called financial services, have made those Indian Ocean nations more vulnerable to manipulation by outside powers than any country around the South China Sea would ever be. Vastly different historical backgrounds and the diverse ethnic composition of the Indian Ocean nations are other factors contributing to the complexity of the region. All the island states have long histories of political instability and exploitation by colonialists, pirates, mercenaries, fraudsters and tricksters, and, more recently in the case of the Maldives, threats posed by Islamic extremists.

And then there is the presence of Western powers, which want to defend their possessions and interests without being sure of who, exactly, there regional allies should be. The United States has its massive base on Diego Garcia, the French are holding on to Réunion, Mayotte and Kerguelen, and the Australians are contemplating what to do with Christmas Island and the Cocos (Keeling) Islands. India, of course, is shoring up its naval capacities on the Andaman and Nicobar Islands. In late October 2018, the French president Emmanuel Macron announced that France would send an aircraft carrier to the Indian Ocean in 2019, 'to defend freedom of navigation.'[1] On a trip to Australia in May 2018, Macron had said that no country could be allowed to dominate the region and that France, Australia and India have a responsibility to protect the region from 'hegemony' – a veiled reference to growing Chinese assertiveness in the Asia-Pacific.[2]

But the lack of any cohesive, coordinated policy and a reluctance to identify China as the main adversary have made the situation in the

Indian Ocean far more unpredictable, and therefore potentially more volatile, than in the world's other maritime regions where superpower interests have also collided, including not only the South China Sea but also the East China Sea and the Pacific Ocean.

It is not even clear what China's intentions are behind its Belt and Road Initiative (BRI). Is it a well-laid and finely orchestrated plan to extend Chinese hegemony over much of the developing world, as its critics claim, or, as the Chinese assert, simply an attempt to replace America's worldwide domination with a multipolar order where there is a more efficient allocation of resources and integration of markets which everyone would benefit from?[3] And could China be overstretching itself with what it has said are projects amounting to several trillion dollars?

Originally called the One Belt One Road Initiative, abbreviated OBOR, the plan was first unveiled by Xi Jinping during visits to Kazakhstan and Indonesia in September and October 2013. The first, curious name alluded to the opening of the proposed overland 'Silk Road Economic Belt' connecting China with Europe through Central Asia, and the 'Maritime Silk Road' that the Chinese claim existed in ancient times across the Indian Ocean. But the name was modified to the BRI in 2016 as the Chinese government had come to the conclusion that the emphasis on the word 'one' was open to misinterpretation.[4]

Bloomberg's Yuen Yuen Ang argues that the modus operandi for the BRI 'is typical in China, where the central government often issues broad directives and expects lower-ranking officials to figure out how to fulfil them.'[5] The hallmark of such communist-style mass campaigns, she maintains, is that 'everyone pitches in with frenzied enthusiasm and little coordination. Vast resources and human capital are mobilised toward one goal. Banks, businesses and officials across the country participate en masse, rather than dividing up responsibilities, as local governments rush to meet what they see as their superiors' wishes.'[6]

The BRI should also be seen in the broader context of being China's 'third revolution.'[7] The first was when Mao Zedong and his communist party emerged victorious from the Chinese civil war and proclaimed the People's Republic on 1 October 1949. China was no longer 'enslaved' by foreign powers – as the communists had claimed it was – and Mao managed to unite the country by occupying Tibet, which China had long claimed though the Tibetans had a different view on the question of sovereignty, integrating the mainly Muslim region of Xinjiang, which until then had been ruled by local warlords, and defeating other warlords elsewhere in the country. The second revolution occurred after the death of Mao in 1976, when the reformist 'capitalist roader' Deng Xiaoping seized power, introduced free-market reforms and turned China into an industrial powerhouse. And now it is the turn of Xi Jinping whose vision is to cement China's status as a world power.

Xi was born on 15 July 1953, four years after the end of the Chinese civil war, or revolution as the communists would call it, in Fuping county, Shaanxi province. His father, Xi Zhongxun, had fought alongside Mao against the Japanese and later the nationalist Chinese Guomindang. He was a member of the central Committee of the Communist Party of China (CPC) and served for a while in the 1950s as vice-premier under Zhou Enlai. But the older Xi was purged and arrested during the Cultural Revolution in the 1960s while the younger Xi was sent to a small village in Yan'an to be 're-educated.'[8] In rural Yan'an, Xi appears to have spent most of his time shovelling dung and arguing with his peasant boss. His older half-sister, who was also there, could not stand the abuse and hanged herself. Xi ran away and hid out in Beijing for a while before being arrested and sent to a work camp. But he must have been well behaved this time, because in 1975 he was allowed to study chemical engineering at Beijing's prestigious Tsinghua University.

After the death of Mao in 1976 and the return to power of Deng, the older Xi was rehabilitated and the younger Xi began to rise in the political hierarchy. In 1985, as part of a Chinese delegation that went to the United States to study agriculture, he stayed with an American family in Iowa, which was his first experience of life outside China.[9] In 1997, he became an alternate member of the CPC central committee, and although he did study Marxism-Leninism-Mao Zedong-Thought at the School of Humanities and Social Sciences, also at Tsinghua University, his role model was the pragmatic reformer Deng rather than the fanatical revolutionary Mao. As governor of Fujian in 2000, he encouraged Taiwanese businessmen to invest in the province. He left Fujian in 2002 to become party chief in Zhejiang province, where he oversaw spectacular economic growth. During that time, he supported promising local entrepreneurs, including Jack Ma, whose Alibaba later grew to become a global company rivalling Amazon.[10]

After that, his rise was even more rapid – and he soon reached the very top of China's hierarchy in 2007 when then Chinese president Hu Jintao wanted to crack down on corruption in Shanghai. Xi was appointed local party chief tasked with clearing up the mess, which he did with utmost efficiency. In the same year, he was promoted to be a member of a standing committee that was going to lead China for the next five years.

Xi then began to travel outside China, and while visiting Mexico in 2009, he met a group of overseas Chinese and explained to them why China had not been affected by the global financial crisis. The greatest contribution towards the whole human race, made by China, Xi said, was to save its 1.3 billion people from hunger – and he went on to blast what he saw as meddlesome foreigners: 'There are some foreigners who have eaten their fill and have nothing better to do than point their fingers at our affairs. China does not, first, export revolution, second, export poverty and hunger, or third, cause unnecessary trouble for them. What else is there to say?'[11]

On 15 November 2012, Xi was elected general secretary of the CPC and, during a visit to the National Museum of China, he brought up the theme of China's 'rejuvenation' calling it 'the greatest dream for the Chinese nation in modern history.'[12] As China scholar Elizabeth C. Economy wrote in her book about Xi and his third revolution:

> The site of Xi's speech at the National Museum was not accidental. While much of China's history is marked by revolution, political and social upheaval, and discontinuities in leadership and political ideologies, the museum celebrates the ideal continuity in Chinese history. Quoting from both Mao and ancient Chinese poets, Xi used the museum as a backdrop to make clear the linkages between an imperial China and a China led by the Communist Party.[13]

Then, in March 2013, Xi became the president of China and later that year set forth his OBOR/BRI, which would show the greatness of the Chinese nation on the world stage. It could be argued that the idea was not entirely new. The curious monument at Jiegao on the China-Myanmar border was erected in the early 1990s and showed that China definitely had a plan to extend at least its economic influence down to the Indian Ocean. But Xi gave it a new meaning. He turned a plan for trade expansion into a grand strategy to dominate the world.

But, typically, five years after it was launched, no Chinese ministry has been assigned to plan or monitor the ambitious BRI initiatives, or even to draw up plans for future projects. Or, as Yuen Yuen Ang points out in her study of the BRI, 'top officials still haven't defined what constitutes a BRI project or who qualifies as a participant in the initiative. As a result, every investment project, whether public or private, profit-making or money-losing, honest or dishonest, claims to be part of the bandwagon.'[14] The *New York Times* reported on 1 August 2018 that attempts were being made to win friends with grandiose schemes, including plans for an indoor ski slope near the beaches of Australia's Gold Coast, a spa with Chinese medicine in the Czech Republic, and cultural centres and amusement parks in the Philippines, Indonesia, Vietnam Italy, Hungary and Serbia.[15]

In a 2016 article, Yang Minghong, a Chinese scholar at Sichuan University in Chengdu, tried to point out the differences between America's Marshall Plan to rebuild Europe after World War II and China's BRI, arguing that the Marshall Plan was 'closely connected with the Cold War' and it enabled the United States to 'intentionally penetrate its political ideology to the European countries through economic aid and development.'[16] No one doubts that the Marshall Plan was launched during the initial stages of the Cold War and one of its aims was to consolidate West European resistance to the eastern, Soviet Bloc. But to claim that the US tried to impose democracy on Europe's democracies, or Germany which had been a democracy before a totalitarian regime took over, is utterly absurd. The BRI, by contrast, Yang argues is a benign international aid plan that 'will not promote the development of the Cold War pattern' but 'should be jointly built through consultation to meet the interests of all.'[17]

The problem for China is that not everyone in Southeast Asia and the Indian Ocean region sees it that way. Few Southeast Asian leaders dare to oppose China openly – but Malaysia's prime minister Mahathir Mohammed has no such qualms. At the end of a five-day visit to China in August 2018, Mahathir, standing next to China's premier Li Keqiang at a press conference in Beijing, did not mince his words. He shocked his

Chinese hosts by declaring that 'we do not want a situation where there is a new version of colonialism happening because poor countries are unable to compete with rich countries, therefore we need fair trade.'[18] He was referring specifically to a number of BRI-related infrastructure programmes in Malaysia, and declared that billions of dollars worth of China-backed projects would be cancelled. 'It's about pouring in too much money, which we cannot afford, cannot repay, and also because we don't need those projects for Malaysia at this moment,'[19] Mahathir told the audience at the press conference in Beijing.

Mahathir not only cancelled infrastructure projects but also canned plans to build a new multibillion-dollar 'Forest City' for up to 700,000 residents on reclaimed land near Singapore. According to Mahathir, it was 'built for foreigners, not built for Malaysians.'[20] Mahathir obviously saw it as a Chinese city in Malaysia and declared that foreigners would not be allowed to buy residential units there, which, in effect, ditched the project.[21]

Mahathir, who was 93 at the time, had made a stunning political comeback during elections that were held in Malaysia in May that year. He had served as prime minister from 1981 to 2003 at which time he oversaw the country's transformation from a middle-developed country dependent on tin and rubber to a newly industrialised, multi-sectored market economy. But he was hardly known for his tolerance of dissent. He was a true authoritarian who stifled the free press and did not hesitate to send critics, among them his deputy Anwar Ibrahim, to jail for what most neutral observers saw as trumped-up charges.

But the corruption of a government led by Najib Razak, the prime minister who lost the May 2018 election, became too much for him to bear, and he turned against the party he had once led, the United Malays National Organisation and allied himself with his old foe Anwar Ibrahim. Najib had visited China in late 2016 and scored several deals – those Mahathir later cancelled. But Najib's downfall was mostly due to a major scandal involving the looting of Malaysia's sovereign wealth fund and accepting huge monetary 'gifts' on the order of US$700 million from Saudi Arabia. The money, Najib claimed, was thanks for fighting the Islamic State. But Najib has no record of having been involved in such a fight and the money went into his personal bank account.[22]

There are striking similarities here between Mahathir and the Maldives' Maumoon Abdul Gayoom, another elderly politician who returned from retirement to join the opposition against a corrupt regime that had lost the support of the people. Like Gayoom, Mahathir also has a daughter with more liberal views who might have influenced him to stand up for high moral principles. And, like Gayoom, Mahathir began his political career as a dissident. His first book, *The Malay Dilemma*, was published in 1970 and was highly critical of Abdul Rahman, then Malaysia's prime minister, but also had a fiercely nationalistic message.[23]

Mahathir argued for affirmative action to be taken to enable the indigenous Malays to break the dominant role the Malaysian Chinese, descendants of immigrants, played in the country's economy. *The Malay Dilemma* was banned by the authorities and it was not until the early 1980s, after he had become prime minister, that it could once again be bought in the country's bookstores. Mahathir's aversion to Chinese economic domination at home could have been a contributing factor to his remarkably frank outpouring of opinions in Beijing in August 2018. But whatever the reason for what he did and said, his words echoed concerns that are not uncommon in the region.

The warnings in 2018 by the Asian Development Bank's Takehiko Nakao and Christine Lagarde of the International Monetary Fund (IMF) about a dept trap are being taken seriously by social activists, economists, academics and even governments in the region. The Hambantota port and airport project in Sri Lanka is held up as an example of how it can go fundamentally wrong when a country relies on heavy borrowing from China, is unable to repay the debt, and ends up losing everything. Even China's long-time ally Pakistan had to turn to the IMF in October 2018 for a bailout as its foreign currency reserves had dropped to US$8 billion, only enough to pay for two months worth of imports.[24] But even so, China announced at the same time that there would be more projects under the US$60 billion China-Pakistan Economic Corridor project, which would open an overland trade route from China's Xinjiang region down to Gwadar and other ports on the Arabian Sea. Chinese foreign ministry spokesman Lu Kang said that China-Pakistan ties would make headway under the newly appointed prime minister, the former cricket star Imran Khan, who had won the elections in July.[25]

Lessons learned from Hambantota and Gwadar prompted Myanmar in September 2018 to scale back its China-backed Kyaukpyu deepwater port, initially projected at US$7.3 billion, to a more realistic US$1.3 billion, and with the Chinese share of the joint projects reduced from 85 to 70 per cent.[26] Myanmar's heavy dependence on China was highlighted without mentioning it by name when the commander-in-chief of Myanmar's armed forces, senior general Min Aung Hlaing, spoke before the cadets at the country's National Defence College on 8 October: 'Myanmar is an independent and sovereign nation...if a country accepts the influence and interference of another country, the former will not be a sovereign country,'[27]

When China pushed for the construction of a 873-kilometre high-speed rail link connecting Yunnan with Thailand's eastern seaboard, the military government in Bangkok did not reject it, but found ways to stall the plan. A line through Laos is under construction, but without its connection to Thailand, China will not be able to link up with the rest of Southeast Asia and as far south as Singapore, a stated BRI goal for the region.[28] The Thais, it seems, prefer to work with Japan, which offers better quality for its infrastructure projects and is less controversial in today's geostrategic context.

China also sees dangers ahead for the BRI, but of a completely different kind. Wang Yiwei, a Chinese scholar and former diplomat, identifies five such potential risks in an English-language book promoting the BRI.[29] The first two are natural and environmental risks. Natural disasters such as landslides could be a problem when roads are built in mountainous areas. The environment may be affected by extensive mining resulting in water pollution as the result of the opening up of remote areas. Although Wang does not mention it, rising sea levels around low-lying islands such as the Maldives would come under these types of risks as well.

Number three on Wang's list concerns the threat of what he calls 'extremist forces.' He mentions the Islamic State and unidentified 'armed groups in Southeast Asia' as forces that would pose 'a threat to the construction of the Belt and Road.'[30] He believes that the BRI is 'destined to be attacked by extremist forces' because 'the initiative is aimed to achieve regional prosperity and wealth-sharing, while various extremist groups' purpose is to attack existing governments and realise their own dictatorships.'[31]

The only armed rebel groups in Southeast Asia are ethnic insurgents in Myanmar, Muslim and communist forces in the Philippines, and Muslim separatists in southern Thailand. Of those the groups in Myanmar would be of specific concern as they operate in the economically important 'Myanmar Corridor', which would explain China's active participation in that country's peace process. China may have almost full control over the United Wa State Army (UWSA) but less over the Kachin Independence Army and other ethnic groups. Those groups may not pose a threat because most of them are allied with the UWSA, but the activities of Rohingya rebels, some of whom are connected with militant Islamic groups in Bangladesh, Pakistan and Saudi Arabia, have certainly attracted the attention of China's security services.

The main such group, the Arakan Rohingya Salvation Army (ARSA), which carried out the attacks in 2016 and 2017 that led to a massive, brutal response from the Myanmar army, is certainly on Beijing's radar. In March 2018, an unnamed leader of a UWSA-led alliance of ethnic armies in northern Myanmar said: 'ARSA has networked with Uighur Muslim terrorists in Xinjiang Uighur Autonomous Region. So, China issued a warning to the Northern Alliance not to network or cooperate with ARSA.'[32] With Uighur rebels active in Xinjiang, the starting point of the China-Pakistan Economic Corridor, and ARSA in the hills and jungles north of Kyaukpyu, China has good reason to be worried about attacks of the nature mentioned by Wang.

Number four on Wang's list is the 'threat of non-governmental organisations'. According to Wang: 'During the construction of the Belt and Road Initiative, there are possible risks in which non-governmental organisations (NGOs), mainly those from the West, mobilise the masses to protest. China's goodwill move is likely to be distorted by various Western NGOs as regional dominance construction under the "China threat" rhetoric [sic].'[33] He goes on to argue that 'there is a great possibility that China will be accused by NGOs of plundering resources of related countries and damaging the ecological environment. And with that accusation as an excuse, various NGOs are able to mobilise the masses to boycott.'[34]

The way to counter that threat, Wang writes, is to 'welcome local people with an inclusive attitude to extensively participate in the building of Belt and Road…and make local people, particularly the young, understand why their Chinese friends are there, and why the Belt and Road Initiative was proposed, so that they can take the Belt and Road as their own road to pursue.'[35] Others would argue that no evil propaganda by foreign NGOs was needed to convince 'the masses' in Myanmar that the Myitsone hydroelectric project, which was going to flood 766 square-kilometres of virgin forest land, would have been harmful to the environment.

Fifth and last on Wang's list is 'maritime security risk'. In order to minimise threats on the oceans, Wang writes that 'we should establish effective monitoring mechanisms, and address the problem of security force staffing on ships.'[36] He mentions piracy off the coast of Somalia as the main problem – but that, if anything, is an excuse. China's naval presence in the Indian Ocean consists mainly of submarines, which would not be of much use if they were sent there to chase pirates. In October 2018, a Type 039A Yuan class SSK, diesel-electric attack submarine, accompanied by a submarine rescue vessel, was spotted in the Indian Ocean – and in the east, so not anywhere near Somalia.[37]

There is also a sixth risk, which is not among those presented and analysed by Wang. China is not particularly astute when it comes to dealing with countries which hold democratic elections and which are, therefore, vulnerable to shifting political winds. Malaysia, the Maldives, Sri Lanka and even Myanmar offer examples of countries where China has thrown in its lot with one group of rulers only to see them being replaced by another who do not share the views of its predecessors. This, of course, comes from being a one-party state where upheavals among the ruling elite are not uncommon, but power stays within that elite and is not threatened by elections or public opinion.

The BRI may be haphazard, uncoordinated and, as Yuen Yuen Ang argues, lacking a proper plan but the geostrategic significance of China's push into the Indian Ocean should not be underestimated. And number five on Wang's list of risks that could derail the BRI is precisely where China's interests are colliding with those of India, Japan and the West. The Chinese have built a military base in Djibouti, and sent submarines into the Indian Ocean, not because they are worried about pirates. And, at least according to Australian analyst David Brewster, the facility in Djibouti is only the first in a network of military bases that China intends to establish in the Indian Ocean region. He discusses the often-raised possibility of Gwadar, Hambantota and an island in the Maldives being transformed into staging points for the Chinese navy and air force.[38]

Brewster also mentions Kyaukpyu and that 'a Chinese naval base there would be well placed to threaten India's naval dominance of the Bay of Bengal and protect (or threaten) the sea lanes that cross the bay and transit the Strait of Malacca.'[39] But the powerful Myanmar military will most certainly resist any move to include elements consistent with naval requirements, not commercial use, in the Kyaukpyu port project. Paragraph 41 of Myanmar's 2008 constitution, which was drafted under the aegis of the military, also states that 'no foreign troops shall be permitted to be deployed in the territory of the Union.'[40] That, of course, does not exclude Chinese access to signals intelligence information the Myanmar military may pick up on listening stations on the Coco Islands and elsewhere, or the possibility of Chinese naval ships docking and resupplying in Myanmar ports, including Kyaukpyu.

Whenever rumours begin to circulate about the possible construction of more Chinese bases in the region, they are routinely denied by Beijing. And it is certainly correct, as China specialist Tom Miller argues in his book *China's Asia Dream*, that Beijing is far more interested in securing alternative routes for its energy imports and protecting commercial sea lanes than it is in building a new empire.[41] China has understandable military interests in the Indian Ocean, but it knows that it cannot challenge the combined power of the US, Indian, Japanese and Australian navies, which, he opines, are operating more closely than hitherto.[42]

However a desire to protect vital supply lines comes with a concomitant requirement for military protection of such seaways – and even if the navies of friendly countries do operate more closely than was the case a decade or two ago, the alliance to which they belong is highly informal and is by no means equivalent to a proper military pact. India has an independent mind when it comes to Washington's role in the region – it is an equal partner with its own foreign policy preferences, not a subservient ally of the United States – and America's commitment to the defence of the Indian Ocean region is far from clear under its enigmatic new president, Donald Trump.

And where does Australia stand? It remains caught between a desire to protect its fundamental, democratic values – and sovereignty – and a heavy economic dependence on China which is affecting its foreign policy options. In October 2018, the official media outlet *The China Daily* published a blistering editorial criticising Australia, saying that Canberra is walking a 'tightrope' between the United States and China.[43] 'To cover up their real intention of jumping on the US bandwagon to contain China,' the editorial continued, 'Tokyo and Canberra pointed accusing fingers at China's so-called maritime assertiveness... expressing concern about the situation in the East and China seas... Canberra and Tokyo should not allow the recurrence of the Cold War paranoia...they should [beware of] letting the US lead them by the nose as it pursues a confrontational strategy.'[44] The editorial concluded that there is a 'fragile peace' in the region which could be 'shattered by the slightest misstep.'[45] And it is precisely the 'misstep' factor that makes the unsettled situation in the Indian Ocean potentially much more dangerous than that in the closely guarded and monitored South China Sea. And that, coupled with the volatility of several of the small Indian Ocean island states, has brought about a situation where even a minor incident – or accident – could indeed trigger a broader conflict.

Wang made it clear in his list of potential risks facing the BRI that the West is the enemy, even if he mentioned only evil NGOs, which would stir up trouble by falsely claiming that China seeks regional dominance. But Chinese spokespersons have also been more explicit than that. In an editorial published by the official news service *Xinhua* on 29 May 2015, the United States was accused of never missing 'an opportunity to talk about the "China threat"...[and] overlooking China's commitment to peaceful development, the US strategic rebalance toward the Asia Pacific – a euphemism for containing rising powers such as China – only serves Washington's own agenda of expanding its political and military presence in the region.'[46] That does not leave much room for the kind of 'power-sharing agreement' envisaged by Hugh White.[47] Neither a rising China nor the United States under Trump, or even his successors, would be interested in something as unrealistic and unworkable as such a deal.

Other Australian analysts argue that their country will have to choose *between* China and the United States. Benjamin Herscovitch of

China Policy, a Beijing-based advisory firm, and a former Australian government official, wrote in 2015 that 'on a growing number of high-stakes foreign policy questions, Australia simply cannot avoid choosing between China and the United States...instead of vainly hoping that Australia will always be able to simultaneously deepen its ties with China and the United States, Canberra must now grapple with the difficult task of determining precisely when the national interest is best served by siding with Washington when it would be better to follow Beijing's lead.'[48]

That, needless to say, is not official policy, but his views should not be disregarded in a debate where many Australians probably agree with him. On the other hand, Australia's defence commitments are quite clearly laid out in the 2016 Defence White Paper. And alarm bells rang in Canberra in 2018 when the media reported that China had built a new wharf on the Vanuatu island of Espiritu Santo which was far too large for the commercial needs of its 40,000 inhabitants and occasional tourists. The port, built with financial support from China, is one of the largest in the South Pacific and can accommodate three cargo ships and two cruise liners simultaneously.[49] Vanuatu denied that it would allow China to use the port as a military base, but Australia warned the Pacific island nation against any move that would allow a greater Chinese military presence in the region.[50]

Vanuatu is too close to Australia for comfort, so it was not surprising that Canberra reacted publicly as it did. But Australia has not issued any similar warning to states in the Indian Ocean, where China has also helped upgrade ports that could have naval applications. China's military presence in the Indian Ocean can also be downplayed as it is still minor there compared with that of India and the United States. Even France has more troops stationed in the Indian Ocean region than China. But precisely because China's move into the region is an entirely new development, and in all likelihood the beginning of a trend, it is undeniable that it caused a serious conflict of geostrategic interests, which in turn, has led to an arms race in the region. And that is an issue which Australia, after all, has not disregarded.

Consequently, Australia is modernising its naval capacities and the 2016 Defence White paper says that it is in response to the rise of China. Defence installations on the Australian mainland as well as on the Cocos (Keeling) Islands and Christmas Island are being upgraded. India did not, in the end, get a naval base on the Seychelles, but efforts to improve its navy and strengthen its naval firepower are continuing. In August 2018, India fired for the first time three K-15 Sagarika, sea-launched ballistic missiles from *INS Arihant*, the lead vessel of its nuclear-powered submarines. The test took place ten kilometres off the coast of Visakhapatnam, the headquarters of the Indian Navy's Eastern Command.[51] The short-range missiles can carry a payload of 1,000 kilogrammes and weigh almost ten tonnes. As part of the same policy to counter China, India has also deployed additional Russian-made Su-30 fighter aircraft, spy drones and missiles along the Chinese border in the northeastern state of Arunachal Pradesh.[52]

Meanwhile in Djibouti, as Amy Cheng wrote in *Foreign Policy* in July 2018, it was noted that China's 200-acre base includes at least ten barracks, an ammunition depot, and a heliport.[53] Four layers of protective fences surround the perimeter; two inner fences are eight to ten metres tall and studded with guard posts. What is supposed to be a logistical support base for rescue missions and anti-piracy operations looks more like a fortress. It is big enough to accommodate thousands of soldiers – and that is in addition to more than 2,500 Chinese peacekeeping personnel already stationed in South Sudan, Liberia and Mali.

Apart from lending Djibouti money to pay for its share of the new Addis Ababa-Djibouti railway, China has provided or pledged support for the construction of new airports, a new port, an oil terminal and new roads. For all those projects, which are part of the BRI, China has paid nearly US$1.4 billion, which is equivalent to 75 per cent of the country's entire GDP.[54] Already in 2015 Djibouti became the fifth-biggest recipient of Chinese credit despite having one of the smallest populations among all the African countries.[55]

Today, Djibouti is one of several countries on the continent that have fallen victim to China's debt-trap diplomacy. And if Ethiopia manages to find alternative outlets to the sea through Eritrea and Somaliland, the loss of income from the transit traffic will force Djibouti into even deeper dependence on China. Beijing's massive leverage could affect Djibouti's other security relationships and, eventually, force other operators of military bases there out of the strategically important country at the entrance of the Red Sea.[56]

Bruno Maçães, a Portuguese political scientist and senior fellow at Carnegie Europe, argues that as new powers rise and the formerly hegemonic West loses relative power, the world is entering the first period in human history in which modern technology will be combined with a chaotic international arena, in which no single actor or group of actors is capable of imposing order – and he mentions Djibouti with all its foreign bases close to each other as a place where a conflict could break out.[57]

What Maçães describes is actually what has become known as the Thucydides's Trap, a theory proposed by Harvard scholar Graham Allison who hypothesises that war between a rising power and an established power is almost unavoidable, or as Thucydides wrote in *The History of the Peloponnesian War*, that it was the rise of Athens and the fear of that this instilled in Sparta that made war inevitable.[58] At a first glance the historical metaphor may seem far-fetched, but Allison gives 16 historical examples from the fifteenth century to the present of such a situation – and 12 of those led to war.

Among his most recent examples are the 1904–1905 Russo-Japanese war over land and sea power in East Asia, Britain supported by France and Russia against Germany during World War I, and World War II between the United States and Japan over influence in the Asia-Pacific region.[59] Among the four situations which did not lead to war were Britain's and the United States' competition for global economic dominance and naval supremacy in the Western Hemisphere in the early twentieth century, and the Soviet Union's and the United States' struggle for global power in the post-World War II era.

After careful preparations, a rising, newly industrialised Japan went to war with Russia in 1904, winning it, and assuming control over the Liaodong Peninsula and seizing Port Arthur, the South Manchurian Railway and half of Sakhalin from the declining Russian Empire. Japan had already seized Taiwan from China and was in the process of taking over Korea. Proclaiming 'Asia for the Asians' in 1933 Tokyo declared that henceforth Japan would be responsible for the maintenance of peace and order in East Asia – and invaded more than half of China. As a result, relations with the United States, which until 1941 had stayed out of World War II, deteriorated and, in desperation Allison argues, the United States approved a plan to deliver a pre-emptive 'knockout blow' at Pearl Harbor.[60]

World War I was triggered by the assassination of Archduke Franz Ferdinand, the heir to the Austro-Hungarian throne, in Sarajevo on 28 June 1914. The assassin, who belonged to a group of Serbian revolutionaries, sought independence for the Slavic provinces of the Austro-Hungarian Empire, but what could have been seen as a 'misstep factor' – to use Wang's description of an incident that could trigger a wider conflict – became a worldwide war. Austria-Hungary allied with Germany, then a rising power, went to war – while Britain, not actually involved in the conflicts in the Balkans, felt a need to maintain its global naval supremacy. A declining Russia joined Britain and France against Germany, which also produced a situation where Russian as well as German statesmen saw war as the perceived alternative to national destruction. The United States entered the war in 1917 when German submarines began attacking American ships – and ended up surpassing its ally Britain as a world power. The original cause for the war, Austria-Hungary's decision to punish Serbia for its alleged involvement in the assassination of Franz Ferdinand had evolved into something much bigger. And it ended with the dissolution of the once mighty Austro-Hungarian Empire. All that remained after territories had been lost was two much smaller countries, Austria and Hungary.

But the question is, what does all this have to do with the new Cold War between the United States and China, and is Allison's Thucydides's Trap theory really relevant to today's stand-offs in the South China Sea and, particularly, the Indian Ocean? The gist of Allison's argument is that he sets the 'rising power syndrome' against the 'ruling power syndrome' – and that would certainly apply to what is happening today in the Indian Ocean region and elsewhere: a rising, self-confident power challenging the supremacy of an old power that seems incapable of maintaining its preferred world order with itself at the apex.

Trump's slogan, 'Make America Great Again' has its more forceful, internationally important equivalent in Xi's 'Make China Great Again.' And, according to Allison, that means returning China to the predominance in Asia it enjoyed before Western colonial powers entered the scene; re-establishing control over the territories of 'greater China', including not only the self-governing territories of Hong Kong and Macau but also Taiwan; recovering what it sees as its historic sphere of influence along its borders and beyond into neighbouring countries so that those would give China the deference great nations such as itself have always demanded; and commanding the respect of the world's other great powers.[61]

Xi also set out to revitalise the CPC, cleansing it of corruption, to promote economic growth and, equally importantly, to revive Chinese nationalism and instil pride in being Chinese. He has also pledged to reorganise and rebuild the Chinese military so it can, as Xi says, 'fight to win.'[62] Xi's vision is for a nation that is much stronger and more powerful than any of the ancient Chinese empires ever was. And China, he believes, will eventually – but hopefully while he is still the leader of the country – replace the United States as the world's leading economic, political and military power. In March 2018, the National People's Congress, China's parliament, voted to remove a clause in the constitution that prohibits the president and the vice president from serving more than two five-year terms in office, enabling Xi to stay on indefinitely. Only two 'no' votes were cast, with three abstentions, from almost 3,000 delegates.[63] Xi's ambition to remain at the helm till China is the world's number one superpower may also be helped by the absence of any real US strategy to counter Beijing's growing influence in the Asia-Pacific. Trump's only interest seems to be in waging a trade war with China by imposing tariffs on Chinese goods entering the United States.

But there is also another side to Xi's dream of making China great again. He has turned tiny shoals and rocks into sovereign-territory islands in the South China Sea, established China's first overseas military base in Djibouti, and spent billions of dollars on defence research and procurement with the aim of building a world-class military to fulfil his aspiration for China to become the main superpower in the Asia-Pacific region. And then there is the costly BRI. It is built on loans and credits offered to weaker nations, but if they cannot repay the money they have borrowed, China may, at best, end up with more overseas real estate. That in itself would constitute an important strategic gain, though the money will have gone.

Beijing already has a tremendous debt issue as a result of trying to spend its way out of the 2008 economic crisis.[64] At that time, Beijing managed to keep its economy growing during the global slump by resorting to massive bank lending to local governments, which then spent the money on infrastructure projects which may or may not have been much use.[65] It kept GDP growth figures up at impressive levels but has left the country with a massive internal debt problem. Recently imposed US tariffs on Chinese goods will also hurt export-led growth.

There is also the issue of demographics. Due to the one-child policy and an ageing population, China will have an estimated 487 million elderly people by 2050 – around 35 per cent of the population – which have to be supported by a proportionally declining number of people of working age.[66] China has no proper plan on how to deal with that issue, and by any calculation it is an impending economic disaster.

There is the risk of China overstretching its resources and not even Xi can escape the fact that resistance to the BRI is already growing in several countries which should have benefitted from China's largesse. According to Pei Minxin, an expert on governance in China, the country's leaders have failed to appreciate adequately the need to avoid was he calls 'imperial overreach.'[67] Pei argues that 'despite early signs of trouble with BRI – which, together with the Soviet Union's experience, should give the CPC pause – China seems determined to push ahead with BRI, which the country's leaders have established as a pillar of their new "grand strategy".'[68]

At a meeting in Tokyo with five Southeast Asian leaders in October 2018, Japan also offered an alternative to China's BRI. While Japan-led infrastructure development projects in the region predate the BRI, the Japanese government has rebranded its competitive offerings as 'quality infrastructure,' a not-so-veiled reference to China's sometimes shoddy construction schemes.[69] The meeting between Japanese prime minister Shinzo Abe and the leaders of Myanmar, Thailand, Vietnam, Laos and Cambodia was clearly part of an effort to regain lost momentum in the region, where China had in recent years taken over with its cheque-book diplomacy and loans and grants for infrastructure development. Tokyo's reference to 'quality' building also took quiet aim at mounting criticism that China's offerings often amount to debt traps that are structured to extract sovereignty-eroding terms and conditions when borrowers, such as Sri Lanka, are unable to repay what they owe.

Japan has a longer history of building roads, bridges and airports in the region than China. But partly due to its controversial history in Southeast Asia dating back to World War II, Japan has taken a comparatively low key approach to its projects, unlike China's bold and visionary BRI. Unlike Western countries – which have criticised the Myanmar government for its handling of the Muslim Rohingya minority, and even re-imposed some sanctions – Japan, well aware of the fact that such punitive measure would push the country back into China's embrace, has taken a more nuanced approach. Japan has offered money to help solve the crisis and resettle the hundreds of thousands of Rohingyas who are languishing in camps in Bangladesh.

Japan is also able to provide a 'cleaner' partnership than China, which often uses intermediary dubious local contractors and middlemen in countries such as Myanmar. Asia World, which is managed by the son of a now deceased infamous opium warlord, got stakes in the Myitsone hydroelectric project in Kachin State and the Kyaukpyu port project – and was implicated in the oil-racket in Singapore – is only one example. China's preferred local partner in ongoing peace talks between Myanmar and the country's many ethnic rebel groups is Wei Xuegang, an ethnic Chinese who is one of the leaders of the UWSA – and a notorious druglord. Wei was indicted in absentia on heroin-trafficking charges in 1993 by a New York federal court, and again in 2005 for being the mastermind of a methamphetamine-producing network. A Thai court has sentenced him to death, also in absentia, on the same charges. The United States is offering a US$2 million reward for information leading to his arrest – but he is safe and sound at UWSA's Panghsang headquarters on the Chinese border, from where he, under the Myanmar name 'U Sein Win' and in collaboration with Chinese intelligence officers, is directing the Wa delegation to the peace talks with the government.[70]

Japan is seeking closer economic cooperation with India as well as the countries of Southeast Asia. It has pledged to help New Delhi upgrade its extensive but run-down railway network. Promises of more assistance came when India's prime minister Narendra Modi visited Tokyo in November 2016 and managed to sign a deal with Shinzo Abe for help with building six nuclear reactors. It was the first time Japan agreed to such a deal with a country that has not signed the Nuclear

Non-Proliferation Treaty.[71] Japan's participation in the Malabar Exercises is also significant, and follows on from a joint declaration of security cooperation that India and Japan signed in October 2008. The prime ministers were different at that time – Manmohan Singh for India and Taro Aso for Japan – but the message was clear. India and Japan agreed to exchange information and coordinate policy 'on regional affairs in the Asia Pacific region and on long-term strategic and global issues.'[72]

Moreover, Japan has pledged to help implement Modi's 'Act East' policy, which is partly aimed at countering China's influence in Myanmar by opening new trade routes from northeastern India to northern Myanmar towns. And India has steadfastly refused to endorse China's BRI, which it sees as an attempt to encircle India. With the China-Pakistan Economic Corridor on one side and the Myanmar Corridor on the other, that fear is not entirely unjustified as the pursuit of new trade routes is inseparable from the desire to gain political and strategic influence.

The original Silk Road inevitably led to geopolitical rivalries for the control of its valuable trade routes. The contest culminated in the so-called Great Game in the nineteenth century, which pitted the British and Russian empires against each other for control over Central Asia – including Russia's quest to reach the warm-water ports in the Indian Ocean. Today, China is a player not only on land but even more crucially on the high seas, and then primarily in the Indian Ocean. The nineteenth-century Great Game did not lead to an open, military conflict between Russia and Britain; it was a spying game where both sides infiltrated local rulers to enhance their respective interests. In that sense, there are similarities between the old Great Game and the New Cold War. But the differences are also striking. All the countries which are now involved in the contest for power and influence in the Indian Ocean region have access to modern technology and advanced weaponry – and they have permanent military bases spread out over a huge area.

A war could be avoided, not by Hugh White's utopian 'power-sharing agreement', but perhaps through a balance of terror not unlike that of the old Cold War when the West as well as the Soviet Bloc realised that a military conflict would prove too costly and devastating for both protagonists. According to Allison, Xi realises this and has approved another plan proposed by the Chinese military's Strategic Support Force: 'Using laser, electronic, and kinetic weapons to destroy or disable all US military satellites in orbit over the crisis area, and cyber-attacks to cripple American command-and-control systems throughout the Asia-Pacific region. The goal is to deescalate: Xi hopes that the US will be shocked into backing down.'[73]

But that sounds suspiciously like a declaration of war. And how would it possibly affect the US presence in bases like that on Diego Garcia? What about India's military bases and powerful navy? Nor is it enough to look only at what global and regional powers are doing. Internal developments in the small island nations of the Indian Ocean are equally important for the future of the region. And if an armed conflict emerges from either a 'misstep' or a more calculated provocation, it is likely to occur in the Indian Ocean where control over shipping lanes is more important than elsewhere, where divergent interests compete and overlap – and where China's ambitions for regional supremacy are the strongest. For the British Empire, India was its prized possession. For Xi, the Indian Ocean is the pearl he wishes to secure for his growing Chinese empire – irrespective of the cost.

NOTES

INTRODUCTION

1. See Lintner, Bertil, 'Burma: China's New Gateway', *Far Eastern Economic Review*, cover story, 22 December 1994. This was the first piece in the international media to highlight the changes that were taking place on the Sino-Myanmar border in the early 1990s. Not available online.
2. Initially called the 'One Road, One Belt Initiative', or OBOR, it was unveiled by President Xi in September and October 2013 and alludes to 'a Silk Road Economic Belt' and a 'Maritime Silk Road'. By mid-2016, the name had been changed to the 'Belt and Road Initiative'(BRI) to emphasise that the plan encompasses not only one 'belt' and one 'road', but a maze of infrastructural projects all over the region. See https://www.slideshare.net/aung3/one-belt-one-road-greater-mekong-subregioneconomic-corridors-and-myanmar (retrieved on 1 April 2018). See also Shepard, Wade, 'Beijing To The World: Don't Call The Belt and Road Initiative OBOR', https://www.forbes.com/sites/wadeshepard/2017/08/01/beijing-to-the-world-please-stop-saying-obor/#5940638f17d4 (retrieved on 5 April 2018).
3. Pan Qi, 'Opening to the Southwest: an Expert Opinion', *Beijing Review*, 2 September 1985, http://beijingreview.sinoperi.com/en198535/665498.jhtml (retrieved on 20 March 2018).
4. Ibid.
5. See Tian Jinchen, 'One Belt and One Road': Connecting China and the World', paper prepared for McKinsey and Company, 19 April

2017, https://www.mckinsey.com/industries/capital-projects-and-infrastructure/our-insights/one-belt-and-one-road-connecting-china-and-the-world (retrieved on 20 March 2018). Tian mentions how Zhang Qian 'helped establish the Silk Road', but there is nothing about his attempts to reach India.

6. For '60 countries', see ibid.; for US$1 trillion to US$8 trillion, see Hillman, Jonathan E., 'How Big is China's Belt and Road?' paper prepared for the Center for Strategic and International Studies, Washington, 3 April 2018, https://www.csis.org/analysis/how-big-chinas-belt-and-road (retrieved on 5 April 2018.)
7. 'Planned Indian Military base stirs Seychelles controversy', *Agence France-Presse*, 3 March 2018, https://timesofindia.indiatimes.com/india/planned-indian-military-base-stirs-seychelles-controversy/articleshow/63146127.cms (retrieved on 20 March 2018).
8. 'Indian, French Forces to Access Each Other's Naval Facilities in Indian Ocean', *The Wire*, 11 March 2018, https://thewire.in/231531/india-and-france-sign-14-agreements-in-a-move-towards-maritime-cooperation/ (retrieved on 2 April 2018).
9. Ibid.

1. THE NEW CASABLANCA

1. Allison, Simon, 'Djibouti's greatest threat may come from within', *Mail and Guardian*, 2 March 2018, https://mg.co.za/article/2018-03-02-00-djiboutis-greatest-threat-may-come-from-within (retrieved on 5 April 2018).
2. Dahir, Abdi Latif, 'Scramble for Djibouti: How a tiny African country became the world's key military base, *Quartz: Africa*, 18 August 2017, https://qz.com/1056257/how-a-tiny-african-country-became-the-worlds-key-military-base/ (retrieved on 5 April 2018); Oladipo, Tomi, 'Why are there so many military bases in Djibouti?' BBC News, 16 June 2015, http://www.bbc.com/news/world-africa-33115502 (retrieved on 5 April 2018); and Lintner, Bertil, Djibouti: the Casablanca of a new Cold War, *Asia Times*, 28 November 2018, http://www.atimes.com/article/djibouti-the-casablanca-of-a-new-cold-war/?fbclid=IwAR0Q01Q7o9jh1T46uV-JZUX2DwPNkup39Wv-lXJEWnAUYM4DbKlciZ5Nsdo (retrieved on 28 November 2018).
3. 'Djibouti welcomes Saudi Arabia plan to build a military base', *Memo Middle East Monitor*, 28 November 2017, https://www.middleeastmonitor.com/20171128-djibouti-welcomes-saudi-arabia-plan-to-build-a-military-base/ (retrieved on 5 April 2018).

4. Maçães, Bruno, 'The Coming Wars', *Politico*, 15 January 2018, https://www.politico.eu/blogs/the-coming-wars/2018/01/the-most-valuable-military-real-estate-in-the-world/ (retrieved on 10 May 2018).
5. Ibid.
6. 'Chinese-built Ethiopia-Djibouti railway begins commercial operations,' *Xinhua*, 1 January 2018, http://xinhuanet.com/english/2018-01/01/c_136865306.htm (retrieved on 4 May 2018).
7. *Tafsa News*, 'Why Djibouti Is the Loser of Ethiopia-Eritrea New Peace Deal', 12 July 2018, https://www.tesfanews.net/djibouti-loser-ethiopia-eritrea-new-peace-deal/ (retrieved on 15 August 2018).
8. Dahir, op. cit.
9. 'Why China's First Overseas Military base in Djibouti is "Only the Beginning",' *Sputnik International*, 13 July 2017, https://sputniknews.com/politics/201707131055515150-china-military-overseas/ (retrieved on 3 April 2018).
10. Lintner, Bertil, 'China advances, West frets in South Pacific', *Asia Times*, 25 April 2018, http://www.atimes.com/article/china-advances-west-frets-in-south-pacific/ (retrieved on 25 April 2018).
11. 'Chinese Foreign Ministry: Djibouti', *China.org.cn.*, 10 October 2006, http://www.china.org.cn/english/features/focac/183543.htm (retrieved on 3 April 2018).
12. Smith, Jeff M., *Cold Peace: China-India Rivalry in the Twenty-first Century*, Lanham, Maryland: Lexington Books, 2014, p. 236.
13. Ibid., p. 236.
14. Ibid., pp. 237-238.
15. See, for instance, 'Critics silenced ahead of China's move to end presidency term limits,' *ABC News*, 11 March 2018, http://www.abc.net.au/news/2018-03-11/critics-silenced-ahead-of-china27s-move-to-end-xi-term-limits/9536274 (retrieved on 20 March 2018) and Bodeen, Christopher, *Associated Press,* 11 March 2018, http://www.businessinsider.com/china-voted-xi-jinping-to-rule-for-life-2018-3 (retrieved on 20 March 2018).
16. *China.org.cn.*, 10 October 2006.
17. Ibid.
18. Pehrson, Christopher J., *String of Pearls: Meeting the Challenge of China's Rising Power Across the Asian Littoral*, Carlisle, Pennsylvania: The Strategic Studies Institute of the US Army War College, July 2006, http://www.strategicstudiesinstitute.army.mil/pdffiles/PUB721.pdf (retrieved on 10 April 2018).
19. Ibid., p. 21.
20. Pehrson, op. cit,. p. 21.

21. Pehrson, op. cit., p. 23.
22. Tea, Billy, 'Unstringing China's strategic pearls', *Asia Times*, 11 March 2011, http://www.atimes.com/atimes/China/MC11Ad02.html (retrieved on 15 January 2018).
23. Hillman, Jonathan, *How Big Is China's Belt and Road?* Washington: the Centre for Strategic and International Studies, 2018, p. 1.
24. Ibid., p. 2.
25. In Chinese: http://world.people.com.cn/n1/2017/0514/c1002-29273764.html (retrieved on 20 May 2018), also quoted in English translation in Thorne, Devin and Ben Spevack, *Harboured Ambitions: How China's Port Investments Are Strategically Reshaping the Indo-Pacific*, Washington: Centre for Advanced Defence Studies, 2017, p. 12, https://daisukybiendong.files.wordpress.com/2018/04/devin-thorne-ben-spevack-2018-harbored-ambitions-how-chinas-port-investments-are-strategically-reshaping-the-indo-pacific.pdf
26. Ibid., p. 1.
27. Ibid., p. 1.
28. 'China Industrial Park in India Launched.' *Global Times*, 21 June 2016, http://www.globaltimes.cn/content/989639.shtml (retrieved on 25 March 2018).
29. Mitra, Devirupa, 'India Sounds Alarm on Chinese Infra Projects in Neighbourhood', *The Wire*, 14 March 2018, https://thewire.in/diplomacy/china-making-headway-in-infra-projects-in-indias-neighbourhood-foreign-secretary-gokhale-to-panel (retrieved on 15 April 2018).
30. Ibid.
31. Ibid.
32. Ibid.
33. Interview with a financial adviser to the Myanmar government, Yangon, 21 December 2017.
34. Lintner, Bertil, 'Little Laos risks losing it all to China', *Asia Times*, 13 May 2018, http://www.atimes.com/article/little-laos-risks-losing-it-all-to-china/ (last accessed on 15 December 2018).
35. Clover, Charles, 'IMF's Lagarde warns China on Belt and Road debt', *The Financial Times*, 12 April 2018, https://www.ft.com/content/8e6d98e2-3ded-11e8-b7e0-52972418fec4 (retrieved on 15 May 2018).
36. Blau, Rosie, 'Did China discover America?' *The Economist*, 21 May 2015, https://www.1843magazine.com/travel/cartophilia/did-china-discover-america (retrieved on 5 May 2018).

37. 'Indonesia's Balancing Act: A Road With China, a Port With India,' *The Wire*, 18 May 2018, https://thewire.in/diplomacy/indonesia-china-india-modi-belt-and-road (retrieved on 20 May 2018).
38. Ma Huan, *Ying-hai Sheng-lan: The Overall Survey of the Ocean's Shores*, Bangkok: White Lotus, 1997. This is a reprint of a work compiled in 1935 by the Chinese scholar Feng Ch'eng-chun.
39. Seidel, Jamie, 'New quest for Chinese navigator Zheng He's ancient fleet an ominous bid for validation of China's expansionist claims', *news.com.au*, 1 March 2018, http://www.news.com.au/technology/science/archaeology/new-quest-for-chinese-navigator-zheng-hes-ancient-fleet-an-ominous-bid-for-validation-of-chinas-expansionist-claims/news-story/0ed1e754cd927a78569129bf83770478 (retrieved on 20 May 2018).
40. Yamada, Go, 'Is China's Belt and Road working? A progress report from eight countries', *Nikkei Asian Review,* 28 March 2018, https://asia.nikkei.com/Spotlight/Cover-Story/Is-China-s-Belt-and-Road-working-A-progress-report-from-eight-countries (retrieved on 5 April 2018).
41. Interviewed in Go, op. cit.
42. Kaplan, Robert D., 'China's Port in Pakistan?' *Foreign Policy*, 27 May 2011, http://foreignpolicy.com/2011/05/27/chinas-port-in-pakistan/ (retrieved on 12 January 2018).
43. 'Two policemen killed as gunmen attack Chinese consulate in Karachi,' *Agence France-Presse*, 23 November 2018, https://www.afp.com/en/news/15/two-policemen-killed-gunmen-attack-chinese-consulate-karachi-doc-1b176m4 (retrieved on 28 November 2018).
44. Panda, Ankit, 'Armed Insurgents Attack Chinese Consulate in Karachi', *The Diplomat*, 24 November 2018, https://thediplomat.com/2018/11/armed-insurgents-attack-chinese-consulate-in-karachi/ (retrieved on 28 November 2018).
45. 'Karachi attack not to affect China-Pakistan Economic Corridor: Chinese Foreign Ministry spokesman,' Wionews, 23 November 2018, http://www.wionews.com/south-asia/watch-karachi-attack-not-to-affect-china-pakistan-economic-corridor-construction-spokesman-179026 (retrieved on 28 November 2018).
46. Mangaldas, Leeza, 'Trump's Twitter Attack On Pakistan Is Met With Both Anger And Support in South Asia,' *Forbes*, 2 January 2018, https://www.forbes.com/sites/leezamangaldas/2018/01/02/trump-brings-in-the-new-year-with-polarizing-pakistan-tweet/#7460426f2b35 (retrieved on 5 January 2018).
47. Azia, Saba, 'Pakistan-US war of words over Donald Trump's tweet', *Al Jazeera*, 3 January 2018, https://www.aljazeera.com/news/2018/01/

pakistan-war-words-donald-trump-tweet-180102055709366.html (retrieved on 5 January 2018).

48. 'China warns of imminent attacks by "terrorists" in Pakistan,' *Reuters*, 8 December 2017, https://www.reuters.com/article/us-china-silkroad-pakistan/china-warns-of-imminent-attacks-by-terrorists-in-pakistan-idUSKBN1E216N (retrieved on 10 December 2017).
49. Khani, Omer Farooq, 'China halts funding CPEC-related projects under shadow of corruption,' *The Times of India*, 5 December 2017, https://timesofindia.indiatimes.com/world/china/china-halts-funding-cpec-related-projects-under-shadow-of-corruption/articleshow/61936975.cms (retrieved on 10 December 2017).
50. Small, Andrew, *The China-Pakistan Axis: Asia's New Geopolitics*, London: Hurst, 2015, p. 180.
51. Notezai, Muhammed Akbar, 'Islamist Discontent Over China's Treatment of Uighurs,' *The Diplomat*, https://thediplomat.com/2016/06/islamist-discontent-over-chinas-treatment-of-uighurs/ (retrieved on 10 May 2018).
52. 'China urges Pakistan to expel Uighur Islamic militants,' *BBC*, 31 May 2012, http://www.bbc.com/news/world-asia-18276864 (retrieved on 15 May 2018).
53. *China 2017/2018*, Amnesty International, https://www.amnesty.org/en/countries/asia-and-the-pacific/china/report-china/ (retrieved on 21 May 2018).
54. *China: Big Data Fuels Crackdown in Minority Region*, Human Rights Watch, 16 February 2018, https://www.hrw.org/news/2018/02/26/china-big-data-fuels-crackdown-minority-region (retrieved on 5 May 2018).
55. Shih, Gerry and Dake Kang, 'Muslims forced to drink alcohol and eat pork in China's "re-education" camps, former inmate claims,' *The Independent*, 18 May 2018, https://www.independent.co.uk/news/world/asia/china-re-education-muslims-ramadan-xinjiang-eat-pork-alcohol-communist-xi-jinping-a8357966.html (retrieved on 22 May 2018).
56. Gady, Franz-Stefan, 'China-Pakistan Military Relations', *The Diplomat*, 15 June 2017, https://thediplomat.com/tag/china-pakistan-military-relations/ (retrieved on 12 April 2018).
57. Gertz, Bill, 'China eyes Pakistan port', *Washington Times*, 18 October 2017, https://www.washingtontimes.com/news/2017/oct/18/inside-the-ring-china-eyes-pakistan-port/ (retrieved on 22 May 2018).
58. Ibid.
59. Sharma, Mihir, 'View: China's proving to be an expensive date for Pakistan,' *The Economic Times*, 23 May 2018, https://economictimes.

indiatimes.com/news/international/world-news/view-chinas-proving-to-be-expensive-date-for-pakistan/articleshow/64285439.cms (retrieved on 25 May 2018).

60. Ibid.
61. Safi, Michael and Amantha Perera, 'The biggest game change in 100 years: Chinese money gushes into Sri Lanka,' *The Guardian*, 26 March 2018, https://www.theguardian.com/world/2018/mar/26/the-biggest-game-changer-in-100-years-chinese-money-gushes-into-sri-lanka (retrieved on 20 May 2018).
62. Abeywickrema, Mandana Ismail, 'Concern Over Mattala Performance', *The Sunday Leader*, 12 May 2013, http://www.thesundayleader.lk/2013/05/12/concerns-over-mattala-performance/ (retrieved on 22 May 2018).
63. Brewster, David, 'Why India is buying the world's emptiest airport,' *The Lowy Interpreter*. 4 December 2017, https://www.lowyinstitute.org/the-interpreter/why-india-buying-world-s-emptiest-airport (retrieved on 5 May 2018).
64. Ibid.
65. Ibid.
66. Ibid.
67. Ibid.
68. 'How Beijing won Sri Lanka's civil war,' *The Independent*, 22 May 2010, https://www.independent.co.uk/news/world/asia/how-beijing-won-sri-lankas-civil-war-1980492.html (retrieved on 20 May 2018).
69. 'China to develop Bangladesh industrial zone as part of South Asia push,' *Reuters*, 4 April 2018, https://www.hindustantimes.com/world-news/china-to-develop-bangladesh-industrial-zone-as-part-of-south-asia-push/story-EJstVJcCGBzTSKfdhzWsCI.html (retrieved on 20 May 2018).
70. Go, op. cit.
71. 'War Chest: US Dominates World Military Spending in 2017,' *Sputnik News*, 2 May 2018, https://sputniknews.com/military/201805021064098631-World-Military-Spending-Riyadh-Surpasses-Moscow/ (retrieved on 10 May 2018).
72. Maçães, op. cit.
73. Ibid.
74. Johnson, Reuben F., 'US warns pilots of laser attacks in Djibouti,' *Jane's Defence Weekly*, 27 April 2018, http://www.janes.com/article/79630/us-warns-pilots-of-laser-attacks-in-djibouti (retrieved on 23 May 2018).
75. Ibid.

76. Connor, Neil, 'Pentagon accuses China of using lasers against US pilots in Djibouti,' *The Telegraph*, 4 May 2018, https://www.telegraph.co.uk/news/2018/05/04/pentagon-accuses-china-using-lasers-against-us-pilots-djibouti/ (retrieved on 10 May 2018).
77. Johnson, op. cit.
78. Ibid.
79. Allison, op. cit.
80. Ibid.
81. Ibid.
82. 'Djibouti', *Freedom House*, 2011, https://freedomhouse.org/report/freedom-world/2011/djibouti (retrieved on 10 May 2018) see also Lintner, Bertil, 'Risks bubbling beneath Djibouti's foreign bases,' *Asia Times*, 28 November 2018, http://www.atimes.com/article/risks-bubbling-beneath-djiboutis-foreign-bases/?fbclid=IwAR1yluJiHHr11Gv33I2V_OYXsCO9FRBtG-n2672OM8UDlxki7YcRYcdHb1c (retrieved on 29 November 2018).
83. 'Djibouti', *Freedom House*, 2012, https://freedomhouse.org/report/freedom-world/2012/djibouti (retrieved on 10 May 2018).
84. Ibid.
85. Allison, op. cit.
86. Ibid.

2. THE MYANMAR CORRIDOR

1. Fuller, Thomas, 'Myanmar Backs Down, Suspending Dam Project', *New York Times*, 30 September 2011, https://www.nytimes.com/2011/10/01/world/asia/myanmar-suspends-construction-of-controversial-dam.html (retrieved on 15 January 2018).
2. Lintner, Bertil. 'The Busy Border,' *Far Eastern Economic Review*, 8 June 1989.
3. For full quote, see Myanmar Press Summary, *Working People's Daily* (Rangoon), Vol. III, No 10 October 1989, p. 14, http://www.ibiblio.org/obl/docs3/BPS89-10.pdf (retrieved on 23 May 2018).
4. For a list of Chinese weaponry delivered to Myanmar, see Lintner, Bertil: 'Lock and Load,' *Far Eastern Economic Review*, 13 September 1990, 'Oiling the Iron Fist,' *Far Eastern Economic Review*, 6 December 1990, and 'Hidden Reserves,' *Far Eastern Economic Review*, 6 June 1991.
5. Ibid.
6. Ott, Marvin, 'Don't Push Myanmar Into China's Orbit,' *The Los Angeles Times*, 9 June 1997, http://articles.latimes.com/1997-06-09/local/me-1645_1_southeast-asia (retrieved on 15 January 2018).

7. For an overview of the 'roadmap', see Arnott, David, *Burma/Myanmar: How to Read the Generals"Roadmap – A Brief Guide With Links to the Literature*, http://www.ibiblio.org/obl/docs/how10.htm and Khin Maung Win, address at a Myanmar Institute of Strategic and International Studies seminar in Rangoon, 27-28 January 2004, http://burmatoday.net/burmatoday2003/2004/02/040218_khinmgwin.htm (both sites retrieved on 15 January 2018).
8. A copy of this confidential report is in the author's possession.
9. Those are direct quotes from the document.
10. See, for instance, Qin Hui's series of articles in *The Economic Observer* in February 2012 titled 'The Mystery of the Myitsone'. English translations of those articles are in the author's possession.
11. Lintner, Bertil, 'The Core Issued Not Addressed,' *The Irrawaddy,* 5 May 2015: 'Insights into the actual situation on the ground has never been the strong suit of foreign peacemakers. The term "military-industrial complex" is often used to describe a network of defence contracts, flows of money and resources among individuals, institutions and various government agencies in the United States. Myanmar now, it seems, has its own "peace-industrial complex" with an abundance of foreign NGOs, supported by massive grants from the European Union, the governments of Norway, Switzerland and Canada, and the involvement of representatives of the UN as well as regional and international bodes.' See https://www.irrawaddy.com/features/the-core-issues-not-addressed.html (retrieved on 5 March 2018).
12. Wee, Sui-lee, 'Myanmar official accuses China of meddling in rebel peace talks,' *Reuters*, 8 October 2015, https://www.reuters.com/article/us-myanmar-china/myanmar-official-accuses-china-of-meddling-in-rebel-peace-talks-idUSKCN0S22VT20151008 (retrieved on 5 February 2018).
13. Quoted in Lintner, Bertil, 'Same Game, Different Tactics: The Myanmar Corridor,' *The Irrawaddy*, July 2015, https://www.irrawaddy.com/news/burma/same-game-different-tactics-chinas-myanmar-corridor.html (retrieved on 12 March 2018). The original *Jane*'s report is available only to subscribers.
14. Ibid.
15. See Kyaw Phyo Tha, "Fear of China Keeps Copper Mine Open: Aung Min', *The Irrawaddy*, 26 November 2012, http://www.irrawaddy.com/news/burma/fear-of-china-keeps-copper-mine-open-aung-min.html (retrieved on 10 January 2018).
16. Sun, Yun, 'The Conflict in Northern Myanmar: Another American Anti-China Conspiracy,' *Asia Pacific Bulletin*, 20 February 2015, https://

www.stimson.org/content/conflict-northern-myanmar-another-american-anti-china-conspiracy (retrieved on 10 January 2018).

17. Quoted in Kyaw Kha, 'Meeting Minutes Reveal Insight into Chinese approach to Burma's [Myanmar's] Peace Process,' *The Irrawaddy*, 22 February 2017, at https://www.irrawaddy.com/news/burma/meeting-minutes-reveal-insights-chinese-approach-burmas-peace-process.html (retrieved on 17 August 2017).
18. Lintner, Bertil, 'Wa rebel group torpedoes Suu Kyi's peace drive,' *Asia Times*, 28 February 2017, http://www.atimes.com/article/wa-rebel-group-torpedoes-suu-kyis-peace-drive/ (retrieved on 10 January 2018).
19. Lun Min Mang, 'Armed ethnic groups congratulate China's Xi on re-election,' *The Myanmar Times*, 21 March 2018, https://www.mmtimes.com/news/armed-ethnic-groups-congratulate-chinas-xi-re-election.html (retrieved on 25 March 2018).
20. See also Lintner, Bertil, "China uses carrot and stick in Myanmar,' *Asia Times*, 28 February 2017, http://www.atimes.com/article/china-uses-carrot-stick-myanmar/ (retrieved on 15 January 2018).
21. Htet Naing Zaw, 'Impossible to Remove Tatmadaw from Politics: Army Colonel,' *The Irrawaddy*. 14 August 2017, https://www.irrawaddy.com/news/burma/impossible-remove-tatmadaw-politics-army-colonel.html (retrieved on 17 January 2018).
22. Dickey, William C. and Nay Yan Oo, 'Myanmar's military holds key to further reform,' *Nikkei Asian Review*, 18 August 2017, https://asia.nikkei.com/Viewpoints/William-C.-Dickey-and-Nay-Yan-Oo/Myanmar-s-military-holds-key-to-further-reform (retrieved on 19 January 2018).
23. For a complete list, see Kalam, Zaid, 'Suu Kyi's lost honours,' *The Daily Star*, 8 March 2018, https://www.thedailystar.net/rohingya-crisis/myanmar-refugee-aung-san-suu-kyi-lost-honours-nobel-peace-prize-oxford-elie-wiesel-ethnic-cleansing-bangladesh-1545265 (retrieved on 10 March 2018).
24. Harris, Kathleen, 'Senate votes to strip Aung San Suu Kyi of honorary Canadian citizenship,' *CBC*, 2 October 2018, https://www.cbc.ca/news/politics/suu-kyi-honorary-canadian-citizenship-1.4847568 (retrieved on 10 October 2018).
25. 'Amnesty International withdraws human rights award from Aung San Suu Kyi,' *Amnesty International*, 12 November 2018, https://www.amnesty.org/en/latest/news/2018/11/amnesty-withdraws-award-from-aung-san-suu-kyi/ (retrieved on 29 November 2018).
26. 'UN human rights chief points to "textbook example of ethnic cleansing" in Myanmar', *UN News*, 11 September 2017, https://news.un.org/

en/story/2017/09/564622-un-human-rights-chief-points-textbook-example-ethnic-cleansing-myanmar (retrieved on 13 September 2017.)

27. Kuhn, Anthony, 'Now a Politician, Aung San Suu Kyi is The Object of Protesters,' *National Public Radio*, 16 March 2013, https://www.npr.org/sections/thetwo-way/2013/03/16/174431490/now-a-politician-aung-san-suu-kyi-is-the-object-of-protesters (retrieved on 5 April 2018).
28. 'Suu Kyi promises Compensation for Copper Mine Villagers,' *Radio Free Asia*, 14 March 2013, https://www.rfa.org/english/news/myanmar/copper-mine-03142013183726.html (retrieved on 5 April 2018).
29. 'China's Xi discussed Rohingya crisis with Myanmar army chief,' *Reuters*, 24 November 2017, https://www.reuters.com/article/us-myanmar-rohingya-china/chinas-xi-discusses-rohingya-crisis-with-myanmar-army-chief-idUSKBN1DO1SK (retrieved on 27 November 2018)í
30. Ibid.
31. 'Myanmar, having warmed to the West, turns to China again,' *Associated Press*, 27 May 2017, https://wtop.com/dc/2017/05/myanmar-having-warmed-to-the-west-turns-to-china-again/ (retrieved on 10 April 2018).
32. Aung Zaw, 'Big Brother to the Rescue,' *The Irrawaddy*, 24 November 2017, https://www.irrawaddy.com/opinion/commentary/big-brother-rescue.html (retrieved on 20 March 2018).
33. Such documents are in the author's possession.
34. 'Kyaukpyu: Connecting China to the Indian Ocean,' *CSIS Briefs*, 2 April 2018, https://www.csis.org/analysis/kyaukpyu-connecting-china-indian-ocean (retrieved on 5 April 2018).
35. See Lee, Yimou and Thu Thu Aung, 'China to take a 70 per cent stake in strategic port in Myanmar,' *Reuters*, 17 October 2017, https://www.reuters.com/article/china-silkroad-myanmar-port/china-to-take-70-percent-stake-in-strategic-port-in-myanmar-official-idUSL4N1MS3UB (retrieved on 10 April 2018).
36. '$20 billion Sino-Burmese railroad abruptly cancelled,' *Go Kunming*, 22 July 2014, https://www.gokunming.com/en/blog/item/3278/20_billion_sino_burmese_railroad_abruptly_cancelled (retrieved on 5 April 2018).
37. Ibid.
38. Bai Tiantian, 'China needs roads, rail to link Yunnan to Myanmar's Kyaukpyu: NPC delegates,' *Global Times*, 7 March 2017, http://www.globaltimes.cn/content/1036494.shtml (retrieved on 5 April 2018).
39. Ibid.
40. Ibid.

41. Smyth, Michael, 'Notorious tycoon from Burma with alleged drug ties welcomed by feds, B.C.' *The Province*, 24 June 2014, http://www.theprovince.com/life/smyth+notorious+tycoon+from+burma+with+alleged+drug+ties+welcomed+feds/9974934/story.html (retrieved on 10 April 2018), see also Fuller, Thomas, 'Profits of Drug Trade Drive Economic Boom in Myanmar,' *New York Times*, 5 June 2015, https://www.nytimes.com/2015/06/06/world/asia/profits-from-illicit-drug-trade-at-root-of-myanmars-boom.html (retrieved on 29 November 2018).
42. Observations by the author during a visit to Kunming, Mangshi and Ruili in March 2018.
43. Fan Hongwei, 'China's "Look South": China-Myanmar Transport Corridor,' *Ritsumeikan International Affairs*, Vol. 10, 2011, pp. 49-50, http://www.ritsumei.ac.jp/acd/re/k-rsc/ras/04_publications/ria_en/10_04.pdf (retrieved on 15 January 2018).

3. INDIA'S ISLANDS

1. Zehmisch, Philipp, *Mini-India: The Politics of Migration and Subalternity in the Andaman Islands*, New Delhi: Oxford University Press, 2017.
2. See, for instance, Lintner, Bertil, 'Arms for Eyes: Military sales raise China's profile in Bay of Bengal,' *Far Eastern Economic Review*, 16 December 1993.
3. Ibid.
4. Chellaney, Brahma, 'Promoting Political Freedoms in Burma: International Policy Options,' in Lagerkvist, Johan (ed.), *Between Isolation and Internationalisation: The State of Burma*, Stockholm: Swedish Institute of International Affairs, 2008, p. 167.
5. For a brief history of the Coco Islands, see Selth, Andrew, *Burma's Coco Islands: Rumours and Realities in the Indian Ocean*, Hong Kong: City University, South-east Asia Research centre, 2008, http://www.cityu.edu.hk/searc/Resources/Paper/WP101_08_ASelth.pdf (retrieved on 10 January 2018).
6. Ibid., p. 6.
7. Selth, Andrew, *Chinese Military Bases in Burma: The Explosion of a Myth*, Nathan, Queensland: The Griffith Asia Institute, Regional Outlook Paper No. 10. 2007, p. 16.
8. Ramachandran, Suda, 'India Bids to Rule the Waves: From the Bay of Bengal to the Malacca Strait, *Asia Times Online*, 19 October 2005, http://www.atimes.com/atimes/South_Asia/GJ19Df03.html (retrieved on 5 May 2018).

9. Chandramohan, Balaji, 'US Courts India in the Indian Ocean,' *Asia Times Online*, 6 May 2010, http://www.atimes.com/atimes/South_Asia/LE06Df02.html (retrieved on 5 May 2018).
10. Dasgupta, Saibal, 'China Gets First-Ever Chance to Enter Indian Ocean for Exploration,' *Times of India*, 2 August 2011, http://articles.timesofindia.indiatimes.com/2011-08-02/china/29842183_1_ore-deposit-mineral-exploration-cnpc (retrieved on 5 May 2018).
11. Ibid.
12. This story is told, and refuted, in P. Mathur, *History of the Andaman and Nicobar Islands*. Delhi: Sterling Publishers, 1968, pp. 13-14.
13. 'India police watch tribal island after killing of American,' Agence France-Presse, 23 November 2018, in *The Daily Mail*, 23 November 2018, https://www.dailymail.co.uk/wires/afp/article-6420573/India-police-watch-tribal-island-killing-American.html (retrieved on 29 November 2018).
14. Referred to at this website: http://www.esa.int/esaEO/SEMQ8L2IU7E_index_0.html (retrieved on 5 May 2018).
15. Mathur, op. cit., pp. 272-273.
16. Ibid., pp. 273-274. After the first Danish missionaries came Moravian Christians.
17. For a colourful description of Ross Island, see Bera, Tilak Ranjan, *Andamans: The Emerald Necklace of India*. New Delhi: UBS Publishers, 2007, pp. 31-41.
18. Mathur, op. cit. pp. 221-222. For an account of the penal colony on the Andamans, see also Phaley, Baban, *The Land of Martyrs: Andaman & Nicobar Islands*. Nagpur: Sarswati Prakashan, 2009.
19. Phaley, op. cit., pp. 60-61.
20. 'With Chinese Submarines Spotted Near Andamans, India Turns to US,' *NDTV*, 2 May 2016, https://www.ndtv.com/india-news/wary-of-chinas-indian-ocean-activities-us-india-discuss-anti-submarine-warfare-1401595 (retrieved on 6 May 2018).
21. Ibid.
22. Gurung, Shaurya Karanbir, '14 Chinese navy ships spotted in Indian Ocean, Indian Navy monitoring locations,' *The Economic Times*, 1 December 2017, https://economictimes.indiatimes.com/news/defence/14-chinese-navy-ships-spotted-in-indian-ocean-indian-navy-monitoring-locations/articleshow/61882634.cms (retrieved on 20 May 2018).
23. Ibid.
24. For a list of joint exercises until 2013, see Smith, Jeff M., *Cold Peace: China-India Rivalry in the Twenty-first Century*, Lanham, Maryland: Lexington Books, 2014, pp. 184-185.

25. Smith, op. cit., p. 181.
26. Green, Michael J., 'Japan, India, and the Strategic Triangle with China,' *Strategic Asia 2011–2012*, http://www.nbr.org/publications/element.aspx?id=529\9 (retrieved on 5 May 2018).
27. *Japan-India Relations*, Ministry of Foreign Affairs, Japan, https://www.mofa.go.jp/region/asia-paci/india/data.html, https://www.mofa.go.jp/region/asia-paci/india/pmv0810/joint_s.html, and https://www.mofa.go.jp/region/asia-paci/india/pmv0810/joint_d.html (retrieved on 2 May 2018).
28. Nagao, Satoru, 'Japan-India Military Partnership: India is the New Hope for Asia,' *Claws Journal*, Winter 2013, p. 69, http://www.claws.in/images/journals_doc/1589692164_SatoruNagao.pdf (retrieved on 20 January 2018).
29. Smith, op. cit., p. 181.
30. Sing, Anup, 'The Dragons Adventure in the Indian Ocean,' in Bajwa, Lt.-Gen. J.S. (ed.), *China: Threat or Challenge?* New Delhi: Lancer Publishers, 2017, p. 165.
31. Nagao, op. cit., p. 72.
32. Wikipedia has very detailed information about the Indian Navy, https://en.wikipedia.org/wiki/Indian_Navy (retrieved on 10 May 2018) and so does the Indian Navy's official website, https://www.indiannavy.nic.in/ (retrieved on 20 May 2018).
33. See https://web.archive.org/web/20120322012643/http://mod.nic.in/reports/cap3.pdf (retrieved on 20 May 2018).
34. 'INS Jalashwa joins Eastern Fleet,' *The Hindu*, 14 September 2007, http://www.hindu.com/2007/09/14/stories/2007091454111600.htm (retrieved on 20 May 2018).
35. Chaudhuri, Pramit Pal, 'Indonesia gives India access to strategic port of Sabang,' *Hindustan Times*, 17 May 2018, https://www.hindustantimes.com/india-news/indonesia-gives-india-access-to-strategic-port-of-sabang/story-KPXWKy7PGAHFUi0jCL26yJ.html (retrieved on 20 May 2018).
36. Ibid.
37. Bhaskar, C. Uday, 'Rising Together,' *Himal*, September 2010.
38. For an excellent account of the Indian communities in Burma, see Chakravarti, Nalini Ranjan Chakravarti, *The Indian Minority in Burma: The Rise and Fall of an Immigrant Community*, London: Oxford University Press, 1971.
39. Quoted in Lintner, Bertil, 'Different Strokes,' *Far Eastern Economic Review*, 23 February 1989, http://www.burmalibrary.org/reg.burma/archives/199701/msg00063.html (retrieved on 15 May 2018).

40. Lintner, Bertil, 'The Islamabad Link,' *India Today*, 30 September 1989.
41. Kuppuswamy, C.S.. 'Myanmar-India Cooperation,' *South Asia Analysis Group*, 3 February 2003, http://www.southasiaanalysis.org/%5Cpapers6%5Cpaper596.html (retrieved on 10 January 2018).
42. Rana, Vijay, 'China and India's Mutual Distrust,' *BBC News*, 21 April 2003, http://news.bbc.co.uk/2/hi/south_asia/2964195.stm (retrieved on 5 May 2018).
43. Kumar, Dinesh, 'Weapons Seized were for North-East Militants,"' *The Times of India*, 13 February 1998, http://www.burmalibrary.org/reg.burma/archives/199802/msg00355.html (retrieved on 10 January 2018).
44. Haksar, Nandita, *Rogue Agent: How India's Military Intelligence Betrayed the Burmese Resistance*. New Delhi: Penguin Books, 2009, p. 19. Haksar's book on the events contains many useful details about the case, but contains inaccuracies in regard to Burmese history. A better account of 'Operation Leach' is in Subir Bhaumik, 'Blood and Sand,' *Sunday*, 31 May 1998.
45. Haksar, op. cit., p. 63. See also Lintner, Bertil, *Great Game East: India, China, and the Struggle for Asia's Most Volatile Frontier*, New Haven: Yale University Press, 2015, pp. 204-206. The accuracy of my account of the events was verified by Col. Grewal himself during a chance encounter in New Delhi in 2009.
46. For a brief biography of B.B. Nandy, see http://en.wikipedia.org/wiki/Bibhuti_Bhusan_Nandy. He is also mentioned in Haksar, op. cit., p. 141.
47. For an overview of this policy shift, see Lintner, Bertil, 'China and South Asia's East,' *Himal*, October 2002, and 'India Stands by Myanmar Status Quo,' *Asia Times Online*, November 14, 2007, http://www.atimes.com/atimes/South_Asia/IK14Df02.html (retrieved on 10 April 2018).
48. Haksar, op. cit., p. 141.
49. For Maung Aye's visits to Shillong and New Delhi in 2000, see 'Maung Aye's Itinerary in India,' *Mizzima News Group*, 15 November 2000, http://www.ibiblio.org/obl/reg.burma/archives/200011/msg00071.html (retrieved on 10 January 2018).
50. Lintner, Bertil, 'India Stays by Myanmar Status Quo,' *Asia Times Online*, 14 November 2007, http://www.atimes.com/atimes/South_Asia/IK14Df02.html (retrieved on 10 Janaury 2018).
51. Ibid.
52. 'India, Myanmar sets $1 bn trade target in 2006–2007,' *The Economic Times*, 15 February 2007, http://economictimes.indiatimes.com/articleshow/1619338.cms (retrieved on 10 January 2018).

53. Rajan, Amitav, 'Myanmar Burning, MEA Told Deora: We Need to Visit But Keep it Low-key,' *Indian Express*, 28 September 2007, http://www.indianexpress.com/news/myanmar-burning-mea-told-deora-we-need-to/222028/ (retrieve don 10 January 2018).
54. 'ASEAN Diplomats Confident Of Trade Boom, *Manipur Online*, 19 September 2010, http://manipuronline.com/headlines/asean-diplomats-confident-of-trade-boom/2010/09/19 (retrieved on 10 January 2018).
55. Lintner, Bertil, 'Mysterious Motives: India's Raids on the Burma border,' *The Irrawaddy*, 30 June 2015, https://www.irrawaddy.com/news/ethnic-issues/mysterious-motives-indias-raids-on-the-burma-border.html (retrieved on 5 May 2018).
56. Observations by the author during a visit to Ruili in March 2018.

4. MAURITIUS

1. For economic growth and GDP per capita, see https://www.ceicdata.com/en/indicator/mauritius/gdp-per-capita (retrieved on 26 August 2018); World Bank data at https://data.worldbank.org/indicator/NY.GDP.PCAP.CD?locations=ZG (retrieved on 25 August 2018).
2. For statistical data about literacy, see https://www.ceicdata.com/en/indicator/mauritius/gdp-per-capita (retrieved on 26 August 2018).
3. For tourist statistics, see https://www.statista.com/statistics/801358/tourist-arrivals-mauritius/ (retrieved on 26 August 2018).
4. 'Chinese firm helps establish smart city in Mauritius as economic ties blossom,' *Xinhua*, 27 July 2018, http://www.xinhuanet.com/english/2018-07/27/c_137352761.htm (retrieved on 25 August 2018) and 'Mauritius airport doubles capacity with new terminal,' Aviation Media, 2 September 2013, http://www.airport-world.com/news/general-news/2975-mauritius-airport-doubles-capacity-with-new-terminal.html (retrieved on 25 August 2018).
5. 'China-Mauritius to Explore new Strategic Partnership,' *Republic of Mauritius*, 21 April 2017, http://www.govmu.org/English/News/Pages/China-Mauritius-to-Explore-new-Strategic-Partnership.aspx (retrieved on 25 May 2018).
6. Ibid.
7. Roche. Elizabeth, 'India woos Mauritius with $500-mn line of credit, maritime security pact,' *Mint*, 28 May 2017, https://www.livemint.com/Politics/KIayyTloo4jsAKpJuF6l5M/India-woos-Mauritius-with-500mn-line-of-credit-maritime-s.html (retrieved on 25 August 2018).
8. Ibid.

9. Metz, Helen Chapin (ed.), *Indian Ocean: Five Island Countries*, Washington: Federal Research Division, Library of Congress, 1995, p. 99.
10. Teelock, Vijayalakshmi, Sooryakanti Nirsimloo-Gayan, Marc Serge Rivière and Geoffrey Summers (eds), *Angaje: Explorations into the History, Society and Culture of Indentured Immigrants and their Descendants in Mauritius, Volume 1: Early Years*, Port Louis, Aapravasi Ghat Fund, 2012, p. 124.
11. Ibid., p. 124.
12. Ibid., p. 128.
13. Teelock, Vijayalakshmi, Sooryakanti Nirsimloo-Gayan, Marc Serge Rivière and Geoffrey Summers (eds), *Angaje: Explorations into the History, Society and Culture of Indentured Immigrants and their Descendants in Mauritius, Volume 2: The Impact of Indenture*, Port Louis, Aapravasi Ghat Fund, 2012, p. 54.
14. Ibid., p. 55.
15. Figures from *Indenture: A Brief History of Indentured in Mauritius and in the World*, Port Louis: Aapravasi Ghat Trust Fund, 2007, pp. 11-17.
16. For detailed statistics, see http://statsmauritius.govmu.org/English/StatsbySubj/Documents/archive%20esi/External%20Trade/Report/1.%20POPULATION%20CENSUS/REPT%200392/REPT_0392_0001.pdf (retrieved on 5 September 2018) and Metz, p. 101.
17. Quoted in Wright, Carol, *Mauritius*, Harrisburg: Stackpole Books, 1974, p. 29.
18. There is an excellent chapter about the Sino-Mauritians in Pan, Lynn (ed.), *The Encyclopedia of the Chinese Overseas,* Singapore: Editions Didier Millet and the Chinese Heritage Centre, second edn, 2006, pp. 351-355.
19. Stoddard, Theodore L., William K. Carr, Daniel L. Spencer, Nancy E. Walstrom and Audrey R. Whiteley, *Area Handbook for The Indian Ocean Territories*, Washington: The American University by the Institute for Cross-Cultural Research, 1971, p. 74.
20. Vine, David, *Island of Shame*, Princeton: Princeton University Press, 2009, p. 7.
21. Ibid., p. 4.
22. Ibid., p. 5.
23. Ibid., p. 8.
24. Early Day Motion 1680: September 16, 2004, Alan Meale, https://www.parliament.uk/edm/2003-04/1680 (retrieved on 30 August 2018).
25. Vine, op. cit., p. 9.
26. Quoted in Doward, Jamie, 'Diego Garcia guards its secrets even as the truth on CIA torture emerges,' *The Guardian*, 13 December 2014,

https://www.theguardian.com/world/2014/dec/13/diego-garcia-cia-us-torture-rendition (retrieved on 10 September 2018).

27. Doward, Jamie, 'British island used by US for rendition,' *The Guardian*, 2 March 2008, https://www.theguardian.com/world/2008/mar/02/ciarendition.unitednations (retrieved on 6 September 2018).
28. Doward, 13 December 2014.
29. 'Mauritius claim to disputed islands concerns Chagos community in Seychelles,' *Seychelles News Agency*, 7 September 2018, http://www.seychellesnewsagency.com/articles/9706/Mauritius+claim+to+disputed+islands+concerns+Chagos+community+in+Seychelles (retrieved on 10 September 2018).
30. Vine, op. cit., p. 175, and Penketh, Anne, 'Exiled islanders set for emotional return to their homeland,' *The Independent*, 30 March 2006, https://www.independent.co.uk/news/world/asia/exiled-islanders-set-for-emotional-return-to-their-homeland-6105199.html (retrieved on 8 September 2018).
31. 'Re-opening old wounds: Chagossians in Seychelles tell of a trip to home islands,' *Seychelles News Agency*, 30 March 2015, http://www.seychellesnewsagency.com/articles/3041/Re-opening+old+wounds+Chagossians+in+Seychelles+tell+of+trip+to+visit+home+islands (retrieved on 8 September 2018).
32. Zephaniah, Benjamin, 'Britain's shameful treatment of Chagos islanders must end,' *The Guardian*, 16 January 2018, https://www.theguardian.com/commentisfree/2018/jan/16/britains-shameful-treatment-chagos-islanders-must-end (retrieved on 5 September 2018) and for court documents, see http://www.bailii.org/ew/cases/EWHC/Admin/2006/1038.html (retrieved on 5 September 2018).
33. Bowcott, Owen, 'Chagos Islanders dispute: court to rule on UK sovereignty claim,' *The Guardian*, 21 April 2014, https://www.theguardian.com/world/2014/apr/21/chagos-islands-diego-garcia-base-court-ruling (retrieved on 6 September 2018).
34. Moyo, Monica, 'Permanent Court of Arbitration finds UK in Violation of Convention of the Law of the Sea in Chago (sic) Archipelago Case,' *Asil Blogs*, 18 March 2015, https://www.asil.org/blogs/permanent-court-arbitration-finds-uk-violation-convention-law-sea-chago-archipelago-case-march (retrieved on 8 September 2018).
35. See https://wikileaks.org/plusd/cables/09LONDON1156_a.html (retrieved on 5 September 2018) and Backford, Martin, 'UK government officials to be cross-examined over WikiLeaks cable,' *The Telegraph*, 26 July 2012, https://www.telegraph.co.uk/news/worldnews/wikileaks/9427615/UK-government-officials-to-

be-cross-examined-over-WikiLeaks-cable.html (retrieved on 5 September 2018).

36. See Rosen, Mark E., 'Is Diego Garcia at Risk of Slipping from Washington's Grasp?', *The National Interest*, 19 September 2017, https://nationalinterest.org/feature/diego-garcia-risk-slipping-washingtons-grasp-22381 (retrieved on 5 September 2018).
37. 'Extended US lease blocks Chagossians' return home,' *Financial Times*, 16 November 2016 (retrieved on 5 September 2018) and Bowcott, Owen, 'Chagos Islanders cannot return home, UK Foreign Office confirms,' *The Guardian*, 16 November 2016, https://www.theguardian.com/world/2016/nov/16/chagos-islanders-cannot-return-home-uk-foreign-office-confirms (retrieved on 5 September 2018).
38. Rosen, op. cit.
39. Chaudhury, Dipanjan Roy, 'India backs Mauritius claim on Chagos Archipelago at International Court of Justice,' *The Economic Times*, 6 September 2018, https://economictimes.indiatimes.com/news/defence/india-backs-mauritius-claim-on-chagos-archipelago-at-international-court-of-justice/articleshow/65694774.cms (retrieved on 10 September 2018).
40. Fatovich, Laura, 'Indian and Chinese Strategic Interest in the Indian Ocean Benefit Mauritius,' *Future Directions International*, 7 June 2017, http://www.futuredirections.org.au/publication/indian-chinese-strategic-interests-indian-ocean-benefit-mauritius/ (retrieved on 25 August 2018.)
41. Wright, op. cit., pp. 156-158.
42. 'Mauritius Eyes Place on Maritime Silk Road,' *Fitch Solutions*, 11 July 2017, https://www.fitchsolutions.com/country-risk-sovereigns/economics/mauritius-eyes-place-maritime-silk-road-11-07-2017 (retrieved on 10 September 2018).
43. Cotterill, Joseph, 'Is Mauritius big enough for China and India?', *Financial Times*, 5 October 2017, https://www.ft.com/content/bb658580-8434-11e7-94e2-c5b903247afd (retrieved on 5 September 2018).
44. Servansingh, Rajiv, 'Economic Diplomacy at Work: Xi Jinping's official visit,' *The Mauritius Times*, 30 July 2018, http://www.mauritiustimes.com/mt/economic-diplomacy-at-work/ (retrieved on 5 September 2018).
45. Li Feng, 'China, Mauritius to turn bilateral friendship into a new page,' *The People's Daily*, 30 July 2018, http://en.people.cn/n3/2018/0730/c90000-9486016.html (retrieved on 10 September 2018).
46. 'China's Belt and Road stirs up local anxieties,' *Nikkei Asian Review*, 24 July 2018, https://asia.nikkei.com/Spotlight/Belt-and-Road/

China-s-Belt-and-Road-stirs-up-local-anxieties (retrieved on 10 September 2018).

47. Ibid.

5. THE FRENCH

1. Figures from *France and Security in the Asia-Pacific*. Paris: Directorate General for International Relations and Strategy, Ministry of Defence, 2015, p. 12.
2. I conducted that interview, which appeared in the 18 November 1995 issue of *Jane's Defence Weekly*. Kerguelen is mentioned in that piece, but, in the actual interview, which took place in Papeete, Tahiti, Vice-Adm. Euverte said more about the strategic importance of Kerguelen, for instance that military ordinance was sent from there to the Gulf.
3. For the early history of Réunion, see Aldrich, Robert and John Connell, *France's Overseas Frontier: Départements et Territoires d'Outre-Mer*, Cambridge: Cambridge University Press, 1992, pp. 29-33.
4. See Doshi, Vidhi, '"I felt abandoned": Children stolen by France try to find their past, 50 years on,' *The Guardian*, 23 October 2016, https://www.theguardian.com/world/2016/oct/22/reunion-france-stolen-children-try-to-find-their-past and Penketh, Anne, 'France faces up to scandal of Réunion's stolen children,' *The Guardian*, 16 February 2014, https://www.theguardian.com/world/2014/feb/16/france-reunion-stolen-children (retrieved on 5 June 2018).
5. *France 24*, 24 February 2012, http://observers.france24.com/en/20120224-three-nights-riots-reunion-island-cauldron-boiling-over-saint-denis-high-cost-of-living-gas-prices-protest (retrieved on 5 June 2018).
6. Sutter, Karl, 'Kerguelen: A French Mystery', Newsletter of the Antarctic Society of Australia, No. 16 (March 1989), pp. 5-20.
7. Ibid., p. 7.
8. Kauffmann, Jean-Paul, *The Arch of Kerguelen: Voyage to the Island of Desolation*, New York/London: Four Walls Eights Windows, 1993, p. 132.
9. Metz, Helen C. (ed.), *Indian Ocean: Five Island Countries*, Washington: Federal Research Division, Library of Congress, 1995, p. 152.
10. Ibid., p. 154.
11. Ibid., p. 161.
12. Ibid., p. 162.
13. 'France's dog of war spared jail,' *BBC News*, 20 June 2006, http://news.bbc.co.uk/2/hi/europe/5097618.stm (retrieved on 10 June 2018).

14. 'Why is China investing in the Comoros?' *CBS News*, 12 November 2014, https://www.cbsnews.com/news/why-china-is-investing-in-comoros/ (retrieved on 20 May 2018).
15. Ibid.
16. 'Xi urges China, Comoros to enhance economic cooperation,' *China Daily*, 4 December 2015, http://www.chinadaily.com.cn/business/2015-12/05/content_22634841.htm (retrieved on 20 May 2018).
17. 'Madagascar: Mining, Minerals and Fuel Resources,' *AZO Mining*, 23 August 2012 (retrieved on 20 August 2018).
18. Ibid.
19. Metz, op. cit., p. 32.
20. For this development, see Metz, op. cit. pp. 12-13.
21. Ibid., p. 14.
22. Ibid., p. 19.
23. For an excellent account of this era, see Dewar, Bob, Simon Massey, and Bruce Baker, *Madagascar: Time to Make a Fresh Start*, London: Chatham House, January 2013, https://www.chathamhouse.org/sites/default/files/public/Research/Africa/0113pp_madagascar.pdf (retrieved on 5 September 2018).
24. Fisher, Daniel, 'The World's Worst Economies,' *Forbes*, 5 July 2011, https://www.forbes.com/sites/danielfisher/2011/07/05/the-worlds-worst-economies/#a9f42895e960 (retrieved on 5 September 2018).
25. Pellerin, Mathieu, *The Recent Blossoming in Relations between China and Madagascar*, Paris: The Institut Français des relations internationales, 2012, p. 10, https://www.ifri.org/en/publications/enotes/notes-de-lifri/recent-blossoming-relations-between-china-and-madagascar (retrieved on 26 August 2018).
26. 'Dominance of Chinese firms in Madagascar sparks social backlash,' *The Straits Times*, 19 December 2016, https://www.straitstimes.com/world/dominance-of-chinese-firms-in-madagascar-sparks-social-backlash (retrieved on 25 May 2018).
27. Ibid.
28. See report from the Hong Kong Trade and Development Council, http://china-trade-research.hktdc.com/business-news/article/The-Belt-and-Road-Initiative/Madagascar-Market-Profile/obor/en/1/1X000000/1X0ADLFU.htm (retrieved on 5 September 2018).
29. See http://www.worldstopexports.com/madagascars-top-import-partners/

30. Wikipedia, using a variety of sources, has a comprehensive list of overseas Chinese at https://en.wikipedia.org/wiki/Overseas_Chinese#cite_note-temporarychinese-86 (retrieved on 25 May 2018).
31. See 'South Africa' in Pan, Lynn (ed.), *The Encyclopedia of the Chinese Overseas*, Singapore: Editions Didier Millet and the Chinese Heritage Centre, second edition, 2006, p. 361.
32. Pellerin, op. cit., p. 4 and Pan, op. cit., p. 347.
33. Pellerin, op. cit., p. 7.
34. Ibid., p. 7.
35. Ibid., p. 8.
36. 'President of Madagascar: Belt and Road Initiative a "visionary strategy",' *Xinhuanet*, 28 March 2017, http://www.xinhuanet.com/english/china/2017-03/29/c_136168310.htm (retrieved on 15 May 2018).
37. 'China welcomes Madagascar to join Belt and Road construction,' *Xinhua*, 6 April 2017, http://www.chinadaily.com.cn/beltandroadinitiative/2017-04/06/content_28814293.htm (retrieved on 10 September 2018).
38. Ibid.
39. 'Madagascar', International Monetary Fund, 2017, http:// www.imf.org/external/pubs/ft/weo/2017/01/weodata/weorept.aspx?pr.x=62&pr.y=9&sy=2017&ey=2021&scsm=1&ssd=1&sort=country&ds=.&br=1&c=674&s=NGDPD%2CNGDPDPC%2CPPPGDP%2CPPPPC%2CLP&grp=0&a= (retrieved on 10 September 2018).
40. Scimia, Emanuele, 'China isn't our target, says French Pacific commander,' *Asia Times*, 25 August 2018, http://www.atimes.com/article/china-isnt-our-target-says-french-pacific-naval-commander/ (retrieved on 25 August 2018).
41. Ibid.
42. 'Emmanuel Macron warns over China dominance in Indo-Pacific,' *Agence France-Presse* in *The Straits Times*, 3 May 2018, https://www.straitstimes.com/asia/australianz/macron-warns-over-china-dominance-in-indo-pacific (retrieved on 5 September 2018).

6. THE SEYCHELLES

1. Quoted in Mockler, Anthony, *The New Mercenaries: The History of the Hired Soldier from the Congo to the Seychelles*, New York: Paragon Publishers, 1987, p. 259.
2. Prokop, Andrew, 'The Secret Seychelles Meeting Robert Mueller is Zeroing in on, explained,' *Vox*, 10 April 2018, https://www.vox.

com/2018/3/7/17088908/erik-prince-trump-russia-seychelles-mueller (retrieved at 18 September 2018.)

3. Ecott, Tim, *The Story of Seychelles*, Victoria: Outer Island Books, 2015, p. 8.
4. Ibid., p. 9.
5. Ibid., p. 11.
6. Ibid., p. 13.
7. Ibid., p. 16.
8. Quoted in ibid., pp. 118-119.
9. Ibid., p. 25.
10. Metz, Helen Chapin (ed.), *Indian Ocean: Five Island Countries*, Washington: Federal Research Division, Library of Congress, 1995, p. 209.
11. 'The Life of Seychelles' Founding President, James Mancham,' *The Seychelles News Agency*, 9 January 2017, http://www.seychellesnewsagency.com/articles/6578/The+life+of+Seychelles%27+founding+president%2C+James+Mancham (retrieved on 5 September 2018), see also Mancham, James R., *Seychelles Global Citizen: The Autobiography of the Founding President of the Republic of Seychelles*, St. Paul, Minnesota: Paragon House, 2009.
12. Mancham, op. cit., pp. 12-13.
13. Ibid., p. 37.
14. Ecott, op. cit., p. 63.
15. Ibid., pp. 55-56.
16. Ibid., p. 57.
17. Ibid., p. 79.
18. Hoare, Michael, *The Seychelles Affair*, New York: Bantam Press, 1986, p. 18.
19. Mancham, op. cit., pp. 148-149.
20. *Soldiers of Fortune: Mercenary Wars*, https://www.mercenary-wars.net/biography/mike-hoare.html (retrieved on 5 September 2018).
21. Hoare, op.cit., pp. 22 and 25.
22. Ibid., p. 27.
23. There are several accounts of the Frothblowers' coup attempt, and apart from Hoare's own in *The Seychelles Affair* there is Brooks, Aubrey, *Death Row in Paradise: The Untold Story of the Mercenary Invasion of the Seychelles, 1981–1983*, Solihull, West Midlands: Helion & Company, 2013. Mockler in op.cit. also has a chapter about the coup attempt, pp. 284-314. See also Mancham, op. cit., pp. 192-193.
24. Labuschagne, Riaan, *On South Africa's Secret Service: An Undercover Agent's Story*, Alberton, South Africa: Galago, 2002, p. 56, and Shaer, Matthew, Michael Hudson, Margot Williams, 'Sun and Shadows: How

an Island Paradise Became a Haven for Dirty Money,' *International Consortium of Investigative Journalists*, 3 June 2014, https://www.icij.org/investigations/offshore/sun-and-shadows-how-island-paradise-became-haven-dirty-money/ (retrieved on 5 August 2018).

25. Mancham, op. cit., p. 192.
26. Hoare, op. cit., pp. 27-28.
27. Quoted in Lelyveld, Joseph, 'Pretoria Jails Famed Soldier After Failed Seychelles Coup,' *The New York Times*, 30 November 1981, https://www.nytimes.com/1981/11/30/world/pretoria-jails-famed-soldier-after-failed-seychelles-coup.html (retrieved on 10 September 2018.)
28. Bermudez, James S., *Terrorism: The North Korean Connection*, New York: Crane Russak, 1990, p. 125.
29. Quoted in Mancham, op. cit., pp. 151-152.
30. Ibid.
31. Ecott, op. cit., p. 91. Ecott refers to Rajiv Gandhi as 'the Indian president', but he was, of course India's prime minister.
32. 'Exiled Seychelles Leader Is Shot Dead in London,' *The New York Times*, 30 November 1985, https://www.nytimes.com/1985/11/30/world/around-the-world-exiled-seychelles-leader-is-shot-dead-in-london.html (retrieved on 15 September 2018).
33. Mancham, op. cit., p. 149.
34. Metz, op. cit., p. 234.
35. Ecott, op. cit., p. 157.
36. Ibid., p. 157.
37. Grant, Euan, 'The Russian Mafia and organised crime: How can this global force be tamed?', *Open Democracy*, 12 October 2012, https://www.opendemocracy.net/od-russia/euan-grant/russian-mafia-and-organised-crime-how-can-this-global-force-be-tamed (retrieved on 5 September 2018).
38. Ellis, Stephen, 'Africa and International Corruption: The Strange Case of South Africa and Seychelles,' *African Affairs*, (1996), issue 95, p. 169, http://francegenocidetutsi.org/EllisStephenStrangeCase.pdf (retrieved on 5 September 2018).
39. Ibid., p. 169.
40. Ibid., p. 170.
41. Ibid., p. 170.
42. Ibid., p. 170 and 'Seychelles Past: The Dark History,' *Seychelles Voice*, 9 October 2016, http://seychellesvoice.blogspot.com/2016/10/seychelles-past-dark-history.html (retrieved on 5 September 2018). *Seychelles Voice* gives the name as The Order of the Knights Hospitalers of Malta for his country, but Ellis's name is the correct one.

43. Ellis, op. cit., p. 176.
44. Ibid., p. 176.
45. Ibid., p. 178.
46. Ibid., p. 178.
47. Thayer, Nate, 'Arms deal on seized weapons,' *The Phnom Penh Post*, 24 February 1995, https://www.phnompenhpost.com/national/arms-deal-seized-weapons (retrieved on 20 August 2018).
48. Information collected by the author in Phnom Penh, mid-1990s.
49. See http://foip.saha.org.za/uploads/images/CaseNo5598_16_FA_20160217.pdf (retrieved on 5 September 2018).
50. Mancham, op. cit., p. 151.
51. 'Seychelles former President launches James Michel Foundation to continue promoting the blue economy,' *Seychelles News Agency*, 10 February 2017, http://www.seychellesnewsagency.com/articles/6752/Seychelles+former+President+launches+James+Michel+Foundation+to+continue+promoting+the+blue+economy (retrieved on 5 September 2018).
52. Shaer, Hudson and Williams, op. cit. Their report for the International Consortium of Investigative Journalists is the most detailed and comprehensive account of the offshore industry in the Seychelles that is available on the Internet.
53. Ibid.
54. Ibid.
55. Ibid.
56. Ibid.
57. Ibid.
58. Ibid.
59. Willacy, Mark, 'Kiribati, Seychelles accused of giving North Koreans passports,' *ABC News*, 5 December 2012, http://www.abc.net.au/news/2012-12-05/an-kiribati-seychelles-accused-of-giving-north-koreans-passports/4409832 (retrieved on 20 August 2018)í
60. Shaer, Hudson and Williams, op. cit.
61. Ibid.
62. Ibid.
63. Ibid.
64. GDP per capita was US$13,997 in 2017, up from US$2,216 in 1961, according to Trading Economics, https://tradingeconomics.com/seychelles/gdp-per-capita (retrieved on 15 September 2018) while the World Bank puts it at US$15,075 in 2016, https://wits.worldbank.org/countryprofile/en/country/SYC/startyear/2012/endyear/2016/indicator/NY-GDP-PCAP-CD (retrieved on 10 September 2018).

65. Chapling, Liam, Hansel Confiance and Marie-Therese Purvis, *Social Policies in Seychelles*, London: Commonwealth Secretariat and United Nations Research Institute for Social Development, 2011, p. 94.
66. Entous, Adam, Greg Miller, Kevin Sieff and Karen DeYoung, 'Blackwater founder held secret Seychelles meeting to establish Trump-Putin back channel,' *Washington Post*, 3 April 2017, https://www.washingtonpost.com/world/national-security/blackwater-founder-held-secret-seychelles-meeting-to-establish-trump-putin-back-channel/2017/04/03/95908a08-1648-11e7-ada0-1489b735b3a3_story.html?utm_term=.4e9c177f4fa0 (retrieved on 25 August 2018).
67. 'Seychelles to Boost Military Cooperation with China,' State House: Office of the President of the Republic of Seychelles,' http://www.statehouse.gov.sc/news.php?news_id=3200 (retrieved on 25 August 2018).
68. Bennett, Jody Ray, 'Seychelles: An Invitation from China,' *Geopolitical Monitor*, 27 December 2011, https://www.geopoliticalmonitor.com/seychelles-an-invitation-for-china-4567/ (retrieved on 25 September 2018).
69. 'Special Representative of the Chinese Government on African Affairs, Xu Jinghu Visited Seychelles,' *Embassy of the People's Republic of China in the Republic of Seychelles*, 18 June 2017, http://sc.china-embassy.org/eng/zsgx/t1488133.htm (retrieved on 25 August 2018).
70. 'Seychelles, India looking for more areas of cooperation,' *Seychelles News Agency*, 10 October 2017, http://www.seychellesnewsagency.com/articles/8039/Seychelles%2C+India+looking+for+more+areas+of+cooperation (retrieved on 25 August 2018).
71. Lintner, Bertil, 'China-India vie for a strategic slice of paradise,' *Asia Times*, 23 November 2017, http://www.atimes.com/article/china-india-vie-strategic-slice-paradise/ (retrieved on 25 August 2018).
72. Saravalle, Edoardo, 'Tourism: China's People Power Tool,' *The Diplomat*, 19 June 2018, https://thediplomat.com/2018/06/tourism-chinas-people-power-tool/ (last accessed on 15 December 2018).
73. Seidel, Jamie, 'China "weaponises" tourism: How Palau may be the model of things to come,' *Reuters*, https://www.news.com.au/travel/travel-updates/china-weaponiss-tourism-how-palau-may-be-the-model-of-things-to-come/news-story/4617b1a1e4657d1434d992031eb58098 (retrieved on 20 September 2018).
74. Simpson, Peter and Dan Nelson, 'China considers Seychelles military base plan,' *The Telegraph*, 13 December 2011, https://www.telegraph.co.uk/news/worldnews/africaandindianocean/seychelles/8953319/

China-considers-Seychelles-military-base-plan.html (retrieved on 25 August 2018).

75. Ibid.
76. Bedi, Rahul, 'India to set up overseas military base on Seychelles,' *Jane's*, 29 January 2018, https://www.janes.com/article/77431/india-to-set-up-overseas-military-base-on-seychelles (retrieved on 25 August 2018).
77. Thande, George, 'Seychelles parliament blocks planned Indian naval base on remote island,' *Reuters*, 22 June 2018, https://www.reuters.com/article/us-seychelles-india/seychelles-parliament-blocks-planned-indian-naval-base-on-remote-island-idUSKBN1JI0UL (retrieved on 20 September 2018).
78. See, for instance, Shubham, 'Is China behind Seychelles' decision to scrap India's military base project?' *OneIndia*, 18 June 2018, https://www.oneindia.com/international/is-china-behind-seychelles-decision-to-scrap-indias-military-base-project-2717719.html (retrieved on 25 August 2018).
79. 'Seychelles opposition boycotts opening of Chinese-built National Assembly building,' *US embassy cable from Mauritius*, 9 December 2009, https://wikileaks.org/plusd/cables/09PORTLOUIS403_a.html (retrieved on 5 September 2018).
80. Ibid.
81. 'Truck drivers protest in Seychelles' capital over exclusion from Chinese project,' *Seychelles News Agency*, 13 February 2018, http://www.seychellesnewsagency.com/articles/8677/Truck+drivers+protest+in+Seychelles%27+capital+over+exclusion+from+Chinese+project (retrieved on 10 September 2018).
82. Hu Qing, 'Sri Lanka, Mauritius, Seychelles routes revived,' *China Daily*, 22 May 2015, http://www.chinadaily.com.cn/m/qingdao/2015-05/22/content_20789485.htm (retrieved on 5 September 2018).
83. Ibid.

7. THE MALDIVES

1. Rasheed, Zaheena, 'Ibrahim Mohamed Solih sworn in as new Maldives president,' *Al Jazeera*, 17 November 2018, https://www.aljazeera.com/news/2018/11/ibrahim-mohamed-solih-sworn-maldives-president-181117111139762.html (retrieved on 29 November 2018).
2. 'An All-Out Assault on Democracy: Crushing Dissent in the Maldives,' *Human Rights Watch*, 16 August 2018, https://www.hrw.org/report/2018/08/16/all-out-assault-democracy/crushing-dissent-maldives (retrieved on 6 October 2018).

3. For an official biography of Maumoon Abdul Gayoom, see https://wn.com/maumoon_foundationge_ihuya_program_03_raeese_maumoon_speech_part_01/politician (retrieved on 5 October 2018).
4. J.J. Robinson, *The Maldives: Islamic Republic, Tropical Autocracy*, London: Hurst, 2015, pp. 138-139.
5. 'Republic of Maldives: Prisoners of Conscience and Unfair Trial Concerns 1990–1993,' *Amnesty International*, 31 May 1993, p. 6. https://www.amnesty.org/download/Documents/192000/asa290011993en.pdf.
6. Lang, Olivia, '"Anni" heralds new era in Maldives,' BBC, 29 October 2008, http://news.bbc.co.uk/2/hi/south_asia/7697283.stm (retrieved on 8 October 2018).
7. Ibid.
8. Robinson, op. cit., p. 2.
9. Ibid., p. 2.
10. https://hottestheadsofstate.com/2010/05/mohamed-nasheed/ (retrieved on 4 October 2018).
11. 'Maldives government highlights the impact of climate change... by meeting underwater,' *The Mail Online*, 20 October 2009, https://www.dailymail.co.uk/news/article-1221021/Maldives-underwater-cabinet-meeting-held-highlight-impact-climate-change.html (retrieved on 6 October 2018).
12. 'Maldives president quits after protests,' *Al Jazeera*, 7 February 2012, https://www.aljazeera.com/news/asia/2012/02/20122765334806442.html (retrieved on 7 October 2018).
13. 'Maldives: 13 year sentence for former president "a travesty of justice",' *Amnesty International*, 13 March 2015, https://www.amnesty.org/en/latest/news/2015/03/maldives-mohamed-nasheed-convicted-terrorism/ (retrieved on 5 October 2018).
14. 'Nasheed to travel to UK for surgery,' *Maldives Independent*, 16 January 2016, https://maldivesindependent.com/politics/nasheed-to-travel-to-uk-for-surgery-121409 (retrieved on 8 October 2018).
15. See Allchin, Joseph, 'Brothers in Corruption: Maldives and Burma,' *Democratic Voice of Burma*, 3 March 2011, http://www.dvb.no/analysis/brothers-in-corruption-maldives-and-burma/14568 (retrieved on 5 October 2018).
16. A copy of the Grant Thornton report, which is internal, is in my possession.
17. Allchin, op. cit.
18. Chakrabarti, Sumon K., 'Isle's oil slick: Maldivian autocrat's family's illegal "oil trade" allegedly worth $800 million,' *The Week*, 20 February

2011, and 'Yameen implicated in STO blackmarket oil trade with Burmese junta, alleges The Week,' *Minivan News Archive*, February 2011, https://minivannewsarchive.com/politics/yameen-implicated-in-sto-blackmarket-oil-trade-with-burmese-junta-alleges-the-week-16046 (retrieved on 5 October 2018).

19. 'Government paying Grant Thornton 4.6 million pounds to halt oil trade investigation,' Minivan News Archive, https://minivannewsarchive.com/politics/government-paying-grant-thornton-4-6-million-to-halt-sto-oil-trade-investigation-65581 (retrieved on 5 October 2018).
20. Chakrabarti, Sumon K., 'Has India lost the mango and the sack in the Maldives?' *News 18*, 2 March 2012, https://www.news18.com/blogs/india/sumon-k-chakrabarti/has-india-lost-the-mango-and-the-sack-in-the-maldives-12668-746548.html (retrieved on 8 October 2018).
21. Ramachandran, Sudha, 'The China-Maldives Connection,' *The Diplomat*, 25 January 2018, https://thediplomat.com/2018/01/the-china-maldives-connection/ (retrieved on 8 October 2018).
22. 'Xi arrives in Maldives for state visit,' *Xinhua*, 15 September 2014, http://www.china.org.cn/world/2014-09/15/content_33510542.htm (retrieved on 5 October 2018).
23. Ramachandran, op. cit.
24. Ibid.
25. 'China-Maldives Friendship Bridge Opens to Traffic,' *Xinhua*, 31 August 2018, http://www.xinhuanet.com/english/2018-08/31/c_137431709.htm (retrieved on 5 October 2018).
26. *Maldives Year Book 2018*, http://statisticsmaldives.gov.mv/yearbook/2018/wp-content/uploads/sites/5/2018/03/10.1.pdf (retrieved on 5 October 2018).
27. Parashar, Sachin, 'China's ocean observatory in Maldives sparks fresh security concerns,' *The Times of India*, 26 February 2018, https://timesofindia.indiatimes.com/india/chinas-ocean-observatory-in-maldives-sparks-fresh-security-fear/articleshow/63072040.cms (retrieved on 5 October 2018).
28. 'China Hits Out At Ex-Maldives President for Criticising its Projects,' *NDTV*, 26 September 2018, https://www.ndtv.com/world-news/china-hits-out-at-mohamed-nasheed-ex-maldives-president-for-criticising-its-projects-1922654 (retrieved on 5 October 2018).
29. Ibid.
30. Ibid.
31. Ibid.
32. Pai, Nitin, 'After Abdulla Yameen, Maldives must now untangle the web of Chinese contracts,' *The Print*, 25 September 2018, https://

theprint.in/opinion/after-abdulla-yameen-maldives-must-now-untangle-the-web-of-chinese-contracts/124107/ (retrieved on 5 October 2018).

33. Long Xingchun, 'China, India should cooperate in Maldives,' *Global Times*, 25 September 2018, http://www.globaltimes.cn/content/1120873.shtml (retrieved on 5 October 2018).
34. Ibid.
35. 'Former Maldives leader Gayoom freed on bail a week after election,' *Al Jazeera*, 30 September 2018, https://www.aljazeera.com/news/2018/09/maldives-leader-gayoom-freed-bail-week-election-180930150231895.html (retrieved on 10 October 2018).
36. Bell, H.C.P., *The Maldive Islands: An Account of the Physical Features, Inhabitants, Productions and Trade*, New Delhi and Chennai: Asian Educational Services, 2004, (reprint, originally published in 1883 by Government Printer, Ceylon), p. 21. For the early history of the Maldives, see also Hockly, T.W., *The Thousand Isles: A Short Account of the People, History and Customs of the Maldive Archipelago*, New Delhi and Chennai: Asian Educational Services, 2014 (reprint, originally published in 1935 in London by H.F. & G. Witherby).
37. Metz, Helen Chapin (ed.), *Indian Ocean: Five Island Countries*, Washington: Federal Research Division, Library of Congress, 1995, p. 258. There are many, some fanciful, accounts of the early history of the Maldives. The Norwegian explorer Thor Heyerdahl in his *The Maldive Mystery* (New York: Ballantine Books, 1987) drew comparisons between some pyramid-like structure he found on one of the islands and ancient pyramids of Mesopotamia and pre-Columbian America. He suggested the first inhabitants of the Maldives were sun-worshippers, similar to the people of ancient Peru and Mexico. But Heyerdahl is not known for being a good historian and travel writer Paul Theroux has compared him to 'a hack writer of detective stories', https://theculturetrip.com/asia/maldives/articles/a-sphere-of-symbols-thor-heyerdahl-s-maldive-mystery/ (retrieved on 8 October 2018).
38. See https://iias.asia/iiasn/iiasn5/insouasi/maloney.html (retrieved on 5 October 2018).
39. Ma Huan, *Ying-yai Sheng-lan: The Overall Survey of the Ocean Shore*, Bangkok: White Lotus Press, 1997 (reprint), pp. 49-50.
40. Ibid., p. 50.
41. Didi, Amir Muhammad Amin, *Ladies and Gentlemen... The Maldive Islands!* Colombo: Evergreen, 1949, p. 12.
42. The best description of the base is on https://en.wikipedia.org/wiki/RAF_Gan (retrieved on 5 October 2018).

43. See O'Shea, Michael, *The United Suvadive Islands Republic: Colonialist Conspiracy or Spontaneous Rebellion? A Study of Maldivian Politics in the Mid-20th Century*, Master of Letters, History Department, University of New England, New South Wales, 1999.
44. Colma, J. *Communication: "What now for Britain?" The State Department's intelligence assessment of the 'Special Relationship'*, Manchester: Salford University, February 1968, http://usir.salford.ac.uk/1712/1/What_Now_for_Britain.pdf (retrieved on 5 October 2018).
45. Fairhall, David, 'Indian Ocean island of Gan returned to Maldives,' *The Guardian*, 15 September 1975, https://www.theguardian.com/world/2015/sep/15/gan-maldives-diego-garcia-island-1975 (retrieved on 10 October 2018).
46. All three quotes from Shaahunaz, Fathmath, 'Three warships of Chinese navy on friendly visit to Maldives,' *The Edition*, 27 August 2017, https://edition.mv/news/4072 (retrieved on 10 October 2018).
47. Shaahunaz, Fathmath, 'Maldives roots for China in South China Sea dispute,' *The Edition*, 4 January 2017, https://edition.mv/news/1987 (retrieved on 10 October 2018).
48. Saran, Shyam, 'Enter the Dragon,' *India Today*, 26 February 2018, https://www.indiatoday.in/magazine/up-front/story/20180226-india-china-maldives-abdulla-yameen-male-mohamed-nasheed-1170909-2018-02-15 (retrieved on 10 October 2018).
49. Ai Jun, 'Unauthorized military intervention in Male must be stopped,' *Global Times*, 12 February 2018, http://www.globaltimes.cn/content/1089435.shtml (retrieved on 10 October 2018).
50. World Bank data, https://data.worldbank.org/indicator/NY.GDP.PCAP.CD?locations=Z4-8S-Z7 (retrieved on 5 October 2018).
51. Bearup, Greg, 'Maldives: Islamist terror could sink Indian Ocean paradise,' *The Australian*, 30 August 2016, https://www.theaustralian.com.au/news/world/maldives-islamist-terror-could-sink-indian-ocean-paradise/news-story/7a80bff385fb3e27ade26a72ce43b3e6 (retrieved on 10 August 2018).
52. Wright, Oliver, 'Islamic State: The Maldives: a recruiting paradise for jihadists,' *The Independent*, 13 September 2014, https://www.independent.co.uk/news/world/asia/islamic-state-the-maldives-a-recruiting-paradise-for-jihadists-9731574.html (retrieved on 10 October 2018).
53. Chauhan, Neeraj, 'After the fall of Raqqa, return of ISIS fighters worries India,' *The Times of India*, 26 October 2017, https://timesofindia.indiatimes.com/india/after-fall-of-raqqa-return-of-isis-fighter-s-worries-india/articleshow/61232251.cms (retrieved on 10 October 2018).

54. Wright, op. cit.
55. Ibid.
56. Boland, Mary, 'Tourists blissfully unaware of Islamist tide in Maldives,' *The Irish Times*, 16 August 2014, https://www.irishtimes.com/news/world/asia-pacific/tourists-blissfully-unaware-of-islamist-tide-in-maldives-1.1898425 (retrieved on 10 October 2018).
57. Robinson, op. cit., p. 167.
58. Ibid., p. 168.
59. Ibid.
60. Ibid.
61. Bearup, op. cit.
62. See https://www.state.gov/documents/organization/171757.pdf (retrieved on 5 October 2018).
63. Buncombe, Andrew, '150 women face adultery flogging on Maldives,' *The Independent*, 22 July 2009, https://www.independent.co.uk/news/world/asia/150-women-face-adultery-flogging-on-maldives-1757150.html (retrieved on 10 October 2018).
64. 'Maldives woman sentenced to death by stoning wins reprieve,' *Agence France-Presse*, 15 October 2015, https://www.telegraph.co.uk/news/worldnews/africaandindianocean/maldives/11940419/Maldives-woman-sentenced-to-death-by-stoning-wins-reprieve.html (retrieved on 10 October 2018).
65. Safi, Michael, 'Maldives blogger stabbed to death in capital,' *The Guardian*, 23 April 2017, https://www.theguardian.com/world/2017/apr/23/maldives-blogger-yameen-rasheed-stabbed-to-death-in-capital (retrieved on 5 October 2018), and Shultz, Kai, 'Maldives, Tourist Haven, Casts Wary Eye on Growing Islamic Radicalism,' *New York Times*, 20 June 2017, https://www.nytimes.com/2017/06/18/world/asia/maldives-islamic-radicalism.html (retrieved on 5 October 2018).
66. Ministry of Defence and National Security, Male, Republic of Maldives: *Announcement*, 13 February 2018, http://www.defence.gov.mv/file.php?fileId=157 (retrieved on 5 October 2018).
67. Chaudhury, Dipanjan Roy, 'India, Maldives sign pact to expand defence cooperation,' *The Economic Times*, 12 July 2018, https://economictimes.indiatimes.com/news/defence/india-maldives-sign-pact-to-expand-defence-cooperation/printarticle/51779405.cms (retrieved on 10 October 2018).
68. 'Minicoy is not part of the Maldives,' http://www.maldivesroyalfamily.com/minicoy_not_maldives.shtml (retrieved on 15 October 2018).
69. Ibid.

70. Ibid.
71. *Bureau of Counterterrorism and Countering Violent Extremism, Country Report 2016: Maldives*, https://mv.usmission.gov/wp-content/uploads/sites/212/2017/07/Country-Reports-on-Terrorism-2016-Maldives.pdf (retrieved on 5 October 2018).
72. Bhadrakumar, M.K., 'Maldives crisis: US-Indian strategic alliance forming,' *Asia Times*, 7 February 2018, http://www.atimes.com/article/maldives-crisis-us-indian-strategic-alliance-forming/ (retrieved on 10 Octonber 2018).
73. Aneez, Shihar, 'Maldives accuses US of intimidation after comments on political prisoners,' *Reuters*, 8 September 2018, https://www.reuters.com/article/us-maldives-politics/maldives-accuses-us-of-intimidation-after-comments-on-political-prisoners-idUSKCN1LN2IR (retrieved on 10 October 2018).
74. *World Military and Police Forces: Maldives, 2013*, http://worldmilitaryintel.blogspot.com/2013/05/blog-post_3049.html (retrieved on 10 October 2018).
75. Rasheed, Zaheena, 'Maldives army seals off parliament, arrests MPs,' *Al Jazeera*, 5 February 2018, https://www.aljazeera.com/news/2018/02/maldives-army-seals-parliament-arrests-mps-180204093020645.html (retrieved on 5 October 2018).
76. Maldives National Defence Force, https://www.webcitation.org/63IBLdclC (retrieved on 10 October 2018).
77. 'Maldives-China Relations,' *GlobalSecurity.org*, https://www.globalsecurity.org/military/world/indian-ocean/mv-forrel-prc.htm (retrieved on 10 October 2018).
78. Ibid.
79. Ibid.
80. Pal, Alasdair, 'Maldives' Chinese debt and political risk could lead to trouble in paradise,' *Reuters*, 18 September 2018, https://www.reuters.com/article/us-maldives-election-debt/maldives-chinese-debt-and-political-risk-could-lead-to-trouble-in-paradise-idUSKCN1LY1QR (retrieved on 10 October 2018).
81. Ibid.
82. See http://www.nationmaster.com/country-info/profiles/Maldives/Economy (retrieved on 5 October 2018).

8. AUSTRALIA'S LITTLE DOTS

1. Babbage, Ross, *Should Australia Plan to Defend Christmas and Cocos Islands?* Canberra: Strategic and Defence Studies Centre, Research School of

Pacific Studies, the Australian National University, 1988, pp. 36 and 40. Also available at http://sdsc.bellschool.anu.edu.au/sites/default/files/publications/attachments/2016-03/045_should_australia_plan_to_defend_christmas_and_cocos_islands_canberra_papers_on_strategy_and_defence_ross_babbage_74p_0731503899.pdf (retrieved on 10 May 2018).

2. Ibid., pp. 32-33.
3. For the history of the Clunies-Ross family, see Clunies-Ross, John C., *The Clunies-Ross Cocos Chronicle*, compiled and self-published in Western Australia by John C. Clunies-Ross, 2009, and Hughes, John Scott, *Kings of the Cocos*, London: Methuen & Co, 1950.
4. Clunies-Ross, op. cit., p. 41 and Hughes, op. cit., p. 44-46.
5. Clunies-Ross, op. cit., p. 38.
6. Hughes, op. cit., p. 56.
7. Ibid., p. 56.
8. Squires, Nick, 'The man who lost a "coral kingdom",' *BBC*, 7 June 2007, http://news.bbc.co.uk/2/hi/programmes/from_our_own_correspondent/6730047.stm (retrieved on 5 September 2018).
9. For a brief history of this epoch in the islands' history, see Adams, Jan and Marg Neale, *Christmas Island: The Early Years 1888–1958*, Chapman ACT: Bruce Neal, 1993, pp. 12-13.
10. Hughes, op. cit., p. 141.
11. For pictures of the Cocos Rupee, see Hughes, op. cit., p. 76.
12. Rees, Jacqueline and Denis Reinhardt, 'End of a dynasty', *Far Eastern Economic Review*, 17 April 1984 (not available electronically).
13. Ibid.
14. Ibid.
15. Chan, Kenneth, *Cocos (Keeling) Islands: The Political Evolution of a Small Island Territory in the Indian Ocean*, p. 15, Honolulu: East West Center, 1987, https://scholarspace.manoa.hawaii.edu/bitstream/10125/21946/Cocos%28Keeling%29Islands1987%5Bpdfa%5D.PDF (retrieved on 5 September 2018).
16. Squires, op. cit.
17. For an account of the mutiny and the Japanese occupation, see Adams and Neale, op. cit., p. 70.
18. Ibid., p. 70.
19. Clunies-Ross, op. cit., p. 129.
20. Kopp, Carlo, 'Strategic potential of the Cocos Islands and Christmas Island,' *Defence Today*, Vol. 9, no 4 (2012), https://www.ausairpower.net/PDF-A/DT-Cocos-Christmas-Mar-2012.pdf (retrieved on 5 September 2018)í

21. See, for instance, discussions on this blog: http://www.vikingsword.com/vb/showthread.php?t=22698 (retrieved on 5 September 2018).
22. The complete text of the defence white paper is available at http://www.defence.gov.au/WhitePaper/ (retrieved on 20 August 2018).
23. *Defence White Paper,* Canberra: Australian Government, Department of Defence, 2016, p. 16.
24. Ibid., p. 16.
25. For a biography of Kang Sheng, see Byron, John and Robert Pack, *The Claws of the Dragon: Kang Sheng, the Evil Genius Behind Mao and His Legacy of Terror in People's China*, New York: Simon & Schuster, 1992.
26. According to several interviews I conducted with the CPB chairman Thakin Ba Thein Tin at the Panghsang party headquarters in December 1986 and January 1987. Thakin Ba Thein Tin told me that he, Ted Hill and Kang Sheng had detailed plans for the revolutionary tide they intended to unleash in Southeast Asia and as far as Australia.
27. Tsai Wei-ping (ed.), *Classified Chinese Communist Documents: A Selection (Chou En-lai's Reports on the International Situation [Excerpts], December 1971 and March 1973)*, Taipei: Institute of International Relations, National Chengchi University, 1978, p. 477.
28. Australian War Memorial website, https://www.awm.gov.au/articles/event/vietnam (retrieved on 14 September 2018).
29. Strahan, Lachlan, *Australia's China: Changing Perceptions from the 1930s to the 1990s,* Cambridge: Cambridge University Press, 1996, p. 294.
30. For a critical account of that period in modern Australian history, see Pilger, John, *A Secret Country*, New York: Alfred A. Knopf, 1991, pp. 142-183.
31. For an interesting eyewitness-account of Pine Gap, see Rosenberg, David, *Inside Pine Gap: The Spy Who Came in From the Desert*, Melbourne: Hardie Grant Books, 2011, written by an American officer who used to work at the station.
32. Lee, Michael, 'Snowden leak reaffirms Australia's four spy installations,' *ZDNet*, 9 July 2013, https://www.zdnet.com/article/snowden-leak-reaffirms-australias-four-spy-installations/ (retrieved on 3 October 2018).
33. Chi Dehua, 'China-Australia trade hits record high in 2017,' *Global Times*, 14 February 2018, https://gbtimes.com/china-australia-trade-hits-record-high-in-2017 (retrieved on 2 October 2018).
34. *Market Profile China*, Canberra: Australian Trade and Investment Commission, 2018, https://www.austrade.gov.au/Australian/Export/Export-markets/Countries/China/Market-profile (retrieved on 5 September 2018).

35. White, Hugh, *The China Choice: Why America Should Share Power*, Collingwood: Black Inc., 2012, p. 11.
36. Ibid., p. 6.
37. Ibid., p. 164.
38. Ibid., p. 146.
39. Garnaut, John, 'The rest of the world is watching how we counter Beijing's campaign of influence,' *The Monthly*, August 2018, https://www.themonthly.com.au/issue/2018/august/1533045600/john-garnaut/australia-s-china-reset (retrieved on 10 September 2018).
40. Ng, Joyce, 'Sino-British Joint Declaration on Hong Kong "no loner has any realistic meaning", Chinese Foreign Ministry says,' *South China Morning Post*, 30 June 2017, https://www.scmp.com/news/hong-kong/politics/article/2100779/sino-british-joint-declaration-hong-kong-no-longer-has-any (retrieved on 10 August 2018).
41. For the full text of the agreement, see http://www.gov.cn/english/2007-06/14/content_649468.htm (retrieved on 5 October 2018).
42. Ibid.
43. Perlez, Jane and Damien Cave, 'As China Rises, Australia Asks Itself: Can It Rely on America?', *The New York Times, 3* December 2017, https://www.nytimes.com/2017/12/03/world/australia/australia-us-china-alliances.html (retrieved on 5 October 2017).
44. Garnaut, op. cit.
45. Remeikis, Amy, 'Sam Dastyari quits as Labor senator over China connections,' *The Guardian*, 11 December 2017, https://www.theguardian.com/australia-news/2017/dec/12/sam-dastyari-quits-labor-senator-china-connections (retrieved on 5 October 2018).
46. Maline, Ursula, 'Chinese businessman Huang Xiangmo's special donations revealed; parties "too reliant",' *ABS News*, http://www.abc.net.au/news/2017-12-12/huang-xiangmos-development-linked-to-greater-sydney-commission/9247860 (retrieved on 5 October 2018).
47. Bourke, Latika, 'Bill Shorten visited home of Chinese donor Huang Xiangmo several months after ASIO party warning,' *The Sydney Morning Herald*, 3 December 2017, https://www.smh.com.au/politics/federal/bill-shorten-visited-home-of-chinese-donor-huang-xiangmo-several-months-after-asio-party-warning-20171203-gzxqps.html (retrieved on 5 October 2018)í
48. Staff writers, 'Chinese donor Huang Xiangmo's $2 million party challenge to Liberal and Labor,' *News.com.au*, 2 March 2018, https://www.news.com.au/national/politics/chinese-donor-huang-

xiangmos-2-million-party-challenge-to-liberal-and-labor/news-story/17d8d657e5347ec173d64cfa8f50cb99 (retrieved on 5 October 2018)í
49. Quoted in Garnaut, op. cit.
50. Ibid.
51. Ibid.
52. Wallace, Charles, 'The art of influence: how China's spies operate in Australia,' *The Sydney Morning Herald*, 3 December 2017, https://www.smh.com.au/public-service/the-art-of-influence-how-chinas-spies-operate-in-australia-20171203-gzxs06.html (retrieved on 5 October 2018).
53. Ibid.
54. Pearlman, Jonathan, 'Foreign students barred from Australian MP internship over spying fears,' *The Telegraph*, 12 July 2018, https://www.telegraph.co.uk/news/2018/07/12/foreign-students-barred-australian-mp-internships-spying-fears/ (retrieved on 5 October 2018).
55. Ibid.
56. McKenzie, Nick, 'Charges loom for ex-intelligence official after ASIO raid,' *The Sydney Morning Herald*, 28 July 2017, https://www.smh.com.au/national/charges-loom-for-ex-intelligence-official-roger-uren-after-asio-raid-20170727-gxjrks.html (retrieved on 6 October 2018).
57. Ibid.
58. Ibid.
59. 'Journalist defends story in libel case brought by billionaire Chau Chak Wing,' *Australian Associated Press*, 14 June 2018, https://www.theguardian.com/media/2018/jun/14/journalist-defends-story-in-libel-case-brought-by-billionaire-chau-chak-wing (retrieved on 5 October 2018).
60. Calmes, Jackie, 'The US Marine Base for Australia Irritates China,' *The New York Times*, 16 November 2011, https://www.nytimes.com/2011/11/17/world/asia/obama-and-gillard-expand-us-australia-military-ties.html (retrieved on 5 October 2018).
61. Nakamura, David, 'US troops headed to Australia, irking China,' *The Washington Post*, 16 November 2011, https://www.washingtonpost.com/world/asia_pacific/us-troops-headed-to-australia-irking-china/2011/11/16/gIQAiGiuRN_story.html?utm_term=.67d016726c07 (retrieved on 5 October 2018).
62. 'Bush's "sheriff" comment causes a stir,' *The Age*, October 2003, https://www.theage.com.au/national/bushs-sheriff-comment-causes-a-stir-20031017-gdwk74.html (retrieved on 5 October 2018).
63. Ibid.

64. Malik, Ashok, 'Under China's shadow, India looks to Australia,' *Yale Global*, https://yaleglobal.yale.edu/content/under-chinas-shadow-india-looks-australia (retrieved on 5 October 2018).
65. Ibid.
66. *Defence White Paper*, p. 62.
67. Murdoch, Scott, 'Angry China rebukes Julie Bishop over East China Sea dispute,' *The Australian*, 7 December 2013, https://www.theaustralian.com.au/national-affairs/foreign-affairs/angry-china-rebukes-julie-bishop-over-east-china-sea-dispute/news-story/4b08fe170b73347b3ef7ce77c05179eb (retrieved on 5 October 2018).
68. Ibid.
69. Murphy, Katharine, 'Chinese premier warns Australia taking sides could lead to a new cold war,' *The Guardian*, 23 March 2017, https://www.theguardian.com/world/2017/mar/23/chinese-premier-warns-australia-taking-sides-could-lead-to-new-cold-war (retrieved on 5 October 2018).
70. Ibid.
71. Ibid.
72. Ibid.
73. White, Hugh, 'America or China? Australia is fooling itself that it doesn't have to choose,' *The Guardian*, 26 November 2017, https://www.theguardian.com/australia-news/2017/nov/27/america-or-china-were-fooling-ourselves-that-we-dont-have-to-choose (retrieved on 5 October 2018).
74. Calvert, Alana, 'You Are Worse Than I Am,' *The Huffington Post* (quoting transcripts published by the Washington Post), 3 August 2017, https://www.huffingtonpost.com.au/2017/08/03/you-are-worse-than-i-am-transcript-released-of-trump-turnbull_a_23063225/ (retrieved on 6 October 2018).
75. Ibid.
76. Smyth, Jamie, 'Battle stations: Asia's arms race hots up, *The Financial Times*, 25 August 2018, https://www.ft.com/content/4492a134-9687-11e8-b67b-b8205561c3fe (retrieved on 30 August 2018).
77. Ibid.
78. *Defence White Paper*, p. 103.
79. 'Defence capability and infrastructure development,' *Parliament of Australia*, 5 April 2017, https://www.aph.gov.au/Parliamentary_Business/Committees/Joint/National_Capital_and_External_Territories/StrategicImportanceIOT/Report_1/section?id=committees%2Freportjnt%2F024077%2F24786 (retrieved on 6 October 2018).

80. Ibid.

9. THE FUTURE

1. 'France to send aircraft carrier to Indian Ocean next year,' *Agence France-Presse*, 20 October 2018, https://economictimes.indiatimes.com/news/defence/france-to-send-aircraft-carrier-to-indian-ocean-next-year/printarticle/66290918.cms (retrieved on 23 October 2018).
2. Ibid.
3. See Ang, Yuen Yuen, 'Needed for China's Belt and Road: a Roadmap,' *Bloomberg*, 27 September 2018, https://www.bloomberg.com/view/articles/2018-09-27/china-s-belt-and-road-initiative-is-a-campaign-not-a-conspiracy (retrieved on 5 October 2018) and Yang Minghong, 'Understanding the One Belt One Road Initiative: China's Perspective,' in Sharma, Bal Krishnan Sharma and Nivedita Das Kundu (eds), *China's One Belt One Road: Initiative, Challenges and Prospects*, New Delhi: Vij Books, 2016, pp. 7-26.
4. For a detailed account of the name change, see Berzina-Cerenkova, Ula Aleksandra, *BRI instead of OBOR: China Edits the English Name of its Most Ambitious International Project*, Riga: Latvijas Arpolitikas Instituts, 28 July 2016, http://www.lai.lv/viedokli/bri-instead-of-obor-china-edits-the-english-name-of-its-most-ambitious-international-project-532 (retrieved on 5 October 2018).
5. Ang, op. cit.
6. Ibid.
7. For an excellent account of China's 'third revolution,' see Economy, Elizabeth C., *The Third Revolution: Xi Jinping and the New Chinese State*, New York: Oxford University Press, 2018.
8. Allison, Graham, *Destined for War: Can America and China Escape Thucydides's Trap?* Melbourne and London: Scribe Publications, 2017, pp. 113-114.
9. 'China's vice-president revisits youth with a trip to the Midwest to meet farming family he stayed with on exchange trip,' *Associated Press*, 15 February 2012, https://www.dailymail.co.uk/news/article-2101652/Xi-Jinping-Chinas-Vice-President-visits-Midwest-farming-family-stayed-exchange-trip.html (retrieved on 15 October 2018).
10. Allison, op. cit., p. 114.
11. Sim Chi Yin, 'Chinese V-P blasts meddlesome foreigners,' *The Straits Times*, 14 February 2009, http://news.asiaone.com/News/the%2BStraits%2BTimes/Story/A1Story20090214-121872.html (retrieved on 5 October 2018).
12. Economy, op. cit., p. 3.

13. Ibid., p. 3.
14. Ang, op. cit.
15. 'China's Plan to Win Friends and Influence Includes Ski Slopes and Spas,' Stevenson, Alexandra and Cao Li, *New York Times*, 1 August 2018 https://www.nytimes.com/2018/08/01/business/china-belt-and-road.html (retrieved on 6 October 2018).
16. Yang, op. cit., p. 11.
17. Ibid. pp. 11 and 13.
18. McGregor, Richard, 'Mahathir, China and neo-colonialism,' *Nikkei Asian Review*, 30 August 2018, https://asia.nikkei.com/Opinion/Mahathir-China-and-neo-colonialism (retrieved on 5 October 2018).
19. Dang Yuan, 'Malaysia's Mahathir dumps Chinese projects amid "new colonialism" fear,' *Deutsche Welle*, 21 August 2018, https://www.dw.com/en/malaysias-mahathir-dumps-chinese-projects-amid-new-colonialism-fear/a-45160594 (retrieved on 5 October 2018).
20. Brewster, David, 'Colonialism with Chinese characteristics,' *Asia-Pacific Policy Society*, 27 September 2018, https://www.policyforum.net/colonialism-chinese-characteristics/ (retrieved on 10 October 2018).
21. Sipalan, Joseph, 'Malaysia says no to foreign homeowners in Forest City project,' *Reuters*, 27 August 2018, https://www.reuters.com/article/us-malaysia-forestcity/malaysia-says-no-to-foreign-homeowners-in-forest-city-project-idUSKCN1LC0AF (retrieved on 10 October 2018).
22. Hope, Bradley, Tom Wright and Yantoultra Ngui, 'Doubts Raised About Claim of Saudi "Donation" to Malaysia Prime Minister Najib Razak,' *The Wall Street Journal*, 26 January 2016, https://www.wsj.com/articles/malaysian-prosecutor-says-saudis-made-legal-donation-to-prime-minister-najib-1453847034 (retrieved on 5 October 2018).
23. Mahathir bin Mohamad (the spelling on the cover), *The Malay Dilemma*, Singapore: Times Books International, 1970. It was published in Singapore when it was banned in Malaysia. It is worth noting that Mahathir's ancestors on his father's side were Indian Muslims from Kerala. His mother was of Malay descent.
24. Andani, Ali Salman, 'Pakistan's IMF plan a symptom of China's dept-trap diplomacy,' *Asia Times*, 15 October 2018, http://www.atimes.com/pakistans-imf-plea-a-symptom-of-chinas-debt-trap-diplomacy/ (retrieved on 18 October 2018).
25. 'As Pakistan Negotiates IMF Bailout, China Says More Corridor Projects Planned,' *Press Trust of India*, 16 October 2018, https://www.ndtv.com/world-news/as-pakistan-preps-imf-bailout-china-says-more-trade-projects-lined-up-1932964 (retrieved on 18 October 2018).

26. Poling, Gregory, 'Kyaukpyu: Connecting China to the Indian Ocean,' *Asia Maritime Transparency Initiative*, 4 April 2018, https://amti.csis.org/kyaukpyu-china-indian-ocean/ (retrieved on 18 October 2018), and Lintner, Bertil, 'Japan offers "quality" alternative to China's BRI,' *Asia Times*, 18 October 2018, http://www.atimes.com/article/japan-offers-quality-alternative-to-chinas-bri/ (retrieved on 18 October 2018).
27. Min Naing Soe, 'If a country accepts influence and interference of other country, the former will not be a sovereign country.' *Eleven Media*, 10 October 2018, http://www.elevenmyanmar.com/politics/15427 (retrieved on 10 October 2018).
28. Crispin, Shawn W., 'China can't always get what it wants in Thailand,' *Asia Times*, 12 September 2018, http://www.atimes.com/article/china-cant-always-get-what-it-wants-in-thailand/ (retrieved on 18 October 2018).
29. Wang Yiwei, *The Belt and Road Initiative: What Will China Offer the World in its Rise*, Beijing: New World Press, 2016, pp. 89-94.
30. Ibid., pp. 90-91.
31. Ibid., p. 91.
32. Lawi Went, 'China Warns Northern Alliance Against Cooperating with ARSA,' *The Irrawaddy*, 2 April 2018, https://www.irrawaddy.com/news/burma/china-warns-northern-alliance-cooperating-arsa.html (retrieved on 10 October 2018).
33. Wang, op. cit., p.92.
34. Ibid., p. 93.
35. Ibid., p. 93.
36. Ibid., p. 94.
37. Unnithan, Sandeep, 'China positions submarine and rescue vehicle in Indian Ocean,' *India Today*, 15 October 2018, https://www.indiatoday.in/india/story/china-positions-submarine-and-rescue-vehicle-in-the-indian-ocean-1368286-2018-10-15 (retrieved on 19 October 2018).
38. Brewster, David, 'China's play for military bases in the eastern Indian Ocean,' *The Interpreter*, 15 May 2018, https://www.lowyinstitute.org/the-interpreter/china-s-play-military-bases-eastern-indian-ocean (retrieved on 5 October 2018).
39. Ibid.
40. *Constitution of the Republic of the Union of Myanmar*, Yangon: Printing and Publishing Enterprise, Ministry of Information, 2008, p. 11.
41. Miller, Tom, *China's Asia Dream*, London: Zed Books, 2017, p. 171.
42. Ibid., p. 171.

43. 'Australia and Japan should not let ally lead them astray: China Daily editorial,' *China Daily*, 11 October 2018, http://europe.chinadaily.com.cn/a/201810/11/WS5bbf41e8a310eff303281e0d.html (retrieved on 19 October 2018). Also quoted in Fernando, Gavin, 'China has issued a direct warning to Australia in a blistering new editorial,' *news.com.au*, https://www.news.com.au/technology/innovation/military/china-has-issued-a-direct-warning-to-australia-in-a-blistering-new-editorial/news-story/2dc17494e63803c4fba6cd7940b44165, 16 October 2018, (retrieved on 18 October 2018).
44. *China Daily*, 11 October 2018.
45. Ibid.
46. 'China Voice: US playing with fire over South China Sea,' *Xinhua*, 29 May 2015, http://www.xinhuanet.com//english/2015-05/29/c_134282034.htm (retrieved on 10 October 2018).
47. White, Hugh, *The China Choice: Why America Should Share Power*, Collingwood: Black Inc., 2012.
48. Herscovitch, Benjamin, 'Australia must choose between China and the US,' *The Weekend Australian*, 16 July 2015, https://www.theaustralian.com.au/business/business-spectator/news-story/australia-must-choose-between-china-and-the-us/2cf0c5d58d55068bacd89c53b964d7d9 (retrieved on 10 October 2018).
49. 'Australia is edgy about China's growing presence on its doorstep,' *The Economist*, 20 April 2018 (retrieved on 10 October 2018).
50. 'Chinese military base in Pacific would be of "great concern", Turnbull tells Vanuatu, *ABC News*, 10 April 2018, https://www.abc.net.au/news/2018-04-10/china-military-base-in-vanuatu-report-of-concern-turnbull-says/9635742 (retrieved on 10 October 2018).
51. Khan, Ahyousha, 'Second Age of Arms Race in the Indian Ocean and India's Test of K-15 SRBM, *South Asia Journal*, 28 September 2018, http://southasiajournal.net/second-age-of-arms-race-in-the-indian-ocean-and-indias-test-of-k-15-srbm/ (retrieved on 10 October 2018).
52. 'India's "Great Wall" Against China Along Border region,' *Sputnik News*, 17 August 2016, https://sputniknews.com/asia/201608171044369064-india-china-border/ (retrieved on 10 October 2018).
53. Cheng, Amy, 'Will Djibouti Become Latest Country to Fall Into China's Dept Trap?' *Foreign Policy*, 31 July 2018, https://foreignpolicy.com/2018/07/31/will-djibouti-become-latest-country-to-fall-into-chinas-debt-trap/ (retrieved on 15 October 2018).
54. Dana, Joseph, 'Will China's dominant position force others out of Djibouti?' *Arab News*, 30 September 2018, http://www.arabnews.com/node/1380096 (retrieved on 10 October 2018).

55. 'Djibouti risks dependence on Chinese largesse,' *The Economist*, 19 July 2018, https://www.economist.com/middle-east-and-africa/2018/07/19/djibouti-risks-dependence-on-chinese-largesse (retrieved on 5 October 2018).
56. Dana, op. cit.
57. Maçães, Bruno, 'The coming wars: The most valuable real estate in the world,' *Politico*, 16 January 2018, https://www.politico.eu/blogs/the-coming-wars/2018/01/the-most-valuable-military-real-estate-in-the-world/ (retrieved on 10 October 2018).
58. Allison, op. cit., p. vii.
59. Ibid., p. 42.
60. Ibid., p. 45.
61. Ibid., p. 109.
62. Ibid., p. 117.
63. Blanchard, Ben and Christian Shepherd, *Reuters*, 11 March 2018, https://www.reuters.com/article/us-china-parliament/china-allows-xi-to-remain-president-indefinitely-tightening-his-grip-on-power-idUSKCN1GN07E (retrieved on 15 October 2018).
64. Pei Minxin, 'China's Ticking Debt Bomb,' *The Diplomat*, 5 July 2011, https://thediplomat.com/2011/07/chinas-ticking-debt-bomb/ (retrieved on 15 October 2018).
65. Ibid.
66. Ibid.
67. Pei Minxin, 'China is losing the New Cold War,' *Project Syndicate*, 5 September 2018, https://www.project-syndicate.org/commentary/china-cold-war-us-competition-by-minxin-pei-2018-09 (retrieved on 10 October 2018).
68. Ibid.
69. Lintner, Bertil, 'Japan offers "quality" alternative to China's BRI,' *Asia Times*, 18 October 2018, http://www.atimes.com/article/japan-offers-quality-alternative-to-chinas-bri/ (retrieved on 18 October 2018).
70. See Lintner, Bertil, 'China is conflicted in Myanmar's wars,' *Asia Times*, 17 May 2018, http://www.atimes.com/article/china-is-conflicted-in-myanmars-wars/ (retrieved on 10 October 2018), and Marshall, Andrew and Anthony Davis, 'Soldiers of fortune,' *Time*, 16 December 2002, http://content.time.com/time/world/article/0,8599,2056076,00.html (retrieved on 10 October 2018).
71. Takenaka, Kiyoshi and Elaine Lies, 'Japan to supply India with nuclear power equipment, technology,' *Reuters*, 11 November 2016, https://www.reuters.com/article/us-japan-india-nuclear-idUSKBN1360YL (retrieved on 10 October 2018).

72. For the full text of the agreement, see https://www.mofa.go.jp/region/asia-paci/india/pmv0810/joint_d.html (retrieved on 20 October 2018).
73. Allison, op. cit., p. 172.

BIBLIOGRAPHY

BOOKS

Adams, Jan and Marg Neale, *Christmas Island: The Early Years 1888-1958*, Chapman, ACT: Bruce Neal, 1993.

Allison, Graham, *Destined for War: Can America and China Escape Thucydides's Trap?* Melbourne and London: Scribe Publications, 2017.

Amtrith, Sunil S., *Crossing the Bay of Bengal: The Furies of Nature and the Fortunes of Migrants*, Cambridge, Massachusetts: Harvard University Press, 2013.

Anderson, Clare, *Legible Bodies: Race, Criminality and Colonialism in South Asia*, Oxford, New York: Berg, 2004.

Aldrich, Robert and John Connell, *France's Overseas Frontier: Départements et Territoires d'Outre-Mer*, Cambridge: Cambridge University Press, 1992.

Babbage, Ross, *Should Australia Plan to Defend Christmas and Cocos Islands?* Canberra: Strategic and Defence Studies Centre, Research School of Pacific and Asian Studies, The Australian National University, 1988.

Bera, Tilak Ranjan, *Andamans: The Emerald Necklace of India*. New Delhi: UBS Publishers, 2007.

Bajwa, Lt.-Gen. J.S. (ed.), *China: Threat or Challenge?* New Delhi: Lancer Publishers, 2017.

Basu, Badal Kumar, *The Onge*, Calcutta: Seagull Books & The ASI, Andaman and Nicobar Island Tribe series, 1990.

Bell, H.C.P., *The Maldive Islands: An Account of the Physical Features, Climate, History, Inhabitants, Productions and Trade*, New Delhi and Chennai: Asian Educational Services, 2004 (reprint, originally published in 1883 in Colombo by Government Printer, Ceylon).

———, *The Maldive Islands: Report on a Visit to Male, January 20 to February 21, 1920*, Colombo: Government Printer Ceylon, 1921.

———, *The Maldive Islands: Monograph on the History, Archaeology and Epigraphy*, Colombo: Ceylon Government Press, 1940.

Bermudez, Joseph S., *Terrorism: The North Korean Connection*, New York: Crane Russak, 1990.

Bertuchi, A.J., *The Island of Rodriguez*, London: John Murray, 1923.

Bera, Dr Tilak Ranjan, *Andamans: The Emerald Necklace of India*, New Delhi: USB Publishers, 2002.

Borton, James, *Islands and Rocks in the South China Sea: Post Hague Ruling*, Bloomington, Indiana: Xlibris, 2017.

Brooks, Aubrey, *Death Row in Paradise: The Untold Story of the Mercenary Invasion of the Seychelles 1981-83, Solihull*, West Midlands: Helion & Company, 2013.

Boussac, Marie-Françoise, Jean-François Salles and Jean-Baptiste Yon, *Ports of the Ancient Indian Ocean*. New Delhi, Primus Books, 2016.

Campling, Liam, Hansel Confiance and Marie-Therese Purvis, *Social Policies in Seychelles*, London: Commonwealth Secretariat and United Nations Research Institute for Social Development, 2011.

Carpin, Sarah, *Seychelles: Garden of Eden in the Indian Ocean*, Hong Kong: Odyssey Guides, 2005.

Cipriani, Lidio, *The Andaman Islanders*, London: Weidenfeld and Nicolson, 1966.

Clunies-Ross, John C., *The Clunies-Ross Cocos Chronicle*, Compiled and self-published by John C. Clunies-Ross, 2009.

Dasgupta, Jayant, *Japanese in the Andaman & Nicobar Islands*, New Delhi: Manas Publications, 2002.

Deignan, H.G., *Burma — Gateway to China*, Washington: The Smithsonian Institution, 1943.

Didi, Amir Muhammad Amin, *Ladies and Gentlemen…The Maldive Islands!* Colombo: Evergreen, 1949.

Economy, Elizabeth C., *The Third Revolution: Xi Jinping and the New Chinese State,* New York: Oxford University Press, 2018.

Ecott, Tim, *The Story of Seychelles*, Victoria: Outer Island Books, 2015.

French, Howard W., *Everything Under the Heavens: How the Past Helps Shape China's Push for Global Power*, Melbourne and London: Scribe Publications, 2017.

Garver, John W. *China's Quest: The History of the Foreign Relations of the People's Republic of China*, New York: Oxford University Press, 2016.

Gordon, Sandy, *Security and Security Building in the Indian Ocean Region*, Canberra: Strategic and Defence Studies Centre, Research School of Pacific and Asian Studies, The Australian National University, 1996.

Grare, Frédéric, *India Turns East: International Engagement and US-China Rivalry*, London: Hurst, 2016.

Gupta, Manoj, *Indian Ocean Region: Maritime Regimes for Regional Cooperation*, New York: Springer, 2010.

Haksar, Nandita, *Rogue Agent: How India's Military Intelligence Betrayed the Burmese Resistance*, New Delhi: Penguin Books, 2009.

Hall, Richard, *Empires of the Monsoon: A History of the Indian Ocean and its Invaders*, London: Harper Collins Publishers, 1998.

Hoare, Mike, *The Seychelles Affair*, New York, London, Toronto, Sydney, Auckland: Bantam Press, 1986.

Hockly, T.W., *The Two Thousand Isles: A Short Account of the People, History and Customs of the Maldive Archipelago*, New Delhi and Chennai: Asian Educational Services, 2014 (reprint, originally published in 1935 in London by H.F. & G. Witherby).

Hughes, John Scott, *Kings of the Cocos*, London: Methuen & Co., 1950.

Husain, Syed Anwar, *Superpowers & Security in the Indian Ocean: A South Asian Perspective*, Dhaka: Academic Publishers, 1992.

Jain, Ravindra K., *Innovative Departures: Anthropology and the Indian Diaspora*, London and New York: Routledge, 2018.

Justin, Anstice, *The Nicobarese*, Calcutta: Seagull Books & The ASI, Andaman and Nicobar Island Tribe series, 1990.

Kaplan, Robert D., *Monsoon: The Indian Ocean and the Future of American Power*, New York: Random House, 2010.

Kauffmann, Jean-Paul, *The Arch of Kerguelen: Voyage to the Islands of Desolation*, New York: Four Walls Eight Windows, 1993.

Kaushiva, Pradeep and Abhijit Singh (eds), *Indian Ocean Challenges: A Quest for Cooperative Solutions*, New Delhi: KW Publishers, 2013.

Kumar, Narender, *Challenges in the Indian Ocean Region: Response Options*, New Delhi, KW Publishers, 2011.

Labuschagne, Riaan, *On South Africa's Secret Service: An Undercover Agent's Story,* Alberton, South Africa: Galago Publishing, 2002.

Lee, Christopher, *Seychelles: Political Castaways*, London: Elm Tree Books, 1976.

Lintner, Bertil, *Great Game East: India, China and the Struggle for Asia's Most Volatile Frontier*, New Haven: Yale University Press, 2015.

Ma Huan, *Ying-hai Sheng-lan: The Overall Survey of the Ocean's Shores*, Bangkok: White Lotus, 1997.

Maloney, Clarence, *People of the Maldive Islands*, Hyderabad: Black Swan, 2013.

Mancham, James R., *Seychelles: Global Citizen, The Autobiography of the Founding President of the Republic of Seychelles*, St. Paul, Minnesota: Paragon House, 2009.

Maniku, Hassan Ahmed, *Gazetteer of the Republic of the Maldives*, Male: TS, 1981.

Mathur, L.P., *History of the Andaman & Nicobar Islands*, Delhi: Sterling Publishers, 1968.

Metz, Helen Chapin (ed.), *Indian Ocean: Five Island Countries*, Washington: Federal Research Division, Library of Congress, 1995.

Miller, Tom, *China's Asian Dream*. London: Zed Books, 2017.

Mockler, Anthony, *The New Mercenaries The History of the Hired Soldier from the Congo to the Seychelles*, New York: Paragon House Publishers, 1985.

Mukerjee, Madhusree, *The Land of the Naked People: Encounters with Stone Age Islanders*, New Delhi: Penguin Books, 2003.

Neale, Marg, *We were the Christmas Islanders*, self-published, 1988.

Phaley, Baban, *The Land of the Martyrs: Andaman & Nicobar Islands*, Nagpur: Sarswati Prakashan, undated.

Rachman, Gideon, *Easternisation: War and Peace in the Asian Century*, London: The Bodley Head, 2016.

Rees, Coralie and Leslie Rees, *Westward from Cocos*, London: George G. Harrap & Co., 1956.

Robinson, J.J., *The Maldives: Islamic Republic, Tropical Autocracy*, London: Hurst, 2015.

Rozman, Gilbert, *Chinese Strategic Thought Toward Asia*, New York: Palgrave Macmillan, 2010.

Saint-Pierre, Bernardin de, *Journey to Mauritius*, Oxford: Signal Books, 2002.

Sanyal, Sanjeev, *The Ocean of Churn: How the Indian Ocean Shaped Human History*, New Delhi: Penguin Viking, 2016.

Scarr, Deryck, *Seychelles Since 1770: History of a Slave and Post-Slavery Society*, London: Hurst, 1999.

———, *Slaving and Slavery in the Indian Ocean*, London: Macmillan Press, 1998.

Scott, Robert, *Limuria: The Lesser Dependencies of Mauritius*, London: Oxford University Press, 1961.

Sharms, Bal Kishan and Nivedita Das Kundu (eds), *China's One Belt One Road: Initiative, Challenges and Prospects*, New Delhi, Vij Books, 2016.

Small, Andrew, *The China-Pakistan Axis: Asia's New Geopolitics*, London Hurst, 2015.

Smith, Jeff M., *Cold Peace: China-India Rivalry in the Twenty-first Century*, Lanham, Maryland: Lexington Books, 2014.

Stoddard, Theodore L., William K. Carr, Daniel L. Spencer, Nancy E. Walstrom and Audrey R. Whiteley, *Area Handbook for The Indian Ocean Territories*, Washington: The American University by the Institute for Cross-Cultural Research, 1971.

Tamta, B.R., *Andaman & Nicobar Islands*, New Delhi: National Book Trust, 1992.

Teelock, Vijayalakshmi, Sooryakanti Nirsimloo-Gayan, Marc Serge Rivière and Geoffrey Summers (eds), *Angaje: Explorations into the History, Society and Culture of Indentured Immigrants and their Descendants in Mauritius, Volume 1: Early Years*, Port Louis: Aapravasi Ghat Fund, 2012.

———, *Angaje: Explorations into the History, Society and Culture of Indentured Immigrants and their Descendants in Mauritius, Volume 2: The Impact of Indenture*, Port Louis: Aapravasi Ghat Fund, 2012.

———, *Angaje: Explorations into the History, Society and Culture of Indentured Immigrants and their Descendants in Mauritius, Volume 3: Post-Indenture Mauritius*, Port Louis: Aapravasi Ghat Fund, 2013.

Vaidya, Suresh, *Islands of the Marigold Sun*, London: Robert Hale, 1960.

Vine, David, *Island of Shame: The Secret History of the U.S. Military Base on Diego Garcia*, Princeton: Princeton University Press, 2009.

Wang Yiwei. *The Belt and Road Initiative: What Will China Offer the World in Its Rise*, Beijing: New World Press, 2016.

Winchester, Simon, *The Sun Never Sets: Travels Through the Remaining Outposts of the British Empire,* New York: Prentice Hall Press, 1985.

Wright, Carol, *Islands: Mauritius*, Harrisburg: Stackpole Books, 1974.

Zehmisch, Philipp, *Mini-India: The Politics of Migration and Subalternity in the Andaman Islands*, New Delhi: Oxford University Press, 2017.

SELECT ARTICLES AND RESEARCH PAPERS

Allison, Simon, 'Djibouti's greatest threat may come from within', *Mail and Guardian*, 2 March 2018, https://mg.co.za/article/2018-03-02-00-djiboutis-greatest-threat-may-come-from-within

Chakrabarti, Sumon K., 'Isle's oil slick: Maldivian autocrat's family's illegal "oil trade" allegedly worth $800 million', *The Week*, 30 February 2011.

CSIS. 'Kyaukpyu: Connecting China to the Indian Ocean', *CSIS Briefs*, 2 April 2018, https://www.csis.org/analysis/kyaukpyu-connecting-china-indian-ocean

Fan Hongwei, 'China's "Look South": China-Myanmar Transport Corridor', *Ritsumeikan International Affairs*, Vol. 10, 2011, pp. 49-50, http://www.ritsumei.ac.jp/acd/re/k-rsc/ras/04_publications/ria_en/10_04.pdf

Hillman, Jonathan E., 'How Big is China's Belt and Road?' paper prepared for the Center for Strategic and International Studies, Washington, 3 April 2018, https://www.csis.org/analysis/how-big-chinas-belt-and-road

Lintner, Bertil, 'Burma: China's New Gateway', *Far Eastern Economic Review,* 22 December 1994.

———, Australia's Strategic Little Dots, *Asia Times*, 25 June 2010, http://www.atimes.com/atimes/China/LF25Ad01.html

———, Same Game, Different Tactics: The Myanmar Corridor', *The Irrawaddy*, July 2015, https://www.irrawaddy.com/news/burma/same-game-different-tactics-chinas-myanmar-corridor.html

———, *The People's Republic of China and Burma: Not Only Pauk-Phaw*, Washington: Project 2049, 2017, https://www.researchgate.net/publication/317167085_The_People's_Republic_of_China_and_Burma-Not_Only_Pauk-Phaw

———, 'China advances, West frets in South Pacific', *Asia Times*, 25 April 2018, http://www.atimes.com/article/china-advances-west-frets-in-south-pacific/

———, 'Djibouti: the Casablanca of a new Cold War', *Asia Times*, November 28, 2018, http://www.atimes.com/article/djibouti-the-casablanca-of-a-new-cold-war/

———, 'Risks bubbling beneath Djibouti's foreign bases, *Asia Times*, November 28, 2018, http://www.atimes.com/article/risks-bubbling-beneath-djiboutis-foreign-bases/

———, Where India quietly watches China at sea', *Asia Times*, December 10, 2018, http://www.atimes.com/article/where-india-quietly-watches-china-at-sea/

Nagao, Satoru, 'Japan-India Military Partnership: India is the New Hope for Asia,' *Claws Journal*, Winter 2013, http://www.claws.in/images/journals_doc/1589692164_SatoruNagao.pdf

Pan Qi, Opening to the Southwest: An Expert Opinion, *Beijing Review*, 2 September 1985, http://beijingreview.sinoperi.com/en198535/665498.jhtml

Pehrson, Christopher J., *String of Pearls: Meeting the Challenge of China's Rising Power Across the Asian Littoral*. Carlisle, Pennsylvania: Strategic Studies Institute of the US Army War College, June 2006, http://ssi.armywarcollege.edu/pdffiles/pub721.pdf

Pellerin, Mathieu, *The Recent Blossoming in Relations between China and Madagascar*, Paris: The Institut Français des relations internationales, 2012, https://www.ifri.org/en/publications/enotes/notes-de-lifri/recent-blossoming-relations-between-china-and-madagascar

Rosen, Mark E., 'Is Diego Garcia at Risk of Slipping from Washington's Grasp?' *The National Interest*, 19 September 2017, https://nationalinterest.org/feature/diego-garcia-risk-slipping-washingtons-grasp-22381

Seidel, Jamie, 'New quest for Chinese navigator Zheng He's ancient fleet an ominous bid for validation of China's expansionist claims', *news.com.au*, 1 March 2018, http://www.news.com.au/technology/science/

archaeology/new-quest-for-chinese-navigator-zheng-hes-ancient-fleet-an-ominous-bid-for-validation-of-chinas-expansionist-claims/news-story/0ed1e754cd927a78569129bf83770478

Selth, Andrew, *Chinese Military Bases in Burma: The Explosion of a Myth*, Nathan, Queensland: The Griffith Asia Institute, Regional Outlook Paper No. 10. 2007.

———, *Burma's Coco Islands: Rumours and Realities in the Indian Ocean*, Hong Kong: City University, South-east Asia Research Centre, 2008, http://www.cityu.edu.hk/searc/Resources/Paper/WP101_08_ASelth.pdf

Shaer, Matthew, Michael Hudson and Margot Williams, 'Suns and Shadows: How an Island Paradise Became a Haven for Dirty Money,' *The International Consortium of Investigative Journalists*, 3 June 2014, https://www.icij.org/investigations/offshore/sun-and-shadows-how-island-paradise-became-haven-dirty-money/

Thorne, Dewin and Ben Spevack. *Harboured Ambitions: How China's Port Investments Are Strategically Reshaping the Indo-Pacific*, Washington: Centre for Advanced Defence Studies, 2017, https://daisukybiendong.files.wordpress.com/2018/04/devin-thorne-ben-spevack-2018-harbored-ambitions-how-chinas-port-investments-are-strategically-reshaping-the-indo-pacific.pdf

Tian Jinchen, 'One Belt and One Road': Connecting China and the World', paper prepared for McKinsey and Company, 19 April 2017, https://www.mckinsey.com/industries/capital-projects-and-infrastructure/our-insights/one-belt-and-one-road-connecting-china-and-the-world

INDEX